Queer in

Translation

Perverse Modernities   A series edited by
Jack Halberstam and Lisa Lowe

Sexual

Politics

under

Neoliberal

Islam

Queer in Translation

Evren Savcı

Duke University Press Durham and London 2021

© 2021 Duke University Press
All rights reserved
Designed by Aimee C. Harrison
Typeset in Garamond Premier Pro, Didot, and Helvetica Neue
by Copperline Book Services.

Library of Congress Cataloging-in-Publication Data
Names: Savcı, Evren, [date] author.
Title: Queer in translation : sexual politics under neoliberal Islam /
Evren Savcı.
Other titles: Perverse modernities.
Description: Durham : Duke University Press, 2021. | Series:
Perverse modernities | Includes bibliographical references
and index.
Identifiers: LCCN 2020019344 (print)
LCCN 2020019345 (ebook)
ISBN 9781478010319 (hardcover)
ISBN 9781478011361 (paperback)
ISBN 9781478012856 (ebook)
Subjects: LCSH: Sexual minorities—Political aspects—
Turkey. | Gender identity—Terminology—Political
aspects—Turkey. | Sexual minorities—Terminology—
Political aspects—Turkey. | Sexual minorities—Religious aspects—
Islam. | Sexism in language—Political aspects— Turkey. |
Neoliberalism—Turkey.
Classification: LCC HQ73.3.T9 S283 2021 (print) |
LCC HQ73.3.T9 (ebook) | DDC 306.7609561—dc23
LC record available at https://lccn.loc.gov/2020019344
LC ebook record available at https://lccn.loc.gov/2020019345

Cover art: Protesters clash with riot police near the Taksim
Gezi Park in Istanbul, on June 1, 2013, during a demonstration
against the demolition of the park. Photo by BULENT KILIC/
AFP via Getty Images.

For Zeliş, Boysan, Ali, and Ayda, who left us too soon.

Contents

Acronyms

ACLU	American Civil Liberties Union
AKP	Adalet ve Kalkınma Partisi (Justice and Development Party)
ANAP	Anavatan Partisi (Motherland Party)
BDP	Barış ve Demokrasi Partisi (Peace and Democracy Party)
BDS	Boycott, Divestment, Sanctions
CHP	Cumhuriyet Halk Partisi (Republican People's Party)
CIA	Central Intelligence Agency
DYP	Doğru Yol Partisi (Right Path Party)
EU	European Union
FETÖ	Fethullahçı Terör Örgütü (Pro-Fethullah Terrorist Organization)
FTM	female-to-male
GIT	Group International de Travail: "Liberté de Recherche et D'enseignement en Turquie" (International Work Group: "Academic Liberty and Freedom of Research in Turkey")
HDP	Halkların Demokrasi Partisi (People's Democratic Party)
IMF	International Monetary Fund
JİTEM	Jandarma İstihbarat ve Terörle Mücadele (Gendarmerie Intelligence and Counterterrorism)
KADEM	Kadın ve Demokrasi Derneği (Woman and Democracy Association)

KİSS	Küresel İncelemeler ve Sınıfsal Stratejiler (Global Analyses and Class-Based Strategies)
LGBTİ	Lezbiyen, Gey, Biseksüel, Transseksüel, İnterseks
LGBTT	Lezbiyen, Gey, Biseksüel, Transseksüel, Travesti
NGO	nongovernmental organization
NTV	Turkish TV channel
OSCE	Organization for Security and Co-operation in Europe
PKK	Partiya Karkerên Kurdistanê (Kurdistan Workers' Party)
RP	Refah Partisi (Welfare Party)
STD	sexually transmitted disease
TEKEL	Tütün, Tütün Mamulleri, Tuz ve Alkol İşletmeleri A.Ş. Genel Müdürlüğü (Tobacco, Salt, and Alcohol Administration)
THY	Türk Hava Yolları (Turkish Airlines)
TOKİ	Toplu Konut İdaresi Başkanlığı (Housing Development Administration)
TÜSİAD	Türk Sanayici ve İş İnsanları Derneği (Turkish Industry and Business Association)
UN	United Nations
YÖK	Yükseköğretim Kurulu (Council for Higher Education)
YTL	Yeni Türk Lirası (New Turkish Lira)

Acknowledgments

It is common for acknowledgments of a first book to start out by recognizing the fact that it takes a village to write a book. I could not agree more, and I will thank my village below, but before I do that, I want to acknowledge the time I was given to write this book—something most of us are given less and less of in an intellectual economy geared to the rapid pace of book production. I was fortunate enough to have a postdoctoral fellowship as well as several years at my first job, where a book was not required for tenure, all of which allowed me to think and rethink and workshop and restructure and rewrite this book into what it has become. I am deeply grateful that life gave me time to think, and I continue to hope that academic life can be restructured in ways that grant all authors the time their books need and deserve.

The first thank-you goes to Sharon Hays, my mentor and dear friend almost since the moment I arrived in the United States. Every day I realize how formative Sharon has been in developing the intellectual I am today and how much I have learned from her about how to marvel at this world even as I am outraged by it.

There are two sets of thank-yous to my two graduate institutions. At the University of Virginia I was lucky to learn from Sarah Corse, Krishan Kumar, Ekaterina Makarova, Rita Felski, Liz Gorman, Bethany Bryson, and Nitin Govil. I also had the fortunate company of wonderful graduate colleagues and friends to think with: Jacob Sargent, Alana Bibeau, Dustin Kidd, Sara Danielson, Jen Silva, and Bethany Blalock. At the University of Southern California I owe many thanks to Mike Messner, Macarena Gómez-Barris, and Jack Halberstam for serving on my dissertation committee. I am thankful to you for all your work in helping me shape my amorphous ideas into a dissertation project, for your respect for and encouragement of interdisciplinary work, for the freedom you gave me to follow my instincts even when I did not yet have the words to make sense of them as a methodology, and for your thoughtful feedback always.

At USC I have also had the privilege to learn from Josh Kun, Tim Biblarz, Pierette Hondagneu-Sotelo, Paul Lichterman, Nina Eliasoph, Ed Ransford, Amon Emeka, Sarah Banet-Weiser, Karen Tongson, Kara Keeling, Sarah Gualtieri, and Nayan Shah. Tim, thank you for coauthoring my very first publication and for teaching me so much in the process. I was also lucky to be in the company of many brilliant graduate students: Cenk Özbay, Glenda Flores, Jess Butler, Ho'esta Mo'e'hahne, Kristen Barber, Demetri Psihopaidas, Jeff Sacha, Brady Potts, Hernan Ramirez, Nicole Willms, Ed Flores, and James McKeever. Outside of my department I'd like to thank in particular Laura Portwood-Stacer, Anjali Nath, Laura Fugikawa, Inna Arzumanova, Meghan Moran, Sinan Birdal, Engin Volkan, Yetta Howard, Jay Sibara, Emily Hobson, Gino Conti, and Deb Al-Najjar for bringing some sunlight (intellectual and otherwise) to that strange journey called graduate school. Cenk, Laura, and Anjali—I am deeply grateful for your lifelong friendship. During the dissertation time and beyond, I am also grateful for the companionship of Kimberly Peirce, who has witnessed the challenges and joys of most of this book.

My deep appreciation goes to Héctor Carrillo and Steve Epstein for having the vision and putting in the time and effort to create the Sexualities Project at Northwestern. Being a fellow at SPAN remains one of the most formative experiences of my career, and there are no words to describe Héctor and Steve's generous mentorship. At SPAN I also had the wonderful intellectual company and friendship of Kirsten Leng. Many other faculty members and graduate students at Northwestern made me feel welcome and provided an invigorating and dreamy intellectual environment. I thank Ann Orloff, who has since become a coconspirator and coauthor, along with the dearest Raka Ray; Özge Samancı, whose creativity, wit, and sense of wonder I got to witness close-up; Mary Weismantel, Jillana Enteen, Bonnie Honig, Jackie Stevens, Mary Dietz, Tessie Liu, Amy Partridge, Rita Koryan, Beth Shakman-Hurd, Jessica Winegar, Brian T. Edwards, Wendy Pearlman, Rebecca

Johnson, İpek Yosmaoğlu, Nicki Beisel, Bruce Carruthers, Jeremy Freese, Gary Alan Fine, Greg Mitchell, Theo Greene, Nisa Göksel, Mert Arslanalp, İmge Oranlı (a DePaul runaway), Nazlı Özkan, Savina Balasubramanian, Ricardo Sánchez, and Pierre Pénet. My time at Northwestern also coincided serendipitously with Meltem Ahıska's year as a visiting scholar. She remains an intellectual inspiration, and I am hopeful she will notice the significant impact that our conversations about Westernization and modernity have had on my thinking.

My first job at San Francisco State University's Women and Gender Studies Program gifted me with a dream feminist department: Julie Hua, Kasturi Ray, Deb Cohler, Jillian Sandell, Nan Alamilla-Boyd, Martha Kenney, and Chris Hansmann—thank you for your friendship and your brilliance. I learned so much from each of you and from our collectivity, and I continue to carry your vision of what a fulfilling intellectual life looks like. Julie, dear friend, I think our paths crossing was preordained since you drew that map of Turkey as a high schooler in Kansas, and I look forward to our letters crossing the country for years to come. Neda Atanasoski, without whom this book would not have existed (and I mean this)—I deeply admire the simultaneity of your firm push and your cheerleading, your brilliance and kindness and generosity. Living in the Bay Area has also meant being in the wonderful presence of James Martel, Paola Bachetta, Sunaina Maira, Minoo Moallem, Caren Kaplan, Omnia El-Shakry, Jessica Fields, Rabab Abdulhadi, and Lucia Volk.

At Yale I am lucky to be surrounded by colleagues with great minds, generous hearts, and fierce politics: Inderpal Grewal, Margaret Homans, Rod Ferguson, Jill Campbell, Laura Wexler, Eda Pepi, Joe Fischel, Andrew Dowe, Ana Ramos-Zayas, Zareena Grewal, Joanne Meyerowitz, Alicia Schmidt-Camacho, Jill Richards, Greta LaFleur, Ali Miller, Rene Almeling, Julia Adams, Jonathan Wyrtzen, Alan Mikhail, Rohit De, Lisa Lowe, Tavia Nyong'o, and Francesco Casetti. A big thanks also to my research assistant extraordinaire, Hazal Başarık, who has been critical in completing the manuscript.

I have been a member of several writing groups over the years, and I am thankful to my colleagues who have read drafts of parts of this book and have proven over and over again that writing life does not have to be lonely: Jyoti Puri, Vrushali Patil, Emily Mann, Patrick Grzanka, Ghassan Moussawi, Sinnika Elliott, Jessica Fields, Darius Bost, Nan Boyd, Deb Cohler, and Marc Stein. My ongoing Gender, Power, Theory workshop brings together amazing feminists who keep my faith in sociology alive. There are too many members to name, but a special thanks to Ann Orloff and Raka Ray for initiating and to Poulami Roychowdhury and Abigail Andrews for carrying on the collective.

I also had the privilege to present and workshop sections of the book at various talks and workshops over the years: at Harvard Divinity School's Sexuality and Religion Workshop; at the Comparative and Interdisciplinary Approaches in the Field of Turkish Studies workshop at Northwestern; at the Translating Transgender Workshop at the University of Arizona; at the Conversations in Humanitarianism and Religion Workshop at the University of California, Riverside; at the Philology and Sexology: Initial Thoughts and Queries workshop at the University of Toronto; at the Turkey's Queer Times Workshop at Sabancı University, Yale Sociology's Comparative Research Workshop, and at Harvard's Black, Brown and Queer+ Collective. I am thankful to the invitations and invaluable feedback of Mark Jordan, Sinan Ciddi, Kent Schull, Brian Baer, Klaus Kaindl, David Gramling, Susan Stryker, Neda Atanasoski, Mariam Lam, Durba Mitra, Zohar Weiman-Kelman, Dina Georgis, Anjali Arondekar, Heather Love, Carolyn Dinshaw, Omnia El-Shakry, Cenk Özbay, Kerem Öktem, Julia Adams, Phil Gorski, and Ahmed Ragab. My book has also benefited immensely from talks I gave at Southern Illinois University–Carbondale, UC Davis, UC Berkeley, Williams College, CSU Los Angeles, Baldwin Wallace University, Kent State University, NYU, the University of Pennsylvania, the University of Zurich, Trinity College, UC Irvine, Sabancı University, the University of Chicago, and the University of Rhode Island. In particular, I am thankful to Kristen Barber, Baki Tezcan, Sunaina Maira, Omnia El-Shakry, Cihan Tuğal, Gregory Mitchell, Molly Talcott, Josh Stacher, Begüm Adalet, Gayatri Gopinath, Helga Tawil-Souri, Lisa Duggan, Sara Mourad, Amelia Carter, Sa'ed Atshan, Zeynep Pamuk, Rob Corber, Zayde Antrim, Vijay Prashad, Kifah Hanna, Paola Bachetta, Fatima El-Tayeb, Jin Haritaworn, Ayşe Gül Altınay, Hülya Adak, Ateş Altınordu, Seçil Epik, Kristen Schilt, Alana Bibeau, and Rosaria Pisa for inviting me and engaging with my work.

Funding for my research and writing has been provided by the Sexualities Project and the Keyman Center for Modern Turkish Studies at Northwestern, by a SFSU Presidential Award, and by the Yale Frederick W. Hilles Publication Fund.

Neda Atanasoski, Inderpal Grewal, Serena Bassi, and Gül Özyeğin have read the entire manuscript cover to cover and provided invaluable feedback. I am also grateful for the careful read and detailed suggestions of Duke University Press's two anonymous reviewers. I owe thanks also to Aslı Zengin,

Sharon Hays, Durba Mitra, Hentyle Yapp, S. Freeman, and Heather Berg for reading chapters and supporting the project.

Courtney Berger has been the best editor I could have asked for. Her faith in this project has been an invaluable source of strength and motivation. Sandra Korn and Lisl Hampton have been the most diligent in assisting me throughout this process, and I thank Leslie Watkins for the copyedits. My gratitude goes out also to the Duke University Press Editorial Board for their comments, and to Jack Halberstam and Lisa Lowe for including *Queer in Translation* in Perverse Modernities—it is a dream come true to be included among books that have been instrumental in my own queer studies formation.

Finally, my dear friends, thank you for being my home and for continuously reminding me of what truly matters: Sinan Göknur, Zeynep Falay, Zeynep Postalcıoğlu, Aslıhan Ünaldı, İdil Özkan, Bahar Ünsal, Osman Erden, Tevfik Eren, Ceyhun Burak Akgül, Leslie Krespin, Burçin Yardımcı, Ayşecan Aral, Ayşe Tümerkan, İpek Bozkurt, Gülgün Özek, Nilay Özlü, Ayşe Hortaçsu, Harun Tekin, Can Yücaoğlu, Özgür Kuru, Esra Ünsal, Zeynep Çelen, Yeliz Şahin, Dino Şirin, Tuna Erdem, Seda Ergül, Baran Ergenç, and Adar Bozbay. A special thanks to Aslı Özyenginer, whose passionate soul and kind and generous heart I am very privileged to know. Perhaps the biggest fortune of my life is being the daughter of parents whose extraordinary love, care, and trust have made me the thinker and the person I am today. Thank you for everything—certainly for the leap of faith when you found out I was leaving computer engineering for gender studies. This book exists because of your belief in me. Feeling my brother Onur's love and pride in me has sustained me over time, and I can only hope I am as good a sibling to him as he has been to me. Finally, Serena Bassi: Thank you for showing me what love, companionship, and intellectual comradery look like and for turning life into the most magical adventure I could ever have imagined.

Introduction

During the 2000s Turkey experienced both the rise of robust and varied LGBT (lesbian, gay, bisexual, trans)[1] movements across the country as well as the rise to power of the so-called moderate Islamist party, Adalet ve Kalkınma Partisi (AKP; Justice and Development Party).[2] While many liberal democracies might view these developments as contradictory forms of social change, a sizable portion of Turkey's Left-leaning liberals initially welcomed both as signs of the increasing cultural liberalization of a nation with a patriarchal, heteronormative, militarist, and strictly secular history—a history that had rendered unimaginable both strong LGBT movements *and* robust parliamentary representation for the Muslim voter base.[3] Also strikingly new in the Turkey of the early 2000s: The AKP clearly departed from previous Islamist parties with its pro-West, pro-globalization, and pro–big business stance. Soon after being elected to office in 2002, the party went to work trying to fulfill the Copenhagen criteria for membership in the European Union, in the process being especially attentive to ethnic and religious rights.[4] It was in this climate, and under the AKP regime, that the annual LGBT pride march, the first of which took place in 2001, grew significantly.[5] Queer activists had been forming formal and informal associations since the early 1990s, and that visibility and organizing activity increased in the 2000s as the nation's "sexual others" became loud and clear in their demands for social justice.

In late June 2015, however, thirteen years after the AKP's rise to power, police attacked people gathering for the LGBT pride march, using tear gas and water cannons to prevent crowds from gathering in Taksim Square or entering the adjacent İstiklal Street. The following year, both the trans and LGBT marches and related press releases were banned for alleged security reasons, and those who tried to gather, chant slogans, or even clap and whistle were again met with police violence and detentions.[6] While such police repression of dissent was no longer considered out of the ordinary after the infamous Gezi Park riots of 2013, where tens of thousands protesting the proposed redevelopment of the public park into a shopping mall were attacked for days with water cannons, tear gas, and plastic bullets, the police had nevertheless not interfered with the pride march of 2013 or 2014.[7] By 2015, however, the exception made for pride seemed to be over, and LGBT marches were now considered to be security concerns alongside other protests and demonstrations.

How does one make sense of these stark shifts, from exciting democratization to the authoritarian crushing of any and all dissent, all within less than a decade? *Queer in Translation* argues that the answers to this question lie in the marriage between neoliberalism and Islam as devised by the AKP regime. The party has not only embraced a neoliberal order, which has resulted in increasing levels of precarity as well as securitization, but also conjured a particular regime of morality that cannot be reduced to the logic of neoliberalism or to that of Islam alone.[8] This regime of morality is precisely what makes sexual politics and discussions about sexual minorities in Turkey a fruitful place from which to draw the contours of what I call, following other scholars of Turkey, neoliberal Islam.[9] LGBT politics in particular emerges as a site where the effects of the existing regime of morality, as well as resistance to it, crystallize. In the following chapters I discuss the various ways in which neoliberal Islam at times foreclosed and, at other times, produced dialogues about justice in Turkey, and how at times it made solidarities unimaginable and, at others, produced a set of conditions that made them unavoidable.[10]

Yet the key intellectual contribution of *Queer in Translation* is not establishing the truth or detailing the mechanisms of neoliberal Islam. Rather, I am interested in the productive paradox that neoliberal Islam posits to queer studies as the field has taken significantly different critical and epistemological positions vis-à-vis the disparate aspects of this political-economic-religious order: On the one hand, queer studies has been deeply critical of neoliberalism and its taming effects on sexual dissent. On the other, Islam in queer studies is often analyzed as the target of Western imperialism, and discussions about Islam are located in contexts of Muslim-minority populations, Muslim immigrants, Islamophobia deployed in homonationalist justifications of the US war on terror, or the continued Israeli occupation of Palestine.[11] This tendency results in most discussions of neoliberalism being confined to US and Western European contexts and in situating Islam, whenever it is addressed, as the subjugated other of Western modernity.[12]

These diametrically opposed treatments of neoliberalism and Islam in queer studies are symptomatic of a key epistemic problem in the field—that of reading nonnormatively gendered and sexualized subjects elsewhere through the paradigm of anthropological difference. This results in positioning queers in the non-West either as authentic local subjects or as modernized, globalized, and therefore inauthentic.[13] Sexual liberation movements that organize in the so-called Third World under any variation of the moniker LGBT have been rendered particularly suspect in queer studies, as the sexual identities they embrace and the liberation politics they practice are often imagined to shore up Western imperial claims about non-Western cultures as backward, nondemocratic, and homophobic. This is especially true of the Muslim world, since recent imperial wars waged against the Middle East have been justified among conservative and liberal queer organizations alike with arguments about state homophobia and violence in these societies.[14] The significance of queer critique aimed at the deployment of liberal LGBT rights to justify imperial wars and Islamophobia notwithstanding, the authentic/colonial binary that underlies this scholarship has made it difficult to theorize the *complexities* of both what circulates under the signifier Islam and of sexual political movements in Muslim-majority countries.

I offer a way out of the epistemological bind that neoliberal Islam poses to queer studies through two interrelated arguments. First, I make a historical/geopolitical one: A historically situated ethnographic study of the contemporary Turkish Republic offers a way out of this queer bind by helping contextualize Islam as a lived reality grounded in political economy and government rule.[15] Second, I make a methodological proposition of *translation* as a way to counter and move past the binaries of colonial/authentic, modern/traditional, and global/local, building on my emphasis on grounded fieldwork.

Turkey throws a particular wrench in the ongoing reproduction of the colonized East/colonial West divide as the descendant of an empire as well as thanks to its current imperial aspirations as exemplified in its military invasion of Syria.[16] With its history of repressive secularism and its present of repressive Sunni Islamism, the republic interrupts the representation of Islam as the victim other of the imperial West.[17] Neoliberal Islam in particular intervenes in the divides of traditional/modern, cultural/economic, and public/private but also in authentic/colonial and East/West—binaries that I suggest continue to haunt sexualities and queer studies scholarships in geographies that are considered to lie outside the West. Further, the positioning of Muslims as victims of colonial modernity and of Islam as *the* current alternative to Western liberal cultural and political economies continues to reproduce Islam not only as homogenous but also as radical alterity to Western modernity. This has not only intellectual but also political implications that we need to confront: The framework of Islam as a victim of Western imperialism is not only a reproduction of the timeless image of Islam as culture, but it also corresponds to the rhetoric used, for instance, by the Islamic State in its imperial war against non-Muslims as well as non-Sunni Muslims, most prominently in Iraq and Syria.[18] While the main goal of this book is to illustrate the complexities of sexual politics under neoliberal Islam, it also recounts stories that, perhaps inevitably, will demonstrate the multiplicity of Islam among those who live it and speak on its behalf, despite the Turkish government's increasing efforts to homogenize and monopolize its meaning.

The methodological solution I offer to this epistemological problem is that of translation. I trace the travel and translation of modern political languages around gendered and sexual minorities, such as "gender identity," "sexual orientation," "hate crimes," "homophobia," and "LGBT rights," within the context of contemporary Turkey and analyze how they enter public political discussions in order to understand the contours and the effects of neoliberal Islam as well as its internal contradictions and unexpected outcomes that make room for resistance.[19] Critical translation studies is helpful in moving away from the colonial/authentic binary because the field deeply historicizes and denaturalizes the link between language and culture and opens up a way to rethink what seems to be the perpetual unspoken equation of language = culture = difference = decolonial. My goal here is not to vacate discussions of linguistic travel out of power but to insist that we understand both language and power historically and in ways that do justice to differences that can get subsumed under the sign of postcolonial and decolonial localities, which are increasingly burdened by decolonial expectations of the Global South.[20] In so doing, I hope to further the queer studies project of analyzing regimes of normativity and respectability in light of imperialism and the global political economy on two fronts: First, by grounding religion, and in my case (Sunni) Islam, in its political economic context, I aim to unburden it from its assigned role as an alternative to political modernity and the imperial West in discussions of sexual orders.[21] And second, by introducing translation studies to queer studies, I hope to interrupt the unspoken English norm in a field where language and discourse have been central to understanding the workings of normativity and power and also to rethink the implications of queer theory's homolingual address for our theories about universality and particularity.[22]

In tracing the travel and translation of the sexual politics vocabulary to Turkey, I purposefully move away from discussions of sexual subjectivity, such as gay, lesbian, or trans, and focus on other terms that are imagined to define or delineate issues around modern sexualities, such as gender identity, sexual orientation, outness, or hate crimes. I do so because, for one, as I outline in the conclusion, the existing paradigms through which sexualities in the non-West are analyzed end up entangled with the binary of authentic/colonial as long as they center on sexual subjectivity. This is because once sexual subjectivity is epistemically centered as the marker of modernity, other indications of it, such as neoliberal capitalism, factor into analyses *only* insofar as they tell us something about how they shape sexual subjectivity. This inevitably recenters the formation of sexual subjectivity as the only meaningful response to modernity. I will show that this is true even for scholarship that has diligently demonstrated that categories of traditional/modern, imported/indigenous, and global/local are inadequate for understanding the complexities of various contemporary sexual and gendered formations or for making sense of the ways in which the subjects who would fall into the various categories experience the world.[23]

The second reason for my moving away from subjectivity has to do with the ways in which an understanding of sexuality as a set of discourses and Foucauldian "subjectless" critique have circumscribed *how* we approach the very question of subjectivity. As I will discuss in more detail below, the focus on the discursive misses out on the hermeneutic dimension of language and meaning. It also risks flattening out the messiness and complexity of personhood. As an effect of subjectless critique, queer studies has failed to sufficiently theorize the social, which is often conflated with the normative, as exemplified in the anti-social turn in queer studies.[24] The social is precisely that messy space between subjectivity and subjectlessness that my analysis aims to capture: where things do not align, subjects are improperly hailed and misinterpellated, language is opaque, and meanings are multiple and contradictory—where subjects are also persons.[25] In *Ghostly Matters*, Avery Gordon invites us to think about the complexity of personhood; this means, among other things, that our categories will always fail to capture the messiness of the social. "It has always baffled me," she writes, "why those most interested in understanding and changing the barbaric domination that characterizes our modernity often—not always—withhold from the very people they are most concerned with the right to complex personhood."[26] I move away from categories of sexual subjectivity in my attempts not to deny complex personhood to people who identify with such categories as gay or lesbian *and* my simultaneous desire not to overemphasize agency in ways that reproduce the structure/agency binary. In fact, I turn to translation as methodology precisely in an attempt to afford more hermeneutic complexity to terms like *outness*. For instance, in chapter 2, where I recount the narratives around a young gay man's murder, I show through the story of Ahmet's outness, which inevitably is entangled with his gayness, that neither *out* nor *gay* captures the complexity of his social existence. Ahmet's relationship to his sexuality and its social life exceed both of these terms and yet are in relationship to them and certainly do not constitute radical and authentic alternatives. As I will discuss, critical translation studies is particularly helpful in dealing with the mess of the social because it understands meaning as always fractured, complex, and, well, messy. And to risk stating the obvious: That meaning and language are social, that they are slippery, complex, and multiple, does not mean that they stand outside regimes of power.

In the conclusion I return to the question of *why* queer studies literature on the non-Western other has centered subjectivity in order to think through the underlying theory of modernity that has informed the field as well as to reflect on where that leaves queer studies vis-à-vis the issue of cultural difference. In what follows, I will first chart out queer studies' disparate analyses of neoliberalism and Islam, which I understand to be a symptom of the field's approach to cultural difference, and which has implications for how sexual politics are theorized elsewhere. I then turn to translation as methodology to discuss how the understanding of language and meaning in translation studies can intervene in the homolingual address of queer studies and its epistemic outcomes, especially regarding authenticity/coloniality and tradition/modernity. I conclude with a discussion of the setting of the stories that follow, that is, the AKP's neoliberal Islamic regime. I situate this formation historically in order to not present the AKP government as a novelty or an exception, and discuss the moral regime of neoliberal Islam as the backdrop against which sexual politics in Turkey unfolded.

Homonormativity, Homonationalism, and the Sticky Problem of Neoliberal Islam

Neoliberalism and its effects on queer politics have been a central concern for queer studies since the early 2000s.[27] In fact, the political economic and geopolitical turn in queer studies has been a most welcome shift in analyses of neoliberalism *and* of contemporary sexual subjectivities and politics. For one, feminist and queer literature insisted on the inseparability of the economy and the state from the cultural, suturing the various and at times contradictory uses of the term *neoliberalism* to mark economic, political, social, and cultural changes during late capitalism.[28] Lisa Duggan, for instance, has warned against the supposed economic/cultural divide perpetuated by the neoliberal logic that *depoliticizes* neoliberalism's redistribution of resources along class, racial, gendered, and sexual lines while positioning identity politics as a matter of special interest groups, which are then pushed outside of the realm of the economic.[29] Duggan maintains, "The goal of raising corporate profits has never been pursued separately from the rearticulation of hierarchies of race, gender, and sexuality in the United States and around the globe. Neoliberals . . . make use of identity politics to obscure redistributive aims, and they use 'neutral' economic policy terms to hide their investments in identity-based hierarchies."[30]

Second, queer studies scholars have illuminated neoliberalism's cultural effects on gay and lesbian politics of hailing self-responsibilizing and (economically, sexually, and politically) respectable citizens, leading them to conceptualize the changes in what used to be more radical sexual politics as homonormativity.[31] Homonormativity captures how the infiltration of progressive movements with the values, logic, and vocabulary of neoliberalism has resulted in the contemporary mainstreaming of LGBT politics in the United States, where an emphasis on privacy, domesticity, and individual freedom has produced such political goals as legalization of gay marriage, acceptance of gays and lesbians in the military, and increasing demands for antidiscrimination and hate crime laws.[32] While this neoliberal brand of identity/equality politics has usually been discussed as a depoliticization of the queer movement and its marriage with consumerism and domesticity, scholars have also documented instances where neoliberal queer values are employed in the name of being more political. Radical transformative politics are increasingly replaced by an emphasis on multiculturalism and diversity, both of which matter as long as they are predictable, marketable, and profitable, marking queers of color and working-class queers as those who cannot be the representatives of diversity politics, as they often lack the diversity skills garnered through corporate diversity workshops taught by diversity experts or, alternatively, during expensive college education.[33]

Liberal notions of freedom dominate mainstream LGBT politics, yet liberal freedom comes with a system of constraints as well as costs associated with it. The principle of calculating the cost of manufacturing freedom is called security.[34] Thus, not unlike neoliberal straight life, neoliberal queer life is one that both demands to be *recognized* for its power of consumption, its respectability, and its family forms, and needs to be *protected* from homophobia, whether engaging in local leisure or travel. This has led to several key developments. For one, it has served an increasing gay(-led) gentrification of inner cities, displacing immigrant communities or bodies of color as sources/locations of homophobic violence.[35] Second, it has swayed the agenda of many LGBT organizations toward demanding federal-level hate crime laws, which critics maintain feeds the prison-industrial complex and the increasing criminalization of poor communities of color.[36] Third, this demand for protection has served the production of certain sites, such as Tel Aviv, as gay meccas, that is, safe spaces for gay tourism where homophobia is allegedly properly policed by the state.[37] This, as scholars have argued, conceals the racism of the Israeli state and its ongoing settlement in and attacks on Palestinian territories.[38] Finally, gay (neo)liberalism seeks the right not only to be protected but also to protect. This latter desire has put the gay military conscription on the US LGBT agenda, resulting in the repeal of the Clinton-era don't-ask-don't-tell policy in 2010 and, more recently, the acceptance of transgender people to serve in the military.

It is in this literature on queer securitization where Islam and Muslim subjects make an appearance, either in critiques of the positioning of homophobic, usually hypermasculinized Muslim men as the threat to gay freedom par excellence or in analyses of discourse on Muslim gays and lesbians in need of rescue from their homophobic cultures. In other words, scholars maintain that the increasing need for protection among homonormative gays has produced an amorphous Muslim culture, and geographies and subjects associated with it, as the location of homophobia and thus as the very thing from which they need protection.[39] In perhaps the most classic work of this archive, Jasbir Puar has argued that this logic, which she terms homonationalism, ranks nations according to their levels of modernity and democracy based on rights and protections for gays and lesbians.[40] She maintains that the mistreatment of gays and lesbians in the so-called Muslim world is employed as a reason why the war against Muslim terrorism is simultaneously a war for/of gays and lesbians. Israeli pinkwashing works as an exemplary mechanism that relies on and further perpetuates this logic, where Israel's human rights violations against Palestinians are concealed by its self-proclaimed progressive position on gay and lesbian rights. The logic of homonationalism situates Tel Aviv as a gay mecca and the nation as the only democracy in the Middle East, exemplifying how gay rights can cover for racial settler colonial projects. Puar's analytic helps shift the focus from the biopolitical distribution of resources to worthy subjects to holding the biopolitical in tension with the necropolitical. This critical shift, in turn, helps us understand how some queer lives today are folded into proper citizenship and on whose behalf death and death-like conditions are unleashed onto disposable bodies and populations. Rejecting the suggestion that all queers always fall outside of reproductive nationalisms and therefore outside of the investments of biopolitics, Puar asks, "How do queers reproduce life, and which queers are folded into life? . . . Does this securitization of queers entail deferred death and dying for others, and if so, for whom?"[41]

Puar's timely and critical intervention has given rise to a body of scholarship that has analyzed the emergence of saving Muslim gays and lesbians as a homonationalist and homoimperialist agenda, especially in the United States, Western Europe, and Israel.[42] There is no doubt about the significance of this work, given the rising fascism and anti-Muslim xenophobia in the United States and Europe that repeats such old tropes as a "clash of civilizations" and the radical unincorporability of an ominous Islam.[43] However, while extremely helpful, generative, and politically urgent, this focus on Islamophobia, homonationalism, and pinkwashing as experienced and performed in Euro-American contexts inevitably frames Islam based on its discursive and symbolic production through an Orientalist, Islamophobic world order.[44] How can we think about the effect of political Islam in Muslim-majority contexts in general and in the case of Turkey under neoliberal Islam in particular, where the dynamics of which lives are folded into national belonging and which lives are cast out as moral or national others are complicated by the coming together of these two systems? This framework, which critiques Islamophobia as an outcome of neoliberal securitization and rescue regimes, turns into a paradox in a context where Muslims are not embodied in the minority, the immigrant, or the victim of Islamophobia and are not signs, figures, or discursive others.[45] How does one step outside this seeming paradox and think about sexual politics under neoliberal Islam from within queer studies, given that neoliberalism has been its ultimate object of critique and Islam its object of rescue? What happens when two structures that have been discussed separately in terms of their influence on sexual politics—neoliberalism and Islam—coincide and create new and complex moral regimes that neither theories of neoliberalism nor discussions of Islam and sexuality are equipped to properly address?

Perhaps this is one reason why the burgeoning field of queer studies in Turkey has not engaged with much of the literature on homonationalism or homonormativity. In recent years, a significant number of articles and volumes have appeared that analyze the role of sexualities and genders that fall outside respectable normativities in Turkey.[46] Most of this rich research and writing has focused on various forms of queer and trans subjectivities and identifications, queer (readings of) art and cultural production, and subcultural formations.[47] Thus far the effects of neoliberalism on gender and sexual formations[48] and the intersection of Islam and queer sexualities[49] have not received much attention.[50] This is partially because Turkish sexual liberation movements have not (yet) faced the same challenges of neoliberal incorporation as the ones located in the United States or Western Europe.[51] It is also because as subjects living and theorizing in a Muslim-majority country with an Islamist authoritarian government, these scholars *experience* Islam as a multifaceted, complex, and contradictory formation, as well as very differently from immigrant minorities in US and European contexts.[52] In other words, homonationalism and pinkwashing do not provide the most immediately relevant frameworks for thinking about neoliberalism as experienced in a Muslim-majority country, under an authoritarian rule that heavily relies on Islam as its moralizing discourse.[53]

A newly emerging queer studies literature in the United States analyzes sexual regimes in the Middle East with an eye to biopolitical forms of control.[54] This scholarship decenters US imperialism as the central or only concern, eschews easy formulations of sovereign/nonsovereign, and does not exceptionalize the precarity of queer life, and yet it interrogates the deployment of sexuality in various bio- and necropolitical configurations.[55] Paul Amar, for instance, has shown that sexuality and morality have become parts of the discursive mechanism for the Egyptian human security state.[56] In this refreshing work that thinks about sexual politics without reducing it to identity politics, Amar argues that human security governance aims "to protect, rescue, and secure certain idealized forms of humanity identified with a particular family of sexuality, morality, and class subjects, and grounded in certain militarized territories and strategic infrastructures."[57] Similarly, Sima Shakhsari's work that critiques the emergent neoliberal entrepreneurial

Iranian queer subjects in the post-9/11 North American knowledge market, where narratives of Islamic repression coming from reportedly native informants are highly valuable, disrupts frameworks that would understand Iranian subjects simply as victims of neoliberal modernity.[58]

My work seeks to contribute to this emerging scholarship and to the queer critique of neoliberalism at large by focusing on the Turkish case. I also seek to contribute to the queer and trans studies literatures in Turkey—while thus far questions of neoliberalism and Islam have not occupied the central agenda of this scholarship, how to understand the existing neoliberal authoritarian Islamist AKP regime, how to strategize for resistance, and how to work in solidarity toward inhabitable futures for all are questions with which many, including queer studies scholars and queer activists in Turkey, are grappling. While I position my central intellectual intervention in North American– and Western European–based queer studies, I am hopeful that the stories I unfold here will contribute to queer studies in Turkey by providing relevant and helpful examples of both the dead ends and the possibilities— "ways to imagine different aspirations for our political projects"—that emerge in the cruxes and fissures of the contradictions of neoliberal Islam.[59] I will speak to the particular ways in which the AKP's neoliberal Islam challenges these disparate treatments of neoliberalism and Islam in queer studies below. For now, however, I turn to critical translation studies to lay out the role that language and translation play in this book.

Translation as Queer Methodology

Despite queer studies' commitment to critiquing identity and universalism and the field's recognition of the constitutive powers of language, it is only very recently that queer studies scholars have recognized the English-centeredness of much of the literature.[60] With the exception of categories of sexual identity, such as gay and lesbian, which act as signs of modernity = cultural imperialism par excellence, many of the concepts employed by queer studies, such as affect, temporality, toxicity, failure, or hope (this last one usually as a bad queer theory object), assume an unspoken universality.[61] This is made possible in particular by failing to situate the terms in the English language and, therefore, assuming their translatability both linguistically and metaphorically.[62] Such grounding of linguistic concepts in the materiality of language becomes especially important if we are to follow the queer theoretical proposal that language is not simply an expression or a representation but is constitutive of "the real."[63]

My aim is not only to point out the specificity of English as a language that dominates queer studies' epistemological unconscious over and against other languages but also to underline the homolingual address that queer theory and queer studies inevitably engage in as a result and to invite a re-thinking of the particular theories of language that animate the field. Naoki Sakai maintains that the homolingual address imagines the world made up of communities of languages (a United Nations model of languages, if you will), where languages are supposed to be easily identifiable as autonomous and distinct from each other.[64] As opposed to this unspoken homolingual address that dominates most fields of inquiry and forms the "modern regime of translation," critical translation studies scholars remind us that language, as an object with particular attributes and constituting comparable entities, is itself a historical construct.[65] Linguistic practices without proper names were deemed deviations as a result of Romanticism and disqualified as proper language.[66] Moreover, the nationalization of languages and the formation of what was considered a mother tongue occurred as a result of the formation of nation-states—further establishing monolingualism and reifying the nation and its citizens' relationship to it.[67] A distinct national language worked to establish the nation as authentic,[68] accompanied by the erasure and, at times, ban of indigenous languages or their reduction to dialect.[69] Therefore, it is useful to keep in mind that what we recognize today as languages are them-selves products of a political history of modernity. As a result, arguments that equate the appearance of new names for sexual subjectivity in a particu-lar language (say Turkish) as a colonial effect inevitably naturalize the said national languages as indigenous, thereby erasing the polyglot histories of these spaces as well as ongoing struggles to maintain them, which in the case of Turkey include speakers of Kurdish, Armenian, Circassian, Zazaki, Laz, Greek, Arabic or Serbo-Croatian, and Ladino.[70]

My understanding of language and the use of *translation* to understand the emergence of new sexual and gender idioms in contemporary Turkey owes a great debt to translation studies. Sakai has argued for the past two decades that we need to think about translation as a social practice, thereby undoing the false binary between language and practice.[71] Departing from Sakai's question, "What sort of social relation is translation in the first place?," a number of critical translation studies scholars urge us to question the modern regime of translation and its role in contemporary global capitalist modernity.[72] They suggest that understanding translation as "a transfer of message from one clearly circumscribed language community into another" presumes languages as homogenous and distinguishable entities, between which translation is supposed to act as a filter.[73] Likening this presumed linguistic equivalence to the capitalist equivalence of commodities, Jon Solomon calls this modern system "translational accumulation."[74] Translational accumulation assumes equivalence and commensurability between languages and systems of signs, where linguistic difference, assumed to be a gap, is traversed by translation.[75] The contemporary international system constituted by nation-states is shored up by national languages as markers of national, and presumed cultural, difference. In other words, the modern regime of translation shores up anthropological difference by equating nation, culture, and language—the very structure that makes the universalism/cultural imperialism versus particularism/cultural authenticity double bind possible.

Instead of abandoning translation as a concept and episteme altogether, translation studies scholars suggest that we think of translation as outside the homolingual address, which ahistoricizes and naturalizes languages.[76] What does it mean then to employ translation critically as a lens without repeating the regime of anthropological difference? Following translation theorists, I employ translation as a methodology to think about the question of difference without reproducing the universalism/particularism binary. I suggest that we not use the term to indicate a seamless move from one language to another in order to bridge the linguistic gap and find common ground but, instead, to indicate *social disjunctures*.[77] "Translation can inscribe, erase, and distort borders. . . . [T]ranslation deterritorializes languages and . . . shows most persuasively the unstable, transformative, and political nature of border, of the differentiation of the inside from the outside, and of the multiplicity of belonging and nonbelonging."[78]

This definition of translation led me to look for social disjunctures in the understandings and uses of the concepts I was following—for instance, if not all subjects who employed the term *LGBT rights* meant the same thing when they expressed support for, or objection to, LGBT rights, what kinds of social and political outcomes would such disjunctures have?[79] Using translation as a methodology led me to pay ethnographic attention to various, and at times conflicting, meanings and political positions that the same terms could evoke—such as *sexual orientation*, *gender identity*, *LGBT rights*, *hate crimes*, *homophobia*, and *outness*. This methodology also inevitably complicates the local, which is often homogenized in its opposition to the global. Not only is this a problematic binary because it has mapped onto others, such as colonial versus authentic, but also because it perpetuates the false assumption that careful attention to the particular is an intellectual and a political solution to the homogenizing forces of globalization—which is often understood in critical scholarship as universalism working as cultural imperialism.[80] I join Sakai in cautioning us not to forget that particularism is complicit with universalism.[81] In other words, our critiques of universalism will not go very far if they are invested in producing and sustaining cultural and linguistic particularity. Understanding not only culture but also language as nonstatic, grounded, and historically changing and as a practical human activity that is deeply intertwined with the material production of the world allows us to see that it is precisely in those moments that trouble both the meanings of vocabularies of gender and sexuality and the political regimes that employ them that we can discover productive spaces for thinking and being otherwise. Understanding how new forms of oppressive systems coalesce and erode our capacities to *think* of a different world is crucial not only to grasp the power of language and knowledge but also to start imagining life differently.

Therefore, emphasizing the English-centeredness of queer studies in a study of the travel and translation of concepts of nonnormative genders and sexualities is *not* to ask for a heightened linguistic sensitivity, an invitation to remember that English is not the only language through which subjects are constituted and make sense of their experiences (and with which scholars make sense of the world).[82] Such an emphasis would mean that we should consider how vocabulary in different languages might inform different ways of knowing and being, which always risks repeating the homolingual address, thus leading to a problematic nativism and cultural relativism against which transnational feminists have long warned us.[83] This is because the (national) language as a unified entity of the homolingual address works as a key mechanism of the production of cultural particularity and because (cultural) particularity is co-constitutive with universalism. Thus, my emphasis on the English-centeredness of queer theory is instead an invitation for queer studies to consider *how homolingualism has shaped its epistemological unconscious* and to start thinking about language heterolingually as well as historically.

On the one hand, the homolingual address informs queer studies' unquestioning equation of (national) language with (national) culture (if there is no indigenous vocabulary of X somewhere, X must not be indigenous to their culture) and erases the political histories of linguistic erasures and suturing. On the other, the Foucauldian theory of modernity posits subjectivity as the key marker of modernity and thus the existence of modern (linguistic) categories of identity as the marker of colonial erasure of authentic culture.[84] I return to this focus on sexual subjectivity over other markers of modernity in the conclusion, but for now I ask: What if we think of language not simply as textual and constitutive but as historically changing and practical human activity?[85] If we follow the translation studies insight that we accept every address as requiring an act of translation (and not assume that communication automatically happens between two subjects who share the same linguistic community), then translation as an episteme indeed interrupts Foucauldian discourse, which dispenses with the hermeneutic dimension of understanding.[86] In other words, understanding language as a historical, practical human activity helps us think about whether certain addresses arrive at all but also about *how* exactly those addresses arrive at their destination.[87] Understanding language as practical human activity helps us both consider discourses in action/practice and not project language beyond history.[88] Further, language as a practical human activity enables us not to neglect the issue of access to language, which is often a deeply classed (and in many occasions a racialized) matter. The move away from an emphasis on sexual subjectivity as *the* determinant of modernity also provides a way to think about collectivities, solidarities, and social change.

Well over a decade ago, David Eng, Jack Halberstam, and José Esteban Muñoz stated:

> Such a politics must recognize that much of contemporary queer scholarship emerges from U.S. institutions and is largely written in English. This fact indicates a problematic dynamic between U.S. scholars whose work in queer studies is read in numerous sites around the world. Scholars writing in other languages and from other political and cultural perspectives read, but are not, in turn, read. These uneven exchanges replicate in uncomfortable ways the rise and consolidation of U.S. empire, as well as the insistent positing of a U.S. nationalist identity and political agenda globally. We propose epistemological humility as one form of knowledge production that recognizes these dangers.[89]

While the invitation to epistemological humility is most welcome, queer studies can go further than to merely reproduce the same center, though this time with humility. One way to do this is by bringing translation studies to bear on queer studies, which can have the effect of finally rendering queer studies more heterolingual. This would complicate the various coarticulations of sexual epistemologies with colonialism, imperialism, or neoliberal capitalism as they are currently imagined to happen both within and through English-language terminology as well as homolingually. What ethnography can contribute to the effect translation studies can have on queer studies is to complicate the local and thereby prevent reductions of the local to the cultural and to the linguistic. Such reductionist accounts themselves always already rest on assumptions about the unity of national languages and the historical erasures that have followed from them—dynamics that queer studies has always been committed to dismantling.

Below I outline key features of the AKP's neoliberal Islam in order to show the impossibility of understanding Islam in today's Turkey as pure, authentic, victimized, or alternative to Western modernity. It is also not possible to understand it as singular or as disentangled from neoliberalism. I trace the historical links between neoliberalism and Turkish moderate Islam, which is increasingly being used by the AKP regime to justify growing inequalities and precarities by producing immoral others. This will help us see why frameworks of homonationalism or homonormativity fall short in capturing the relationship between sexual liberation movements in Turkey and neoliberal Islam.

The Rise of the AKP and the Moral Politics of Neoliberal Islam

Lest readers think that the marriage of neoliberalism with Islam is an AKP invention, it is important to note that the introduction of neoliberalism *and* a particular public moderate Islam to Turkey both date to the military coup of September 12, 1980.[90] While the economic liberalization program of Turkey had been devised several months prior to the coup, the military junta was central to ensuring the continuity of the economic reform package known as the January 24th Decisions. Up until then, the Turkish economy had been a state-led, closed-market system with an emphasis on national production and consumption combined with strict import regulations. The military coup not only enforced the beginnings of the neoliberalization of the economy through IMF- and World Bank–supported structural adjustment policies, but it also preempted any organized resistance to this process by banning many forms of political organizing, including by labor unions, and jailing union leaders.[91] Turkey as a result became one of the key testing grounds for the joint IMF–World Bank approach.[92]

If economic neoliberalization was one significant outcome of the 1980 coup, its other key effect was the introduction of Islam and, more specifically, what was referred to as *Türk-İslam sentezi* (Turkish-Islamic synthesis) as a social glue, a remedy to political rifts in the country.[93] This remedy was intended to end the political divisions between communists and the fascist ultra-Right that had escalated to a violent conflict at the time, especially in order to replace "the left-wing ideas and discourse of Turkey's youth with a more cohesive religious culture."[94] This move was also done in conjunction with the US war against the perceived communist threat and ultimately led to the crushing of the Left and the strengthening of the center Right in Turkey. Yet the project of Turkish-Islamic synthesis that aimed at the Islamicization of public and social life had to be carefully managed. This was due to both the military-backed *laiklik* (Turkish secularism; from the French *laïcité*) principle of the constitution and the necessity of preventing Islam's radicalization, as in the Iranian case.[95] In fact, during this period the success of the Iranian Revolution resulted in the United States' encouragement of liberal Islamist projects all over the Middle East.[96] In this context, "in sharp contrast to the leftist overtone of Islam in Iran (led by Shariati), Islamism in Turkey developed along with an expanding free market."[97] With support from the 1980s government, the military encouraged the building of mosques and the expansion of religious education. Mandatory religious education was added to public school curricula in 1980. In the decade following the elections in 1983, the Turkish government opened 124 new preacher schools. Between 1973 and 1999 the number of mosques in Turkey increased by 66 percent with the construction of 29,848 new mosques.[98] Religious orders and brotherhoods also boosted their activities in this period, setting up Quran courses; reading groups; charity foundations; women's, youth, and mutual-support associations; and student dormitories.[99] Thus it is impossible to understand Islam in contemporary Turkey apart from these histories of de-leftification and de-radicalization.[100]

Also referred to as the Turkish model, Islamic liberalism in Turkey—the "marriage of formal democracy, free-market capitalism, and a (toned down) conservative Islam"—took off especially in the 1990s as a result of the failure of center-Right parties to address problems of the urban poor as well as the intensifying war between the Turkish Armed Forces and the Kurdish guerrilla PKK (Kurdistan Workers' Party) starting in 1994.[101] In a country where the Left was severely dismantled after the 1980 coup, both of these developments contributed to the weakening of the center-Right, paving the way for Islamist parties on the right to rise to power. The first major success of Islamist parties during this period, the triumph of the RP (Welfare Party) in the 1994 municipal elections followed by their success in the 1995 general elections, was due to their political discourse that emphasized social justice, critiqued pro-West big business and the capitalist banking system, and effectively delivered much-needed services, in addition to their Islamist discourse.[102] The party's municipal governments were lauded not only for their efficiency but also for their commitment to aiding the urban poor living in proliferating *gecekondu* (squatter) neighborhoods without proper infrastructure, lacking access to jobs with decent pay and benefits.[103] Recep Tayyip Erdoğan's performance as the successful and charismatic mayor of Istanbul during the early RP government, delivering roads, bridges, green spaces, and, in some cases, jobs set him up as a promising political candidate to run the country—especially in the context of a neoliberal understanding of politics as "a technocratic endeavor: rational, sterile, and free from the messiness of ideology and ideological struggles."[104] When the military forced Prime Minister Necmettin Erbakan to resign in 1997 and banned him from formal politics for five years, citing growing Islamist insurgency, Erdoğan emerged as the undisputed new leader of Islamist politics.[105]

In 2001 Erdoğan formed the AKP, which came to power in the 2002 elections as the first single-party government following a series of failed coalitions, and at the tail of the major 2001 economic crisis.[106] The young leadership of AKP positioned the new party as democratic, secular, pro-Western, pro-state, and pro-capitalist, and the neoliberalization of the country sped up under AKP leadership.[107] Unlike the previous Welfare Party–led coalition, AKP wholeheartedly embraced and followed the IMF- and World Bank–induced austerity measures, and within the first several years of the new government Turkey experienced significant economic growth.[108] The party also discursively solidified its (neo)liberal position by distancing itself from military rule and by rhetorically aligning the Kemalist raison d'état with military authoritarianism and a closed-market economy. This position implied that (military) violence, authoritarianism, and lack of freedom rested with the statist economy of the Kemalist era and that the AKP-led neoliberal economy equaled freedom and was made possible by its non-militaristic/non-fascist/nonauthoritarian regime. As I detail in chapter 4, in his speeches Erdoğan frequently aligned himself with the two prime ministers who have been key liberalizers of the economy, Turgut Özal in the 1980s and Adnan Menderes in the 1950s, creating a genealogy of economic liberalism as progress. He also narrated the progress of the Turkish economy as historically under attack by forces he claimed were plotting against the nation.

AKP distinguished itself from previous Islamist governments not only in its alliance with Western big business but also in its acceleration of the EU accession process by passing packages of laws to fulfill the Copenhagen criteria.[109] A significant early legislative overhaul resulted in changes to the penal code, including the removal of references to such concepts as morality, chastity, honor, or virginity; the criminalization of marital rape; and the recategorization of sexual assault under crimes against the individual instead of crimes against public morality.[110] Capital punishment, which has strong historical ties to military coups in Turkey, was banned.[111] The AKP's discourse of democracy also delved into ethnic rights. Despite the government's failure to prevent the assassination of Armenian-Turkish journalist Hrant Dink and even though the nationalist faction within the party had blocked the first attempt to hold a conference on the Armenian genocide, at the time my fieldwork began in summer 2008, the Kurdish opening, the Armenian opening, and the Alevi opening were all important discussion items on the national agenda.[112] There was also talk of a headscarf opening that would allow women to wear the Islamic headscarf in public universities and offices, which was outlawed at the time.

It was in this climate, and under the AKP, that the LGBT pride march, which had been held annually starting in 2001, grew significantly in size. In summer 2008 the AKP was in the midst of their democratic openings and showed no signs of the authoritarianism, rampant privatization, and precaritization of life and labor that would follow. As previously noted, their policies were initially welcomed by many Turkish Left-leaning liberals. And while such moves as the Kurdish opening were indeed reminiscent of political strategies that have been critiqued as the multicultural incorporation of difference in Euro-American contexts, in a country where uttering the Kurdish language in the parliament had led to deputy Leyla Zana's ten-year imprisonment, the AKP's diversity politics were hard to dismiss.

Thus, the picture at the start of my research was of a moderate Islamist party that was pro-West, pro-business, and fully in compliance with the IMF and the World Bank, as well as EU demands, and of an LGBT movement that was flourishing. This was not an uncomplicated terrain, however; in fact, in chapter 1 I detail the complex entanglements of the headscarf opening with LGBT rights in ways that foreclosed the establishment of alliances among activists. Nevertheless, it was a hopeful atmosphere and, according to several LGBT activists, a welcome change from the center-Left Cumhuriyet Halk Partisi (CHP; Republican People's Party). These activists found CHP to be staunchly secularist (*laïcist*), which, among other things, meant that the party had relied on the Turkish military purportedly to protect democracy, including in the form of military coups. The strong anti-militarism of LGBT activists contributed to their alignment with AKP, as the party not only ended capital punishment (which, as noted, is strongly associated in Turkey with military coups), but it also expressed the desire to transform the nation's culture of military custody.

If AKP's cooperation with the EU, the IMF, and the World Bank is one reason for the impossibility of understanding Islam in contemporary Turkey through a romanticized notion of the local and as disentangled from a transnational political economy, another one can be found in the AKP's neoliberal packaging of Islamic difference in the 2007, UN-backed neoliberal branding project Alliance of Civilizations. Islamic civilization has been proposed as a true alternative to Western civilization by Ahmet Davutoğlu, one of the masterminds behind the AKP, who has served in various high-ranking positions, including chief adviser to PM Erdoğan, minister of foreign affairs, and prime minister.[113] The Alliance of Civilizations project sought to promote "tolerance, respect, dialogue and cooperation" in the global fight against terrorism, turning the clash of civilizations logic on its head while nonetheless relying on the same neat distinctions between East and West and reifying an ahistorical culture of each.[114]

A number of scholars have analyzed the various economic and social effects of neoliberalism in Turkey: from the privatization of various public goods, such as telecommunications, petrochemicals, and other industries, to the weakening of labor unions, the rise of informal and precarious labor, the shrinking of social security and pension systems, the transformation and incorporation of radical Islamists into a neoliberal mold, and the Islamic charity fixation on social welfare.[115] I return to these issues in greater detail in chapters 3 and 4, when I analyze the intense privatization and urban redevelopment under AKP-led neoliberalism as well as the moralization and securitization of the revolts against them. Here I will briefly provide a couple of examples of how the economy, security, and Islamic morality are woven together in order to lay out the terrain on which the sexual politics detailed in the following chapters unfolded. These examples illustrate what I consider to be the two key distinctions of the morality politics of the AKP's neoliberal Islam. For one, the binaries evoked and utilized by neoliberalism (deserving/undeserving; legitimate/illegitimate; morally upright/questionable; responsible/irresponsible) are animated by an alleged Islamic morality. For another, using this vocabulary of Islamic morality, the AKP has extended the meaning of marginality onto a wide range of bodies and subjectivities instead of limiting it to the lower ranks of society, a development that has had an important impact on how the politics of normality is understood and countered in Turkey.

As discussed at the beginning of this introduction, between 2008 and 2015 Turkey went from supporting a growing LGBT movement to attacking participants at the 2015 pride march. Then, in 2016, both the trans and the

LGBT marches were banned, and anyone who tried to participate was again met with police violence and detentions. Security measures were not only applied to the pride march and LGBT events—security emerged as an overarching framework through which increasing precarities resulting from rapid privatization and financialization were to be contained. Those suspected to be security threats to the nation and the national economy, which are often conflated in the AKP's rhetoric, were also rendered as *morally* suspect. For instance, during the Gezi Park uprisings, in his attempts to delegitimize the protesters, Erdoğan wrongfully claimed that they had entered the Dolmabahçe Mosque with shoes on and had drunk beer inside.[116]

I write about the employment of Islamic morality in order to securitize and contain the Gezi Park uprisings in more detail in chapter 4. For now, I note that Gezi provides a perfect example of how the logic of the market, the logic of security, and the discourse of Islamic morality (often proposed as national values) are openly tied together in AKP officials' and especially Erdoğan's rhetoric. This connection serves to reinforce economic obligations as well as economic betrayals as deeply moral ones.[117] This was evident in pro-AKP media as well as in the rhetoric of AKP politicians claiming that Gezi constituted a movement started by innocent environmentalists who wanted to protect the park but was taken over by anti-government political factions that provoked everyone in the squares and the streets to demand the government's resignation. By positioning those critical of the government as simultaneously *morally* and *politically* suspect, the government's rhetoric collapsed the two categories, delegitimized the political demands of the demonstrators, and justified the securitization of the protests. At the same time, it was precisely this *morality* politics that expanded the meaning of marginality to cover ever-expanding crowds that helped many previously disparate groups see the links between their marginalization and oppression and to reject the government's call to respectability.

Inderpal Grewal has argued that contrary to arguments that neoliberalism has waned, we are experiencing a more "advanced" stage of it, which "enables its contradictions to be resolved by neoliberal and militarized means, that is, through the work of securitized, exceptional citizens."[118] Following Grewal, I suggest that if neoliberal capitalism is a system that produces increasing precarity for larger groups of people (through the disappearance of the middle class, the rise of surplus existence, the disappearing of welfare and related social safety nets, the rising dispossession and indebtedness, and the crushing of labor unions), and if it justifies such inequality via moralizing mechanisms (the categorization of deserving versus undeserving, the rise of respectability politics, the increasing individualization of responsibility, and an emphasis on self-sufficiency and self-entrepreneurialism), then in the case of Turkey, Islamic morality factors as the key mechanism through which neoliberalism is "domesticated"[119] and through which the government distinguishes between the deserving and the undeserving, the good moral citizens and the bad immoral elements conspiring with foreign powers for the government's downfall, and between those who need to be securitized and those who will assist in that securitization. Similar to Grewal's "exceptional citizens" in the United States, in chapter 3 I discuss the employment of "deep citizens" in Turkey, those who help impose state ideologies of morality and execute violence on behalf of the state.[120]

At the same time, I am not arguing that securitization constitutes a brand-new state logic or practice in Turkey. In fact, the language of terrorism and the Turkish state's war against Kurds have been ongoing for over three decades. Under neoliberalism, however, old forms of securitization are in fact garnering new neoliberal logics. Security is marketed to populations not only through the old discourses of national unity but also as a necessity when the national economy is under attack—this line of reasoning is especially applicable to economies that rely on foreign investment and tourism and, thus, political stability. In a system of market veridiction, where the robust economy already tells us that AKP is the right government for Turkey, this weaving together of economy and security implies that protecting the economy might also require protecting the Turkish government and vice versa. In other words, the fight against Kurds or any other so-called terrorists or lobbies is now a national duty not simply for security for security's sake but so that the Turkish economy will continue to prosper.

As AKP continues to discursively nationalize and moralize the economy, it continues to privatize public goods. When citizens object to such privatization they are deemed enemies of the state, which is no different from being enemies of the national economy and of religion. They are not only traitors seeking the downfall of the nation, and therefore questionable national subjects; they also are declared morally suspect, where the contours of morality are weaved with a formal and generic understanding of Islam (indicated by such actions as taking one's shoes off upon entering a mosque and not drinking alcohol inside). This weaving together of the economy and Islamic morality are also illustrated in instances of Erdoğan attributing the deaths of hundreds of miners at the Soma mine explosion not to unsafe labor conditions, but to the *fitrat* (Allah-given nature) of mining. *Fitrat* also served to remind feminists, who protested Erdoğan's claim that women who are not mothers are incomplete, that it was in the *fitrat* of womanhood to bear children.[121] His continued demand that all families bear at least three children was simultaneously explained by the God-given nature of womanhood *and* Turkey's need for a young population for a strong economy. At the same time the Turkish state continues to kill Kurdish children, who are imagined as future impediments to the Turkish economy and therefore a threat to the state, Turkish mothers are invited to bear children for the future of the same Turkish economy as good national subjects, but also as good Muslims, who are told by Erdoğan not to worry about finances, as Allah will provide the *rızık* (livelihood) of every child.[122]

Despite Turkey's attempts to brand its Ottoman past as well as its current moment as a tolerant civilization throughout which different ethnic and religious groups peacefully live side by side, Kurds are joined today by many others in the securitized category of the terrorist.[123] During the AKP's seventeen-year reign, various political groups have been charged with terrorism, which has only intensified since the July 2016 coup attempt. Among those deemed terrorists, in addition to political Kurds, are those who speak up against the state violence targeting Kurds, such as Academics for Peace, and also the radical Left, Gülenist religious Right, as well as various members of the military, the judiciary, and the education sector. As of April 2020, the government had arrested over 90,000 people and purged 150,348 civil servants.[124] Among those cast out as unrespectable, immoral subjects are women who seek abortions or refuse motherhood, women who laugh out loud in public, students living in coed housing, bachelors, citizens who consume alcohol or tobacco, journalists who critique the government, and anyone deemed to be in opposition to Erdoğan's rule. This deployment of marginality through discourses of terrorism *and* immorality is continually justified by the rhetoric of Turkey's strong economy, which is under national and international attack and demands the securitization of those elements seeking its downfall.

I am not arguing that this expansion of marginality is unique to Turkey. The world is experiencing a rise in authoritarian and fascist regimes in which premises of liberalism and respectability as usual no longer apply.[125] What I offer instead is an invitation to hear the stories that follow as illustrative of complex contradictions of neoliberalism in general and of neoliberal Islam in particular. These contradictions at times perpetuate the regimes that produce them and at others interrupt them. The stories that follow illustrate the complex and occasionally unexpected outcomes of such expanding characterizations, as they focus on the shifting meanings of morality and marginalization in relationship to the state and the economy. They also demonstrate that neither LGBT activists' initial excitement about the AKP and their democratic openings nor their subsequent alienation from and critique of its conservative, authoritarian, and racist rule can be understood through colonial mimicry or the frameworks of Islamophobia or homonationalism. Finally, it is worth noting that the Turkish model is not representative of all of the operating logics of various forms of neoliberal Islam. I suggest, however, that there are lessons to be learned from this case about why it might matter to contextualize both neoliberalism and Islam, even as theory (queer or otherwise) might entice us toward abstraction.

Queer in Translation

When I embarked on this project in 2008, many of the current political realities of Erdoğan's regime were either nonexistent or nascent and barely recognizable. LGBT political organizing was vibrant; new solidarity associations were forming all over the country and not just in urban centers. Political, or personal, disagreements between different organizations never seemed to get in the way of solidarity. The pride march, with an entire week of events leading up to it, seemed to attract larger crowds every year. It is only fair to say that, under those circumstances, I did not set out to study neoliberal Islam, inasmuch as it was not yet a term widely used by scholars to talk about the political regime in contemporary Turkey. Interested in queer political organizing, I had set out to analyze how LGBT activists understood their political goals and commitments. As I quickly realized, understanding queer politics required coming to terms with the effects that newly emerging vocabularies were having on the articulation of political imaginaries and desires. Thus, I followed not one organization but events and cases that emerged while I was in the field that told stories of how vocabularies such as LGBT rights, gender identity, sexual orientation, homophobia, and hate crimes were used in public and political discussions. As a result, each of the chapters features a case study tracing the translation of these idioms and showing that translation as a transnational queer methodology can help us analyze the social disjunctures that at times are produced and at other times heightened by the emergence of new vocabularies. The particular debates that unfold in each chapter are also inevitably affected by and thus shed light on how Islam and neoliberalism are conjoined in contemporary Turkey.[126]

My first summer of fieldwork also was the beginning of Turkish government officials making references to demands by LGBT organizations. In chapter 1, "Subjects of Rights and Subjects of Cruelty," I trace the terms

LGBT *rights* and *homophobia* as they began to be voiced in public political debates; also at that time, the headscarf issue was being debated as a woman's human right rather than a religious right, an aspect of the various liberal openings the AKP was introducing as part of the EU accession process. These liberal human rights discourses ultimately worked to position Muslim headscarf activists against LGBT activists by confronting the former over whether they supported LGBT rights, thereby testing their sincerity in claiming their own human rights. By rendering their complex positions—which did not follow an easy for-or-against (LGBT rights) political formula—as homophobic, these debates foreclosed solidarities between headscarf activists and LGBT activists in protesting increased neoliberal state violence. Thus, I show that even dominant and universalizing discourses such as human rights are not something to which every subject who decides to engage with them is granted equal access (the right to claim human rights is not equally distributed, if you will). At the same time, Muslim women's positions on the issue of LGBT rights ultimately illuminate that it is not only human rights discourses but also their Western critiques that travel transnationally in these debates. Finally, I discuss the potential of what I call a *politics of cruelty*, whereby subjects *oppose* cruelty as an alternative framework for social justice to liberal rights–based politics. I do not romanticize this view as a perfect solution, especially because, as I show, the question of the current relationship between the state, public space, and religion are shot through with modern and liberal understandings of these terms not only for secular but, also, Muslim subjects.

Another story that erupted during that first summer and that unfolded in complex and unpredictable ways was the murder of a twenty-six-year-old gay man, Ahmet Yıldız. Following the story of his murder introduced me to the bear subculture of İstanbul, of which Ahmet had been a participant. Chapter 2, "Who Killed Ahmet Yıldız?," examines the travel of the concepts of *outness* and *chosen families* through the story of Ahmet's murder. I show that the positioning of Ahmet's life as an unfulfilled desire for an out-and-proud existence and his murder as an honor killing worked to nationally reify the Eastern Kurdish regions of the country as feudal and traditional and traveled internationally to tell the story of what happens to gay people in backward Muslim countries. These narratives in turn relegate family violence to geographies imagined as Muslim and uphold both Western family romance and the myth of the West as a location of stranger danger. Turning to the only witness of the murder case, a Muslim single mother, reveals other sexual others of the Turkish state who are not easily folded into the neoliberal logic of minority groups needing protection. It also reveals alternative Muslim approaches to homosexuality and sin that are not encountered in transnational gay accounts of the story. Finally, I use Ahmet's story to problematize the newsworthiness of the eventful death of a young gay Kurdish man and the valorization of gay (Kurdish) lives in the context of slow deaths that have been and continue to be administered to many Kurdish citizens all over the country by the neoliberal Sunni state.

There may have been no better witnesses than trans sex workers to two important transformations introduced by neoliberal Islam in Turkey: urban redevelopment projects and transformation of the police force. Chapter 3, "Trans Terror, Deep Citizenship, and the Politics of Hate," traces the travel of the term *hate crime* by focusing on the spatial exclusion of transvestite and transsexual sex workers from public space; it also demonstrates how changes in the police treatment of sex workers speak to larger changes in national politics. In addition, it shows how violence against trans sex workers illuminates a new relationship that is mediated by the state, citizens, and violence. Both this new relationship, which I call *deep citizenship*, and the demands of trans women sex workers for a hate crime law challenge current theories that fail to see how a neoliberal state does not always concentrate the means of violence. Understanding *hate* as a structuring element of neoliberal Islam that renders lives precarious, trans women seek not to punish individual haters but to use the term as a means of understanding vulnerabilities as shared, collective realities. They also understand hate as a mirror of the logic of terror, a mechanism of rendering subjects as criminal and monstrous, which I show has extended from so-called Kurdish terror, leftist terror, and transvestite terror in the 1990s to much larger publics today. Holding an investment in life and a divestment from hope together in tension, trans women's analyses demonstrate that asking for legal change can have meanings beyond the purchase of respectability politics on citizen-subjects.

In chapter 4, "Critique and Commons under Neoliberal Islam," I return to the question of possibilities for political solidarities and resistance. One of the first things that struck me as I started my research was how politically knowledgeable and savvy LGBT activists were regarding the global political economy and neoliberal funding structures yet still reproduced class divisions that were not necessarily accounted for by neoliberal notions of respectability. Focusing on the tensions between LGBT activists and the clients of a women-only (and mostly queer) bar, I show how the thing that was experienced as a political/apolitical divide between activist and non-activist LGBT groups in Istanbul was in fact a *class divide* based on cultural capital and informed by the travel of Western theories on *gender identity* and *sexual orientation*. I juxtapose this moment of failed coalition building with the solidarity LGBT activists and non-activists established during Gezi Park uprisings in 2013, when many citizen-subjects were officially cast as unrespectable others. Rejecting the neoliberal Islamic state in its call for conservative consumer respectability, and turning the park into a commons for several weeks, helped queer and non-queer subjects move past class, ethnic, and religious divides to imagine new ways of living together. It also resulted in new ways of understanding past divisions as produced by structures that worked not for, but against, the people. I contrast these two cases of the relationship of apolitical subjects to politics to point out both the limits of critique as a Left political mode of engagement and to emphasize the promises and potential of the commons. While I underscore the limits of the Gezi commons in accounting for the larger effects of class, I end by recognizing the political potential of this imperfect collectivity in resistance for redefining life to make it worth living.

One

Subjects of Rights and
Subjects of Cruelty

On March 7, 2010, the Turkish daily *Hürriyet* ran a profile on Selma Aliye Kavaf, then the AKP's head of the Ministry of Women and Family Affairs, to honor International Women's Day.[1] Published under the heading "Homosexuality Is an Illness, and It Should Be Cured," the piece opened with journalist Faruk Bildirici's note that he had felt obliged to do a profile on the minister ever since her first public statements about feeling irritated by seeing sex scenes on TV shows. It then summarized Kavaf's life under thirteen headers, ranging from her family background to her work experience, from previous political engagements to personal inspirations and her marriage. Her conservative politics were underlined throughout the page, exemplified in her admiration for Margaret Thatcher as well as in her critique of women's rights NGOs, which the minister found to be too quick to call any and all men's behavior abuse. Yet the heading "Sexual Orientation" stood out compared to the rest. "I believe that homosexuality is a biological degeneracy, an illness," the minister claimed. "I think it is something that should be cured. Therefore, I do not approve [of] homosexual marriages. There is no work being done about them [homosexuals] in our ministry. Neither have we received any requests. We are not saying there are no homosexuals in Turkey. These cases exist."[2]

Constituting the first public declaration by a minister of the Turkish Republic that homosexuality is an illness—an announcement exacerbated by the fact that this small section of the interview evoked the headline of the entire profile—this news report created a moment the nation had never before experienced. What followed next, however, was perhaps even more unexpected: After some initial criticisms targeting the statement, on March 21, 2010, a group of Islamic NGOs publicly read an open letter expressing their support for Minister Kavaf.[3] While this endorsement, signed by 21 associations and an umbrella organization comprising another 160 groups, might have been somewhat less surprising in the later years of the AKP government, during its first term the party had tried to distance itself from previous Islamist parties (see the introduction). At the time of Kavaf's interview, government officials rarely referenced Islam in their discourses. As a result, while the minister's statement raised questions about the place of homosexuality in national politics, the reaction of the NGOs, many of which had formed as Islamic human rights associations, extended the debate to the place of homosexuality and of democratic rights in Islam.

What had incited the minister to make such an unexpected statement and compelled these NGOs to publicly endorse it? Although LGBT activists had presented a petition stating that gender identity and sexual orientation should be included in the new constitution's antidiscrimination clause as part of the AKP's various democratic openings, the issue of homosexuality did not seem to be anywhere on the AKP agenda. Neither was it anywhere on the agendas of the listed NGOs, which had been formed in the late 1990s to overturn the headscarf ban for students at public universities and employers in all public offices. In this chapter I will recount the events leading up to Kavaf's statement to analyze this particular incitement to discourse. Paying attention to the disjunctures produced by the translation of LGBT rights to the context of Turkey, I will highlight the failures of neoliberal incorporation of difference in the case of Turkish headscarf rights and LGBT rights. Such disjunctures resulted not only along what may be expected lines between secularists and Islamists, or LGBT activists and headscarf activists, but also among Muslim activists themselves over the meanings of justice, cruelty, and rights in the context of difference, thereby revealing increasingly transnationalized understandings of all of these terms and undoing the presumed stability of the local against a totalizing global. Instead of debating the presumed colonial effects versus the authenticity of LGBT rights discourses, I argue that analyzing the uses of LGBT rights in the context of neoliberal Islam makes it possible to highlight not only the existing divergences but also various foreclosed solidarities between headscarf and LGBT activists.

I show that the equivalence established between LGBT rights and the headscarf right through a human rights framework in the context of Islamist AKP's neoliberal multiculturalism and democratic openings and against the historical background of staunch secularism, ultimately led to the treatment of LGBT rights as a litmus test for headscarf activists—a test promoted by suspicious secularists to see whether the commitment of headscarf activists to democratic rights and liberties was sincere and thus to establish whether they deserved their own democratic rights. A reduction of these events to the question of what Islam thinks about homosexuality is deeply misguided, as this chapter will illustrate. This is both because the transnational economic and political developments at the time, especially the EU accession process, deeply shaped these discourses and because various Islamic actors and headscarf activists displayed differing views on the issue of homosexual rights. At the same time, framing the series of events as a product of discursive colonialism and its associated epistemic violence is equally misguided. This is because it was not only LGBT activists but also headscarf activists who used a rights framework to discuss particular incidences of state and social violence taking place at the time. In fact, as we will see, even the criticisms leveled against this framework as not being the proper Islamic reaction employed hybrid arguments of Islamic authenticity, on the one hand, and poststructuralist critique and queer theory, on the other. I do not make this last point to discredit these interventions as inauthentic or insincere but to underline the obvious limits of authenticity as an evaluative framework in modern neoliberal societies.

In fact, as the following pages will show, sincerity itself—as a form of authenticity—worked as a political category and was used to call into question the commitment of headscarf activists to justice for all. I illustrate that sincerity emerges in this context not simply as a secular management of religious piety to ensure its proper containment within the depoliticized private realm but also as a framework that calls into question the religious sincerity of headscarf activists by emphasizing the importance in Islam of justice for all. As some secularist thinkers, journalists, and politicians questioned whether headscarf activists were "Muslims to themselves" (*kendine Müslüman*) only, they married political sincerity with religious sincerity by calling into question the commitment of Muslim headscarf activists to democratic rights *and* to an accurate understanding of Islam. I maintain that instead of selectively questioning the sincerity of political subjects, listening carefully to the voices that failed to support LGBT rights without rushing to deem them homophobic opens up room to think about social justice in different terms. More specifically, I investigate the political promises and limits of the discourse emergent at the time that emphasized *opposition against* cruelty toward all, over and against *support for* abstract liberal rights. While I show a number of merits of a politics of cruelty that could work to forge solidarities between differently targeted social groups by state violence, I also emphasize that contemporary interpretations of Islam that arose during the debates on homosexuality leave unanswered important questions about the public/private divide. As I will discuss, the question of the secular privatization of religion needs to be put in conversation with contemporary articulations of Islam in a world already divided into public and private spheres.[4] These debates showcase the limits of both a purely secular and a purely Islamic response to the issue of state violence and demand a historicized approach to both categories. I suggest that this task proves to be exceedingly important given increasing violence in Turkey perpetrated by a government that justifies its actions in the name of Islamic morality and consolidates its voter base with a discourse of standing up for believers.

Turkish Secularity and Modernity

In order to understand the headscarf debates that unfolded in Turkey in the period from 2008 through 2010, we need to briefly revisit the historical significance of *laïcité* (secularism) in Turkey and the special role the headscarf was made to play in this history. The Turkish Republic is a Muslim-majority, constitutionally secular country, founded in 1923 as the descendant of the Ottoman Empire. The nation was founded after a quarter century of political turmoil in the region, a lost world war, a period of occupation by the Allied Forces, and a war of independence that led to the formation of the republic by the military leader Mustafa Kemal Atatürk and his cadre. "Reaching the level of contemporary civilizations" was the overarching goal of this newly established republic as set forth by Atatürk, and what was meant by "contemporary civilizations" was European civilization.[5] This goal was to be achieved through a series of fundamental reforms in the political, social, and cultural realms of the new nation-state.

Many of these reforms aimed at shrinking Islam's centrality to the cultural and social fabric of the nation as a way to erase old forms of authority associated with the Ottoman Empire.[6] They included such changes as the secularization of the country through the removal of the caliphate—the spiritual leadership of the Muslim world that had resided with the Ottoman Empire since 1517—and the outlawing of *tekke* and *zaviye* (religious orders) and their leaders; changing the alphabet from Arabic to Latin; changing from the Islamic calendar and the old weights and measures to Western ones; reorganizing the work week, such as shifting the official day off from Friday (the day of collective prayer at mosques) to Sunday in order to become compatible with the Western business world; strongly encouraging a Western "civilized" dress code; and secularizing, centralizing, and nationalizing education.[7] These reforms of the public space cast the nation's other mostly as its Islamic past. Not only were many of the reforms targeted at changing the Islamic ways of governing, dressing, educating, and living (implying that they were unfit for the modern world), but they also identified an open enemy/traitor. During the war of independence (1919–23), the last sultan-caliph had reached an agreement with the occupying forces to destroy the Kemalist resistance then building up in Anatolia. In 1920 the sultan asked the şeyhülislam[8] to issue a fatwa declaring holy war against the insurgents, which helped situate Islam of the center as a key enemy of Kemalist nationalism. Yet Atatürk did not stop at condemning the sultan-caliph and the şeyhülislam; he also took an uncompromising position against popular Islam, furthering a double-casting of Islam as the other: While Islam of the center represented treason, popular Islam was cast as backward, and religious sects called *tarikats* were cast as centers of superstition, passivity, and laziness that were standing in the way of enlightened modernization and progress.[9]

The rhetoric of civilization played a key role in justifying the desirability of all these changes, and as with many other nation-building projects, the emancipation of women was cast as a key marker of the level of civilization attained by the republic. Atatürk was adamant about civilizing women, even more than he was about civilizing men. Women's suffrage, a secular dress code, women's increased access to the public sphere, including institutions of education and the labor force, are listed among important accomplishments of the new regime.[10] In brief, the construction of a national identity in Turkey by partially overwriting Islam combined with positioning the so-called republican woman as the ultimate symbol of the civilized new nation doubly positions women who embrace an Islamic life, choose to cover their heads, and critique the secular state as a failure of the national project and as the ultimate terror of the republic. Turkish feminists have produced important criticisms of this era's gains for women (referring to it as state feminism) and have unearthed the Kemalist government's lack of support for independent feminist organizing during the early years of the republic. However, their analyses for a long time did not extend to questioning the symbolic burden of the headscarf and the institutional barriers experienced by women who veil.[11] The secular rhetoric surrounding women with headscarves in Turkey continued to cast them as either naive victims of their oppressive male kin or as terrorist minds/bodies working to replace the secular order with an Islamic one.[12]

Yet the Turkish headscarf problem started taking its contemporary shape when, in 1987, it was officially banned from being worn on public university campuses and when, on February 28, 1997, the ban began to be more strictly enforced. In February 1997 the National Security Council identified the headscarf as one of the main indicators of what the councilor referred to as the Islamic threat and called for the enforcement of the headscarf ban in public spaces, including public schools and offices as well as universities. It was during this period that Virtue Party deputy Merve Kavakçı entered the parliament wearing a headscarf and was forcefully removed from the building, ultimately losing her Turkish citizenship.[13] In 1997 Necmettin Erbakan, who was then prime minister and leader of the Islamist RP (Welfare Party), was forced to resign by the armed forces. One of the resolutions Erbakan was asked to sign along with his resignation was the "enforcement of the attire law," and as a result, many public universities began to actively police students wearing the headscarf, banning them from campuses.

This led to strong protests by covered women demanding the fulfillment of their right to education as well as by some feminist groups that felt the headscarf had become an issue of women's educational rights.[14] During the initial removal of students with headscarves from college campuses and at protests held in front of various university entrances, instances of the use of force by university security and of police brutality were documented. I want to underline here the significance of the positioning of headscarf wearing as a national security concern at the time. At the end of the chapter I will return to the question of securitizing headscarf-wearing college students at one point in time and LGBT events at another, by secular and Islamist-leaning governments, respectively, which is more productively understood as a matter of authoritarian security states and not through a religious/secular binary.[15] When the protests against the ban proved ineffective in changing the legislation or in softening the attitude of university administrators, many veiled students chose to wear hats or wigs atop their headscarves in order to be able to continue attending classes, and others went abroad to finish their college education.[16] The ban on the headscarf at public universities also resulted in the formation of various Islamic charity associations, such as Ak-Der, Mazlum-Der, and Özgür-Der, which positioned themselves as human rights organizations against cruelty, specifically targeting inequalities resulting from the headscarf ban. These associations would later become central figures in the backlash against homosexuality by participating in the declaration to support Minister Kavaf.

(Un)Reasonable Citizens, (Un)Reasonable Demands

As noted above, summer 2008 was a time of AKP's democratic openings. Having governed for the previous six years, AKP had started taking a series of democratic steps in trying to solve some of the painful and long overdue issues of the republic. These included, for instance, initiating the first official Kurdish television station and taking steps toward mutual border openings, referred to, respectively, as the Kurdish opening and the Armenian opening. AKP was also considering a headscarf opening to repeal the headscarf ban on public university campuses and passing legislative packages to fit the Copenhagen criteria for EU accession. Yet AKP's most hotly debated undertaking was the party's proposal to redraft the constitution, which had been drafted in 1980 by generals of the Turkish Armed Forces who had staged the last military coup. Many secularists agreed with CHP's (Cumhuriyet Halk Partisi [Republican People's Party]) fears that the civil constitution was merely a facade for the AKP to lay down the groundwork for strengthening their hold on power,[17] but a significant segment of anti-militaristic progressives, whether aligned with AKP politics or not, were agreeable to the idea of a civil constitution. Many LGBT activists were among the latter group due both to their anti-militaristic politics and also because of their hopes for an LGBT opening. Istanbul-based Lambdaistanbul (LGBT Solidarity Association) as well as Ankara-based KaosGL and Pembe Hayat (Pink Life associations) started a signature campaign asking that *cinsel yönelim* (sexual orientation) and *cinsiyet kimliği* (gender identity) be included in the new constitution.[18]

Yet both the redrafting of the constitution and the government's gestures toward a potential headscarf opening were unnerving to many secularists. Especially prominent was the fear that lifting the ban at universities would create a slippery slope: Once veiling on public university campuses was permitted, what would stop Islamists from further demanding that the headscarf be worn at high schools, then at middle schools, and even elementary schools? This fear was informed in particular by the assumption that the headscarf was oftentimes a restraint imposed on women by patriarchal Muslim male kin and, more importantly, by the fear that the mere presence of headscarves would produce what was referred to as neighborhood pressure.[19]

As a result, secularists imagined that if the headscarf were to be officially allowed, young girls would be coerced by their fathers and brothers to cover their heads in order to attend elementary school and that those who did not encounter familial pressure would have to endure it at school from their veiled peers. As voices ranging from skeptical to deeply concerned multiplied, Minister of State Burhan Kuzu felt it was time for a declaration to dissipate such anxieties: "We do not have to respond to every request," he stated, referring to possible future requests for headscarves at elementary schools. "There is a high level of requests from homosexuals for equality and the right to marriage. Are we going to give it to them simply because they are asking for it? We are obliged to act within the responsibilities of [the party in] power."[20]

With these words Kuzu divided headscarf politics into moderate/reasonable versus extremist/unreasonable demands and made a rhetorical move to simultaneously break down the slippery slope continuum that headscarf critics had employed and establish AKP's political position as moderate. He also became the first public figure to compare the headscarf issue to LGBT rights by bringing up LGBT activists' demands for equal rights (and an imaginary request for gay marriage, which at the time was not part of the activists' agenda) when the subject in question was headscarf wearing on public university campuses. The comparison was made to suggest that the hypothetical demand that headscarves be worn at elementary schools and the activists' actual demand for LGBT rights were equally unreasonable, presumably made by unreasonable citizens. Nonetheless, it provided rhetorical ammunition for those who believed that both the government and the women asking for the right to wear the headscarf were what is colloquially referred to as Muslims to themselves (*kendine Müslüman*). This expression suggests self-seeking motives on the part of those viewed as being Muslims to themselves—that they are only after their own rights, liberties, and welfare. It also points out what headscarf critics considered to be a deep-seated *insincerity* by underlining Islam's emphasis on justice and welfare for all. To be a true Muslim, therefore, is to be a Muslim to everyone. In the following months and years, Kuzu's rhetorical move would be turned on its head by secularists, and homosexual rights would become a litmus test for practicing Muslims, especially for women with headscarves—a test to see whether they could be trusted with democratic rights and liberties. Such trust, which lies at the heart of the notion of citizenship and is presumed for most citizens, was not granted to women with headscarves, who were seen as being *kendine Müslüman*, that is, Muslim to themselves. As such, in this contemporary use *against* pious Muslim groups in Turkey, the expression *kendine Müslüman* married religious insincerity with political insincerity, simultaneously dismissing the religiosity and the political motives of Muslim groups, particularly women with headscarves.

Muslim to Oneself or Muslim to Everyone?

A couple of weeks after Kuzu's statement, in mid-February, a group of women with headscarves issued a petition critiquing the "prohibitionist mentality" in the country and located the headscarf ban among a number of other criminalizations and inequalities perpetrated by the state. The petition, entitled "If Freedom Is the Issue, Nothing Is Detail," proclaimed: "We declare in all sincerity as women who experience discrimination because we cover our heads that we will not be happy attending universities with our heads covered until ... [among other conditions] the legal and psychological conditions are established for Kurds and Otherized peoples to feel that they are essential parts of this country; until those actually responsible for cruel unsolved assassinations are brought to justice; legislations are made to end Title 301 trials; ... Alevis' religious worship is no longer reduced to 'cultural activities'; ... the largest obstacle to freedom of science at universities, Council for Higher Education (YÖK), is terminated."[21] Right before closing with Prophet Mohammed's words "The heavens and the earth stand thanks to justice," the petition statement declared: "No freedom is true freedom before the mentality of prohibition (in this country) is brought to a complete end, which is the mentality that helps the continuation of this unjust system through spreading the fear that one of us constitutes a danger for the other and sets us against each other. As people who know what limits on one's freedom means, we will continue to stand against every form of discrimination, infringement of rights, of oppression and imposition."[22] And with these words, women with headscarves positioned themselves as warriors for a just and free world where all oppression and discrimination is understood to be part of the same system and is fought against collectively.

In newspaper interviews that followed, organizers of the petition, Hilâl Kaplan, Havva Yılmaz, and Neslihan Akbulut, voiced a heightened awareness of the Muslim to themselves accusations being aimed at women with headscarves.[23] They clarified that they did not claim "woman with headscarf" (*başörtülü*) as an identity, but they also felt that the solidarity they had been providing to other groups oppressed by the state was rendered invisible and that women with headscarves were easily positioned as insincerely evoking rights, equality, and liberty only to further their own agenda. Yılmaz added: "We participated in many events. I met Neslihan and Hilâl at Hrant Dink's funeral,[24] for instance. Should we talk about that as 'We as women with headscarves walked at Hrant Dink's funeral?!' That would be a cruel thing."[25] The assassinated Armenian Turkish journalist Hrant Dink's funeral in 2007 indeed had become a platform for tens of thousands to march in solidarity against state racism and nationalism with signs that read "We are all Hrant" and "We are all Armenians." This political reaction was due to Dink's trial under title 301 at the time of his murder for allegedly "denigrating Turkishness" in his writing as well as to death threats he had been receiving from nationalist groups, for which he had not been granted state protection despite reporting the incidents. The rhetoric of solidarity voiced through "We are all Hrant" and "We are all Armenians" is a frequently used formulation in protests in Turkey today, but Dink's funeral constituted one of its earliest articulations. Holding together in tension what might be understood as identity politics (emphasizing Dink's Armenianness) with disregarding the identities of those marching as irrelevant, these slogans simultaneously recognized difference as a structure through which uneven life chances are distributed and rejected it as a meaningful way to organize social, political, and economic life. Yılmaz's perception of inserting one's own plight, if not identity, into this rhetoric of solidarity as cruelty reflected this spirit: The march was about the assassination of Dink and the targeting of Armenians in the country and was not to be conflated with or co-opted by any other issue, including their own fight for the right to headscarf.

The women's caution around identity politics was not limited to a political humbleness and an ethic of solidarity, however. Their objection was further elaborated a year later, in the first piece Kaplan wrote for what would become her long-standing column in the daily *Taraf.* In this article, titled "Herkese Müslüman" (Muslim to everyone), Kaplan contrasted identity politics, which she understood to be an effect of modernity through which all subjects are invited to look out for their own good, with what she referred to as *hak. Hak* is a capacious term, derived from Arabic, and in Turkish is used to mean *right*, as in human rights (*insan hakları*), but also *justice* in general, as in the phrase *hak yerini buldu* (justice found its place/was delivered). Hak is also one of the ninety-nine names of Allah, exemplifying and emphasizing the significance of justice in Islam.

Kaplan evoked hak as a totality of justice that cannot be divided into identitarian frames of minority rights. Further, as described above, all three women understood the division operated by minority rights paradigm to be *zulüm* (a cruel thing) and an undermining of a fight for justice and freedom for all, as demanded by their petition. Kaplan further analyzed identity politics in her piece as a tool of the Turkish state to divide citizens into Kurdish versus Turkish, Armenian versus Muslim, Muslim versus secular, Alevi versus Sunni—categories produced by power. "'We' as subjects of cruelty therefore cannot imagine a justice-loving [*hakperest*] horizon and fail to struggle shoulder to shoulder." Thus, she claimed, the first thing from which we needed to liberate ourselves was this language of power. She concluded her piece by defining the kind of Muslim who can engage in such a project as a "Muslim to everyone" (*herkese Müslüman*):

> A Muslim whose fundamental purpose is the establishment of justice in this country, who for that purpose fights not only against authoritarian secularism but also alongside groups who are oppressed by the same laïcism, such as Alevis and non-Muslims; one who distances themselves from institutions and discourses that are products of the Turkish-Islamic synthesis, which utilize Islam in order to nationalize peoples through mandatory religious education or Friday sermons, and as a result empty out Islam and distort its message; and one who has committed themselves to solidarity with all subjects of cruelty [*mazlumlar*] who are wronged by these discourses, starting with Kurds.[26]

Lest readers think the critique of identity politics by these headscarf activists is the reason they did not align with demands for LGBT rights, it is worth emphasizing that their analysis is not a critique of identities as such, since they did not question the existence of, or identification with, such categories as Alevi or Kurd. They also did not mind participating in a march that declared "We are all Armenians." They admitted to their own ambivalence between not accepting women with headscarves (*başörtülü*) as an identity and their simultaneous desire to be *recognized* as Muslim women who stood against the murder of Armenian journalist Hrant Dink. Ultimately, their objection was to a *politics* based on categories due to its divisive nature, a divisiveness devised by the very same nation-state structures we ought to be struggling against—a position very similar to the structural critique of hate by trans sex worker activists discussed in chapter 3. Thus, this call for the subjects of cruelty to work alongside each other against oppressive structures was also an invitation to recognize the illusion of differences, not in order to invalidate the material effects of those differences, but so that "we" (a "we" Kaplan herself put in quotation marks) can work toward a just future that refuses the production of differences by state structures. During the interview, the three women also clarified that their stance differed from those who position the removal of certain constraints as a condition of the removal on others (such as "headscarf ban is problematic, but [Title] 301 should also be lifted"). They asked for each and every one of the state prohibitions on people's lives, thoughts, words, and looks to be ended, unconditionally.[27]

Soon the three petitioners would be invited to a more direct engagement with LGBT politics, when in another interview the journalist brought up Kuzu's statement that had denied LGBT rights and compared it to permitting headscarf wearing in elementary schools. The "freedom for everyone" declaration had remarkably not included any statement on homosexuals. Why had that been the case? "I am glad you asked," Yılmaz responded.

> Homosexuality is not accepted according to Islam. But it is not considered a pathology the way it is in the West. On the contrary, every person has homosexual drives. Islam recommends not to listen to your nefs and not to follow this drive. At the end, Islam, like any other religion, draws some lines and considers certain things to be a sin. I absolutely do not see homosexuality as an illness. I always critique the police oppression of homosexuals, that they are forced into prostitution, that they are imprisoned into this life(style). We did not willingly leave homosexuality out. We even had a workshop on "Islam and homosexuality" before; we are debating this. They should leave us alone; all we want/need to do is to talk and debate about it.[28]

Thus, Yılmaz refused to view homosexuality as an illness, voiced compassion for what she understood to be the unfair living conditions of homosexuals in Turkey, *and* simultaneously positioned homosexuality as a sin, as something that is outside of the boundaries drawn by Islam. While *they* did not willingly leave homosexuality out as an issue of freedom from their statement, the fact that *Islam* left it out of its boundaries of acceptable behavior made it hard to take a firm pro-LGBT-rights stance.

While these Muslim women were being incited to a discourse on homosexuality and were starting to produce a homosexuality-as-sin framework (to which I will later return), that same summer a popular Turkish talk show, *Teke Tek* (One on One), hosted women university students to discuss the headscarf issue on college campuses. The two-and-a-half-hour episode, titled "Türban Tartışması" (Headscarf debate), hosted four women—two with headscarves and two without. While one of the uncovered guests, Özlem Gökçin, took an uncompromising position against headscarves at public universities in the name of secularism, both the (male) host, Fatih Altaylı, and the other uncovered guest, Çiğdem Özkan, seemed more agreeable to removing the ban. They understood the issue as a matter of women's educational rights, stating that men who might be against the secular republic could freely roam campuses while Muslim/Islamist women were marked by their headscarves and, as a result, were not allowed at universities.[29] Yet a clear presumption of the biased worldview of those who wear the headscarf (and of the objectivity of those who do not) permeated their logic. They feared that a teacher with a headscarf might influence their kids at school. Or, they wondered, how could a judge with a headscarf make fair and objective decisions, especially when cases involved uncovered women?[30] As Nuray Bezirgan, one of the veiled guests pointed out, women with headscarves had been subjected to the exact same anxiety for most of their lives, as every schoolteacher who instructed their children and every judge who ruled on their cases had been unveiled.

Such anxieties around whether Muslim women could be trusted to be fair to everyone was fueled by the country's history of staunch secularism and facilitated by the Muslim to oneself discourse that assigned a potential insincerity to pious Muslim subjects seeking religious rights. On the talk show, however, the ultimate test of the religious and political sincerity of the covered guests turned out to be whether they supported rights and liberties for homosexuals. Homosexual rights were first brought up by the unveiled guest Özkan, who started by critiquing the other unveiled guest's statement that a secular life was more desirable because it was more civilized. Such lifestyle hierarchies were unacceptable, maintained Özkan, but then, were Muslims not creating similar hierarchies when it came to homosexuality? "And in Turkey some Islamist groups . . . , they defend the headscarf, but they do not defend a homosexual and see homosexuality as an illness, and there lies the problem, very simple. They see the headscarf as a higher, more important value but [think] of the homosexual as bad, think of them as having an illness."[31] Bezirgan responded that she and other veiled women were concerned about achieving their own liberties first, but she then quickly added that she did not know much about the lives of homosexuals in the country and did not want to comment on an issue she was not informed about. This did not constitute a satisfactory answer, though, as for the remainder of the show the subject of homosexual rights was continuously brought up by Altaylı and Özkan, who finally openly demanded that Bezirgan take a clear stance on this issue. Homosexual rights turned out to be a test she *had to take* and *had to pass*.

What is employed in such exchanges is a rights discourse in which fundamental rights and liberties are treated as a totality. Yet not everyone's relationship to the discourse (and exercise) of fundamental rights and liberties is seen as *equally genuine*. This is because democracy is imagined as a fragile structure that houses its own potential demise, as it may naively grant political access to its enemies who would then use their newfound power to undermine it.[32] Situating democracy as an actor in a script of tragic betrayal by those whom democracy serves casts democracy as a flawless social good that can be related to through either gratefulness or betrayal while overlooking all kinds of nationalist, capitalist, and neoimperialist violence that has been and continues to be enacted in its name. As a result, only some are demanded to produce proof of their sincerity and good intentions in relationship to democracy.[33] Unsurprisingly, the ones who need to prove their sincerity are the ones who do not have their fundamental rights and liberties *yet*. Through producing proof of their sincerity, they also produce proof that they *deserve* the fundamental rights and liberties they are requesting. The logic of Muslim to oneself fuels such debates when women with headscarves are presumed to be fundamentally untrustworthy even, and perhaps especially, as they speak the language of fairness, justice, equality, and freedom. Having shifted from marking selfish individuals to marking devout Muslims as a homogenous group in the Turkish secular imaginary, Muslim to oneself colored debates and made certain secular ears unable to fully hear the painful experiences women with headscarves had had to endure.

It is also worth noting that these discussions were taking place at a time when the plea for headscarf wearing in public universities and offices was no longer framed as an entitlement resulting from a religious obligation, but as a matter of personal choice and human right.[34] In other words, despite the desires of the women behind the freedom-for-everyone petition to not include headscarf wearing as an identity category, woman-with-headscarf, often simply referred to as *türbanlı* (veiled), was shifting from marking religious piety to working as a neoliberal category of difference to be incorporated through politics of multiculturalism. AKP's strong pursuit of the EU membership as exemplified by its various democratic openings as well as outlawing the death penalty were central in positioning human rights as the most readily available venue to activists. Even though (human) rights had become a central framework through which many citizens had understood and imagined justice since the 1980s, it was the first time that headscarf wearing was being incorporated into this framework. At the same time, the disjuncture between human as a universal and Muslim as a particular continued to haunt headscarf activists' attempts to mobilize their demands in terms of rights.

Homosexual Rights as a Litmus Test

When Bezirgan finally asked what kinds of problems homosexuals face in Turkey, Altaylı and Özkan failed to produce any examples except that the Istanbul-based LGBT solidarity association Lambdaistanbul had recently been ordered to close down by İstanbul Valiliği (Istanbul Governor's Office). When Özkan objected, "Excuse me, are there people who are not admitted to schools, or are beaten up by cops, like us, because they are homosexuals? Because I don't see any," she was given a vague response that, yes, some homosexuals were literally lynched. "But those must be a few ignorant people doing that," Bezirgan replied.[35] How did that compare to their own *systematic* suffering, instigated by the very state they were citizens of? She had miscarried due to police violence under detention and had been interrogated for ties to terrorist groups. When she was finally charged with "interrupting others' education" and sentenced to six months in prison, she had to seek asylum and live seven years in Canada to continue her education and flee the oppressive political climate in Turkey after the February 28, 1997, resolutions (referred to informally as the February 28th Resolutions).

Of course, the lives of LGBT persons in Turkey are equally if not more painful, especially trans women sex workers who are continuously subject to heteropatriarchal state violence as well as violence at the hands of (cis heterosexual male) citizens, which I recount in more detail in chapter 3. Their presence could have made for a productive discussion about state violence in Turkey as well as help expand what seemed to be the operating understanding of systematic violence from juridical, codified violence to the violence of normative social regulations. As seemingly no LGBT activist was invited to the show, the systematic pain and suffering that normative structures cause to LGBT subjects and the ways in which they render nonnormative lives unlivable were not part of the conversation. The noncriminalized status of homosexuality, gender nonconformity, and transness in the country, combined with the clear lack of knowledge of Altaylı and Özkan on the topic, made the discussion of homosexual rights even more abstract, one clearly and only employed as a litmus test and not because of a genuine concern for the state of LGBT subjects in the nation.

It was during the same month of the airing of this episode that the Council of Europe's Conference of European Ministers Responsible for Family Affairs took place in Vienna. As Turkey's minister for women and family affairs, Selma Aliye Kavaf also participated at the conference and put reservations on two of the items on the resolution prepared by the participants. First, the statement: "These days the family expresses different life-forms, and children in Europe grow up in different family formations that can change throughout the life course of the child" had to be qualified with "these life-forms vary according to each nation." Second, Kavaf demanded that the item of the resolution suggesting that Council of Europe member countries look into the possible standardization of the rights and legal standing of children living in alternative family formations be supplemented with the phrase "this should be evaluated within national legal frameworks." The reason for the requested change, Kavaf stated, was that the formulation of "alternative families" could open the door to homosexual adoption and added, "We as a country do not accept homosexual marriage, and neither do we accept the institution of homosexual parenting/family."[36]

Kavaf's reservations were of course enabled by an international juridical structure that produces the family as a site of religious and cultural authenticity and difference, unlike, for instance, regulations of international trade. Saba Mahmood maintains that modern family law has occupied an exceptional juridical place since its inception because, unlike other forms of law, it was never expected to be universal.[37] The continued exceptionalization of matters of family, gender, and sexuality, exemplified here by the fact that one *can* put reservations on family-related statements based on culture and tradition, continually produces the family as the site of cultural difference and authenticity. It was these reservations, along with her conservative stance freely expressed in the press regarding romance and sexuality on television,[38] that led to the interview with Kavaf mentioned at the outset of this chapter that was published in the daily *Hürriyet* for International Women's Day in 2010 with the heading "Homosexuality is an illness; and it should be cured."[39]

This historical statement was produced by the complicated position of a government that simultaneously fostered conservative values in many domains, including sexuality, while continuing to put significant effort toward becoming an active member of the EU, inciting in the process various demands for rights and liberties. Therefore, the AKP government found itself continually in conversation with EU demands and, as previously discussed, was presenting democratic openings that very much followed the logic of multicultural inclusion of minorities. This logic of multicultural inclusion faced various issues: While the Kurdish incorporation via legislating a few ethnic civil rights failed to deliver the voter support AKP had wished for and was already short of addressing land-rights issues that were on the forefront of Kurdish separatists' agendas (see chapter 2), the headscarf opening encountered other limits of liberal rights. Exposing the fact that not everyone had equal access to *legitimacy* when they spoke the language of rights, this case illustrates that the issue with the travel and translation of human rights' discourses is more complicated than whether they constitute a Western imperial imposition or a reworked and resignified localized framework. The context of secularist historical fear of Islamicization in Turkey, and contemporary disbelief in the government's democratic changes, extended to questioning the genuineness of headscarf activists when they embraced the language of human rights and tried to explicitly state their support for all kinds of ethnic, religious, and political rights and freedoms. The expression *kendine Müslüman*, which married religious insincerity with political insincerity, simultaneously dismissed the religiosity and the political motives of Muslim groups and particularly of women with headscarves. Thus, this particular translation of human rights as a recognizable liberal framework to demand the right to wear the headscarf did not have the same effect as demanding just *any* other right due both to the political histories of the republic as well as the particularly tenuous period of redrafting of the constitution.

As recalled above, a number of Islamic human rights NGOs that were formed after the February 28th Resolutions produced a declaration of support for Kavaf's stance regarding homosexuality as an illness.[40] This declaration further solidified homosexuality as a litmus test for Muslim subjects' sincerity, among other reasons because the test had *finally* worked to expose pious Muslims' democratic double standards. Critiques targeted one of the associations in particular, Mazlum-Der, which seemingly had earned the trust of secularists as an organization truly dedicated to human rights. News reports and columns with titles such as "Muslims' biggest exam," "Mazlum-Der's litmus test: Homosexuality," "Human rights end at Mazlum-Der when it comes to homosexuality," and "So, you were supporters of *mazlumlar*?" (subjects of cruelty) underlined what was seen as either the failure of Mazlum-Der to truly embrace human rights or the hypocritical stance of the organization exposed at last.[41] The last heading in particular used the idiom *mazlum* in the name of the organization, which translates as "subject of cruelty," and questioned whether the association deserves its name given its failure to serve all those who suffered from various forms of cruelty.

Is It an Illness or a Sin?

There was a second response to the Muslim NGOs' statement, which came from Hilâl Kaplan, one of the three Muslim women who had initiated the freedom for everyone declaration discussed above. In her daily *Taraf* column, Kaplan asked why Muslims would accept a secular scientific framework of homosexuality as illness without questioning the power/knowledge structure that made possible both the initial declaration of homosexuality as an illness and the subsequent removal of it from the category of illness/abnormality in the West.[42] Echoing Yılmaz's position cited earlier, both Kaplan and her husband Süheyb Öğüt argued in different newspaper columns and interviews that homosexuality was natural in Islam *and* a sin but no more a sin than adultery, drinking alcohol, or smoking and, hence, should be treated similarly.[43] They both also insisted that under no condition could cruelty against homosexuals be tolerated within an Islamic framework.

Kaplan openly criticized Muslims' reactions that contained no acknowledgment or critique of the breach of civil rights and the cruelty shown toward homosexuals, such as police or family violence. Yet she also took a firm stance in suggesting that being called homophobic would not deter her from declaring that homosexuality is a sin as a Muslim. Insisting that women with headscarves, who already were sacrificing on so many fronts for their beliefs, including their education, declare support for homosexual rights was, for her, a major inconsistency, and those who made such demands were simply "blackmail democrats."[44] Even in her invitation of Muslims to a more proper and authentic Islamic framework, Kaplan was not a cultural purist: Her column often housed references to Western poststructuralists, psychoanalytic theorists, and theorists of power and sovereignty, such as Michel Foucault, Slavoj Žižek, Carl Schmitt, Georg Lukács, and Theodor Adorno and Max Horkheimer, among others. Undermining simplistic frames of cultural authenticity, her work exemplified that it is not only Western liberal epistemic frameworks (such as human rights) that travel elsewhere but also their critiques that can emanate from the West. In other words, if the demands for the right to wear the headscarf were now infused with liberal human rights' rhetoric and were thus rendered comparable to LGBT rights, Kaplan's objection that invited Muslims to a more authentically Muslim position on homosexuality was shot through with Foucauldian critiques of the history of sexuality and the rise of scientific institutions in the West. These examples clearly complicate liberal/illiberal, secular/religious, traditional/modern, and global/local binaries, yet such complication does not require us to overlook the political stakes of Muslim women's right to wear the headscarf or the AKP's continual use of their plight for its own consolidation of power.

The three responses I have outlined thus far—Muslim women who are unaware of the plight of LGBT subjects and do not make public statements about homosexuality, Muslims claiming that homosexuality is an illness, and Muslims claiming that homosexuality is normal but also a sin—were treated as one group and placed under the rubric homophobia. This particular translation of human rights and homosexual rights into the contemporary Turkish context left no room for a *genuine* and *inhabitable disjuncture* between an Islamic understanding of homosexuality as a sin and a secular human rights framework according to which all people are entitled to inalienable rights.[45] As she anticipated, Kaplan was named "the most homophobic journalist of the year" in the annual Tomatoes with Hormones award ceremony during LGBT pride week in 2010.

Politics of Rights and Politics of Cruelty

At its core, the question of political solidarity is about who we can have political conversations with and what draws the limits of such conversations. What these debates and the increasing amount of authoritarian state violence taking place ever since made clear is that while a politics of rights proved very limited in the context of contemporary Turkey—the insistence on it serving only to prove an already presumed failure of Muslim subjects' political sincerity—a *politics of cruelty* is not only possible and potentially very fruitful but also urgently needed. By politics of cruelty I am gesturing toward a form of political worldmaking that centers *opposition to* all forms of cruelty, which would be different from a politics of rights that centers on liberal recognition, and *support for* rights of juridically recognized subjects. Unlike a "politics of pity" or other forms of sentimental liberal humanism and tolerance, cruelty in these debates was evoked not in liberal, but neither in utterly illiberal terms.[46] The narratives and demands of subjects involved in the headscarf debates traveled between Islamic notions of cruelty and justice (*hak*) and liberal human rights (*insan hakları*) in order to negotiate the need to access public education and workplaces and a simultaneous desire to think about social justice beyond difference. A politics of cruelty would not have classified voices that clearly recognized and objected to state and civilian violence against LGBT people as homophobic and would have found valuable ground for solidarity instead of demanding a gesture of support consisting of an abstract recognition of legal entitlements.

Soon after these events the AKP, which had excited so many with their democratic openings, was reelected to a third term and quickly changed its tune, banning books and officially ordering the destruction of artwork; blocking access to websites; making nonchalant declarations about civilians killed in allegedly anti-terrorism maneuvers in the Kurdish regions of the country; unleashing excessive and fatal police force onto protesters; instigating various conservative sexual measures, including talks about outlawing abortion; and ultimately initiating the mass arrest of journalists, academics, and students (along with military personnel) for conspiring to lead a military coup against the government and/or for aiding and participating in armed terrorist organizations as well as their ideological branches. Perhaps it would have been harder to write off as homophobic those activists who had ambivalent positions on rights yet clear and firm stances against cruelty during the AKP's later, more violent years, because solidarities forged against cruelty would have seemed more pressing. The lost solidarities in this story proved to be especially unfortunate because, going forward, the rhetoric of various AKP government officials, especially Erdoğan, was increasingly aimed at polarizing the public into pious, respectable Muslims, on one hand, and presumably secular and immoral ones, on the other. This polarization was not always successful, as I will discuss in chapter 4. Nevertheless, it did mobilize a loyal voter base for the government. Through monopolizing the definition of Islam and building a moral center around this fabricated core, it also continually marginalized non-Muslims and Muslim minorities within Turkey. This, in turn, has fueled a heightened secular backlash against everything that represents religion and piety such that many secular Turks who were then sympathetic to a woman's right to wear the headscarf are today able to conceive of veiled women only as AKP supporters and, thus, as subjects invested in authoritarian oppression.

This state of affairs suggests that Turkey's queer and feminist politics would benefit from a serious decoupling of the Islamist party in power from multiple groups of women wearing the headscarf, all with different politics regarding secularism, human rights, and the position of women in society. At the same time, I am cautious not to overstate and romanticize the possibilities of a politics of cruelty. While a framework of cruelty based on a nonidentitarian framework of justice/hak has the potential to forge solidarities and alliances, I am not arguing that homosexuality as sin is a more homofriendly stance than homosexuality as illness. Neither do I claim that this framework is more authentic or without its own problems. All of these issues crystallized in a meeting between LGBT activists and Neslihan Akbulut,

Hilâl Kaplan, and Süheyb Öğüt to discuss how they might be able to support LGBT organizations in their fight against state violence without condoning homosexuality.[47]

The meeting, held in April 2008, had been scheduled in the midst of dialogue and solidarity efforts among various feminist, LGBT, and Muslim groups. The Turkish-Armenian journalist Hrant Dink had recently been assassinated, causing a huge social outcry and resulting in the formation of a number of groups, including the January 19th Platform, through which citizens from differing political positions gathered to think about ways of organizing collectively against state-condoned racist violence. Various LGBT and feminist groups had taken a clear stance critiquing the headscarf ban. Conversely, the Istanbul Governor's Office had ordered Lambdaistanbul to close down—while an appeal was in the works, the order constituted a significant source of stress for the activists. Kaplan had conveyed through Cansu, a Lambdaistanbul volunteer she had known through feminist organizing, that, as a group of Muslims, they did not condone the order. They understood that the solidarity association was a means through which activists could fight against state and police violence, and they recognized the efforts to close down Lambdaistanbul as acts of *zulüm* (cruelty). In this, they would support LGBT activists. Yet they would not be able to support their attempts to seek legal rights, since homosexuality was *haram*, according to Islam. Due to the genuine interest in seeking ways to organize together, several Lambdaistanbul volunteers joined Kaplan, Öğüt, and Akbulut at the premises of the Islamist human rights organization Ak-Der to discuss potential ways to act in solidarity.

The conversation revealed both Muslim activists' desire to work with LGBT activists as well as the challenges that their particular understanding of Islam posed to that desire. Led by Öğüt, the group presented what both Lambdaistanbul volunteer Eren and the meeting notes taken by another activist referred to as an "Islamic utopia" in which the violent, interventionist state led by arrogant politicians would be replaced by a system in which every subject would be guided by Islamic ethics and duties and also their own conscience. The secular state would always be more authoritarian, as well as more repressive and controlling, than this new Islamic order because in a secular regime people do not feel humbled in the presence of Allah. Further, they maintained, even when Islam deemed particular acts *haram*, it had utmost respect for *mahrem* (the private sphere). Therefore, even when homosexuality was considered sinful according to Islam, no one should interfere with an individual's private affairs. By demanding legislative changes, LGBT activists were inviting the state into their bedrooms, which was exactly what the secular state wanted. Both Kaplan and Öğüt thought that queer theory supported their critique of identity politics as well as their rejection of a desire to be recognized by the state, citing Judith Butler several times during the meeting.

When LGBT activists asked what they thought about the recent declaration by some *ulama* (Muslim clerics) in Indonesia regarding Islam not having a clear position on homosexuality, the Muslim activists indicated that they did not take the declaration too seriously. The meeting notes state that the *feqh* (Islamic jurisprudence) scholars these Muslim activists follow and trust must be more orthodox than the Indonesian ulama.[48] The queer activists argued that it was impossible to separate the public and the private and to overlook the ways in which the public is already sexualized through the institutions of heterosexual marriage and the family. Under conditions of compulsory heterosexuality, coming out was the only way not to be presumed heterosexual. They pressed further: How could one take a stance against cruelty without also standing against the very structures that produced the conditions of cruelty? Muslim activists did not respond to this directly, according to the meeting notes, but later in the meeting Öğüt declared that in Islam the public sphere is heterosexual.

The meeting notes end with a comment about potential plans to perhaps have a screening of the Parvez Sharma documentary *The Jihad for Love* and invite the Muslim activists to see it. The notes also indicate a desire to introduce them to the gay-identified South African imam Muhsin Hendricks if the pride week committee could manage to fly him out for an event so that the Muslim activists could meet a Muslim scholar who did not believe that homosexuality is haram.[49] While the disagreements in the meeting were real, so was the mutual desire to communicate and seek ways to support each other. Yet positioning the disagreements in terms of incommensurability between homosexuality and Islam reifies both terms. While discussions in the meeting highlighted various positions on homosexuality in Islam on behalf of queer and Muslim activists, the debates on the liberating versus limiting nature of mahrem also deserve a similar complexity since mahrem, understood as private and thus in contradistinction to public, is itself a modern reinterpretation.

Mahmood argues that the simultaneous relegation of gender and sexuality *and* of religion to the private realm by the secular state "has tied up their regulative fates in such a way that struggles over religion often unfold over the terrain of gender and sexuality."[50] It is important to recognize here that

Mahmood is principally concerned with the production of modern notions of "religious minority" and, as a result, "family law," through which religion has historically been put in charge of the family—referred to by Talal Asad as "the secular formula for privatizing religion." In other words, Mahmood maintains that "while religious morality has always been concerned with sexuality, ... their delineation as quintessential elements of private life under secular modernity has created an explosive symbiosis between them that is historically unique."[51] Although the Turkish Republic does not make room for separate family law for religious minorities, it is a secular state that has relegated both religion and matters of gender and sexuality to the private. The modern public/private divide, in other words, is a framework with which many subjects conceptualize the world. While the notion of mahrem could be argued to be authentically Islamic, the ways in which it is imagined to overlap with the modern concept of private, exemplified by Muslim activists' references to the bedroom, are not. Therefore, as Muslim activists argue for an Islamic utopia, they, too, make such arguments as subjects produced by histories of modernization and secularization.

Not only are all subjects products of various histories, but they are also subjects of the unfolding dynamics of power. As the AKP government grew increasingly authoritarian, and the peace process with Kurds was replaced by heavy securitization of all involved in Kurdish politics, Kaplan, who had declared in the freedom for everyone petition that all cruelty in the nation had to stop, "starting with the Kurds," openly aligned herself with the government in her columns condemning Kurdish politicians and portraying them as terrorists. Süheyb Öğüt published a piece in 2015 directly linking the HDP (Kurdish Peoples' Democratic Party) to the armed PKK (Kurdistan Workers' Party) and comparing them to what he understood to be butch lesbians' (failed) phallic performance: "Never mind, these HDP+PKK's look like butches who act like a macho (guy), challenging the State and the majority of people by way of using dildo-like external weapons. There is a 'good girl' woman behind this mask. There is a pathetic servant behind those who work for the Big Other's enjoyment (of secularism, of Israel, of Kemalism)."[52] Their desire for dialogue and solidarity with queer activists, or other subjects of cruelty, seems to be over; in fact, Kaplan has since become a columnist for one of the AKP's daily papers. The same logic that deemed the headscarf as a matter of national security at the end of the 1990s has since been applied to various other others of the nation, securitizing queer events and Kurdish politics alike (discussed in greater detail in chapters 2 and 4). For my purposes here, it is simply worth underlining that with Kaplan and Öğüt's newfound political alignments, it would be all too easy to dismiss these histories of dialogue between Muslim and queer activists as insincere, proving secularists' concerns that the headscarf activists were nothing but Muslims to themselves.

I suggest instead that we read these unfolding conversations not as signs of sincerity or the lack thereof and neither as symptoms of modernity versus tradition, globalization versus local authenticity, or queerness versus Islam. If these discussions make anything clear, it is that the travel and translation of knowledge are not the purview of any particular group. There certainly is no way of knowing the sincerity of any political subject at any given time, and even strong solidarities might wither in time due to conflicting loyalties, interests, or simply the unfolding of history. A dismissal based on insincerity would do injustice to the Muslim voices that at different points have shown interest in organizing collectively against state violence and continue to do so. I do not offer the concept of a politics of cruelty as a perfect solution to violence, and neither do I claim it to be a framework of radical alterity vis-à-vis Western modernity. Instead, I suggest that it be understood as a space of negotiation for solidarities that are necessary for people to collectively live self-determined and dignified lives. As the number of groups targeted with various forms of state violence is on the rise in Turkey, all citizens need to hear different accounts of systemic state and social violence that are injuring many already vulnerable populations. Understanding our social existence as multiple, and being able to have conversations about such vital matters as enduring state violence *and* violences produced by manifold normativities, are at the heart of political existence. Our ability to strategize against oppression and find ways to flourish and thrive depends, at least partially, on our willingness to listen differently.

Two

Who Killed Ahmet Yıldız?

On July 17, 2008, news of the murder of a young gay man in Istanbul hit the national papers. Ahmet Yıldız, a Kurdish physics major at Marmara University, was shot and killed while returning to his car after having purchased some ice cream at Tuana Cafe in Üsküdar. The papers mentioned that Ahmet was *eşcinsel* (homosexual) and had filed an official complaint with the attorney general's office regarding threats he had been receiving from his family a couple of months prior to the murder.[1] On the other hand, the papers noted, the manager of the cafe, Ümmühan Darama, who was shot in one heel by a bullet that initially seemed to have been misfired, might have been the actual target of the gunshots. She had occupied city-level positions with the ANAP (Motherland Party) and was known for her legal battle over an inheritance for her son with ex-partner Mehmet Akarçeşme, who had been murdered in 1996.[2] While some papers referred to her son with Akarçeşme as "out-of-wedlock," others mentioned that Darama and Akarçeşme had an Islamic matrimony (*imam nikahi*).[3] In the initial reports, Darama received more detailed and expansive coverage than did the murdered young man.

A couple of days following the incident, the British newspaper the *Independent* published a full-page article titled "Was Ahmet Yildiz the Victim of Turkey's First Gay Honour Killing?"[4] While the Turkish papers had indicated that Ahmet was a gay man and had been receiving threats from his family, none of them had used the term *honor killing* in relation to his murder. The discourse of Turkey's first gay honor killing spread fast through the Turkish media, and Darama was soon dropped from the story. The fact that Ahmet's family was not claiming his body for the customary Islamic washing and burial also heightened suspicions that, indeed, it might have been his kin who were responsible for Ahmet's murder.[5] Six major Turkish newspapers published close to full translations of the *Independent* piece within the next few days and thereafter referred to the case as an honor killing.[6]

Yet, honor killing was not just a framing device used by the *Independent* to narrate Ahmet's story; it also helped weave together *theories* about national dynamics that the paper argued had led to the event, establishing the symbolic significance of Ahmet's murder. Quoting Ahmet's friends' claim that his only crime "was to admit openly to his family that he was gay," the *Independent* declared that there were bigger powers at play: Ahmet was a victim of "an increasingly liberal society and its entrenched conservative traditions" and frictions between "old mentalities and growing civil liberties."[7] These frictions were due to Turkey's recent liberalization and hence its inevitable transition toward becoming a country that respected civil rights: "Turkey was all but closed to the world until 1980, but its desire for European Union membership has imposed strains on a society formerly kept on a tight leash."[8] The paper then linked Ahmet's murder to other honor killings in Turkey—more than two hundred deaths per year, it reported—and to other geographies marked by lawlessness: "So-called 'honour killings' continue to be a grim reality *wherever conservative social mores resist the rule of law*."[9]

The *Independent* thus conveniently left out the fact that 1980 also marked the last and arguably bloodiest military coup in the Turkish Republic, which had crushed the Turkish Left and introduced (right-wing) Islam, first by the military junta and later by consecutive right-wing governments as the social glue of a society torn by ideological rifts. Also omitted were such details as how the "unleashing" of the nation formerly on a tight leash had involved the liberalization of the Turkish economy, which had resulted in an ever-expanding foreign debt crisis that in 2001 led to a major economic crash.[10] The *Independent* employed a popular neoliberal story line of civil, and in this case gay, rights as signs of democracy and progress. Not captured in narratives that emphasize liberal individual rights are the various forms of violence and "slow deaths" resulting from structural adjustment policies imposed by the IMF and World Bank on so-called failing liberal economies, which result in increasing poverty and indebtedness of the people.[11] The *Independent*'s narrative, based on this narrow (neo)liberal understanding of freedom—individual freedom for recognizable minority subjects and individual rights—also informed the paper's presentation of Ahmet as a young man who just wanted to live a happy, *out* life. It was publicizing one's liberalness in the face of entrenched conservative traditions that was putting LGBT people like him in danger.

Immediately following the *Independent* article, Turkish domestic media reprinted translated excerpts of the piece without any critical engagement with its discourse, reproducing, circulating, and establishing the truth-status of Ahmet's murder as a gay honor killing. Despite a singular moment in one Turkish paper that seemed to complicate the story by citing a Lambdaistanbul activist who had found the *Independent*'s report "rushed" and devoid of clear facts, most other national papers unproblematically adopted the language of honor killings.[12] Through the circulation of these translated excerpts, what was described as the Turkish "national split-psyche" and culture wars also became the national framework through which the tale of the murder was told. Once this vision of Turkey was set up, the cause of Ahmet's murder followed almost naturally: a casualty of the national clash of civilizations. Outness and visibility had caused his death, since publicizing one's liberalness in the face of entrenched conservative traditions was putting LGBT people like him in danger. The suspicions that Ahmet's family was responsible for the murder were further reinforced by interviews with Ahmet's boyfriend at the time of his death, who had confirmed that Ahmet had been receiving threats from his family and that he himself had witnessed Ahmet filing the official complaint with the attorney general's office. When investigative journalists finally uncovered a letter Ahmet had composed for the online bear magazine *Beargi*,[13] they seemed to have found the evidence they had been looking for and cited from it extensively.[14]

Translation beyond the Orient and the Occident

In this chapter I trace the travel of outness to the context of Turkey as well as the transnational circulation of (queer) families of choice and (gay) honor killing as metaphors and frameworks through which Ahmet's story was understood, narrated, and acted on. Before I turn to Ahmet's letter and the discourses of outness, however, a reorientation of the story is in order. At first glance the narrative seems fairly familiar: Turkey is positioned as the Oriental other of Europe—a land of backward traditions, customs, and lawlessness, except for a few subjects who represent a reach for civilization, such as gays desiring outness and all those desiring EU membership. The *Inde-*

pendent works as the mouthpiece of the "Gay International,"[15] spreading the episteme of outness and replacing desiring subjects with legible (and thus imperial) gay subjectivity. These newfound gays then emerge as subjects of pity and rescue. Gay liberalism and homonationalism provide the *Independent* with a media-friendly gay honor killing discourse, according to which murdered gays in the Middle East become ideal subjects of (Western) liberal grief. While the *Independent* itself did not bring up Islam in relation to Ahmet's murder, as I will analyze later in this chapter, the transnational circulation of the story as a gay honor killing and subsequent online tributes to Ahmet elicited responses that positioned Islam as the culprit behind his murder, bringing the story full cycle as a tale of homonationalism and Islamophobia.

Yet I will show that our analysis of the gay honor killing framework would be incomplete without taking into consideration Turkey's long histories of Occidentalism as well as the AKP's neoliberal minority politics in the context of racial nationalism, which helped bolster particular subjects' legibility as victims of violence while making others invisible. For one, in the case of Turkey as opposed to many other countries in the Global South, the discourses of progress employed by the *Independent* receive a further twist since Turkey's geographic location and its history have led the nation to both be imagined *and* imagine and brand itself as a bridge between East and West. This representation of Turkey has historically positioned the country in a perpetually ambiguous relationship to the geographic sites of the East (presumably marked by Asia) and the West (presumably marked by Europe) and to the different temporalities assumed to be associated with these geographies: progress and backwardness.[16] At the same time, as seen in the paper's description of the supposed tensions present in Turkey, the East and the West were simply placed *within* the nation and eternally reproduced. This vision of Turkey as partially Westernized, in transition toward modernity, and about to fully respect civil liberties also informs the national "self-conscious anxiety that it [Turkey] is arrested in time and space by the bridge itself."[17] The image of the bridge that is supposed to take the nation from its backward past toward the emancipated, properly modernized future also marks the static nature of the republic's relationship to the East and West in the global popular imaginary. Turkey is thus doomed with civilizational schizophrenia and defined by a permanent internal clash of civilizations.

This image of Turkey as plagued by internal civilizational conflict is not simply an Orientalist trope, however, but a narrative that has been implemented, deployed, and reproduced in various ways starting from the early years of the republic. The civilizational aspirations of the republic's founder

Atatürk informed a series of reforms that aimed to face the nation away from Islam and toward the West, especially Europe (see chapter 1). An East/West split employed and reified in ideologies of Orientalism and Occidentalism continues to this day to geographically mark populations with civilization and backwardness (which frequently map onto urban versus rural subjectivity), as I will narrate, especially in the nation's relationship to Kurds in the east and southeast.[18] If the Kemalist project constituted a classic modernization effort, which operated with a singular Enlightenment model of modernity, the AKP government's strategy has been one of alternative modernities. Ahmet Davutoğlu—one of the founders of AKP, minister of foreign affairs from 2009 to 2014, and prime minister from 2014 to 2016—had argued in his 1994 book *Alternative Paradigms* that the Islamic paradigm is "absolutely alternative to the Western."[19] Situating Islamic societies as ontologically different and thus on an alternative path to modernity, this claim, with its reliance on a universal/particular binary and simplistic ideas of cultural difference in which culture *and* difference are both conceptualized as ahistorical, is no different in its essence from clash of civilizations arguments.[20]

Perhaps because of its refusal to include capitalism in its theorizations of modernity and culture, the alternative modernities paradigm easily yields to neoliberal multiculturalism.[21] It should come as no surprise then that under AKP rule Turkey has made special efforts to brand and market its Islamic difference. Aslı Iğsız notes that in both the UN initiative Alliance of Civilizations, launched in 2005 and cosponsored by Turkey and Spain, as well as the World Economic Forum meetings in 2006, Turkish government representatives positioned the country as a modernized nation that is part of the Islamic civilization, thus claiming that it "is uniquely positioned to act as a bridge between civilizations, particularly through accession to the European Union."[22] Joining post-9/11 discourses that allegedly seek to promote international peace through a logic of cultural/civilizational tolerance, AKP's alignment of peace, security, and economic stability has been perpetrating its own civilizational violence on "terroristic" (read: Kurdish) bodies and geographies that it deems incapable of civilization or peace. As I will discuss below, honor killings play an important role in marking Kurdish geographies and populations with civilizational lack, doubly rendering Kurds as backward and inevitably colluding with the acts of violence perpetrated by AKP's neoliberal Islam.[23]

The period for which I trace the circulation of these discourses coincided with an increasing emphasis on neoliberal minority rights frameworks in Turkey during the first two terms of AKP governments. This emphasis on liberal minority politics combined with the framework of honor killing performed multiple erasures. For one, Ahmet's Kurdishness faded into the background due to the emphasis on his gayness in both the international and the national media. In other words, it was not only in the *Independent* but also in Turkish media that "gay" was employed as a minority category to exceptionalize the death of a Kurdish gay man by prioritizing individual and eventful death, thus making invisible all forms of state violence and slow deaths unleashed daily on Kurdish populations in Turkey. During the years of the ongoing court case for Ahmet's murder, the failure of the neoliberal incorporation of Kurds into AKP's "new Turkey" through minoritarian civil rights projects, such as education in mother tongue or Kurdish-language TV channels, became obvious, intensifying the militarized violence perpetrated against the Kurdish-majority regions of the country as well as Kurdish politicians and intellectuals.[24] I will conclude the chapter by discussing issues of land rights and separatism that challenge neoliberal ideologies of minority incorporation as well as the alleged decline of the nation-state in the neoliberal era.

Another erasure resulting from the emphasis on liberal minority politics in discussions of Ahmet's murder was in rendering certain subjects as victims and delineating our very capacity to *recognize* subjects that did not fall into existing minority categories. Through the story of Ümmühan Darama, the only witness to the murder, I will illustrate the plight of those who are not coded as minorities, juridically or epistemically, and what acts of violence are left *unrecognizable* if we insist on neoliberal minoritarian frameworks in our search for justice. As social justice movements, including feminist and queer movements, increasingly adopt the liberal and juridical vocabulary and the logic of minorities, subjects such as Darama are rendered invisible not just in the eyes of the law but also in the eyes of social movements that are supposed to be alternatives to mainstream institutions that historically have failed to deliver justice.

Finally, the transnational and national circulation of outness as a gay social good and of honor killing as an Eastern form of crime coupled with the translation and circulation of families of choice come together to perpetuate the understanding of family violence as a sign of backward geographies. This inevitably reifies neoliberal family ideals, where families are imagined as safe havens from the ruthless capitalist public sphere. Furthermore, this particular circulation of outness, honor killing, and families of choice reproduces state violence as a marker of civilization when compared with family violence. Paying attention to the outsourcing of family violence to the East also highlights the constitutive outside of neoliberal normativities of the so-called West, such as the private family, as these are often established over and against nations perpetually marked as the locations of unruly family structures. In other words, I suggest that our discussions of neoliberalism need to become specific and transnational at once: While neoliberalism is influenced by its historical and political circumstances and cannot be treated as a totality that sweeps the world in exactly the same way, it is also important not to overlook the fact that those particularities unfold and take shape in the context of transnational connections. This means, among other things, that national narratives and ideologies unfold in the context of persisting civilizational logics and discourses.

The disjunctures produced by the travel and translations of outness, queer families (of choice), and honor killings provide us with insights into the limits of neoliberal identitarian minority politics both by exposing other sexualities and intimacies that are rendered illegible through them and by the structural violence targeting populations that refuse (the very terms of) such neoliberal handouts. Yet, despite the Orientalist framings of the honor killings I discuss and despite my problematization of the valorization of Ahmet's gayness over his Kurdishness, I find that we would be mistaken to treat this as a story of authentic versus imperial sexualities perpetrated by some ominous "Gay International."[25] The accounts by Ahmet's friends, as well as Ahmet's own story of coming out, provide complex narratives regarding their sexualities and their relations with their families in the context of their subcultural affiliation as bears. These narratives indicate neither a dismissal of outness as a Western imposition nor an understanding of their families' (expected or experienced) reactions to their sexualities as a symptom of their backwardness. It would be difficult and in fact cruel (to use a key term of chapter 1) to argue that epistemic and other forms of violence flow only in one direction in the case of the murder of a young gay man. What kinds of responses and analyses can we provide that take various forms of localized and transnational power dynamics into consideration without forgetting that hegemonies are scattered?[26] How do we understand translation not as a flawless bridge or as total impossibility but as a mode of analysis that opens up ways of seeing the very conditions under which it unfolds?

Rethinking Outness and Neoliberal Family Values

Outness was a major narrative in the news coverage of the murder case (Ahmet was killed by his family because he was gay and because he had come out to his parents) as well as in activist circles and among Ahmet's friends, most of whom belonged to the bear subculture. The *Independent* had framed Ahmet's death as a result of conflicts between traditional and liberal tendencies in Turkey, and there were two key terms the paper highlighted to illustrate the alleged tensions: "Ahmet Yildiz's crime, his friends say, was to admit openly to his family that he was gay." Outness and family came together in this narrative as representatives of the liberal and the traditional but also as elements rendered meaningful vis-à-vis each other. Ahmet's crime, after all, was not coming out to just anyone but coming out to his family. Discursively positioning outness as a crime, the *Independent* simultaneously affirmed the backwardness and perversity of systems under which outness was punished (as opposed to just systems under which the murder would be the crime) and its own liberal position—a position with which the paper's readership and indeed all liberal subjects were assumed to align. Foreshadowing claims of simultaneous lawlessness *and* an autonomous logic of law of the family structures that must have led to Ahmet's murder as a punishment of the crime of outness, the *Independent* doubly affirmed neoliberal definitions of the family and gayness.

The two terms that the *Independent*'s narrative brought together in order to shed light on Ahmet's death, *outness* and the *family*, also constitute two terms widely discussed in queer studies. On one hand, outness and the epistemology of the closet that informs it have been subject to queer critique perhaps more than any other concept that has been produced by modern regimes of sexuality and adopted by LGBT movements. Dating back to Michel Foucault's analysis of modern subjectivity that understands the confessional urge as central to "scientia sexualis" and its regimes of truth, most of this body of work operates with the Foucauldian definition of modernity, where power is theorized as first and foremost productive of sexual (and other) *subjectivities*.[27] Not only does this confessional relationship to sexuality produce it as a form of truth waiting to surface, but by demanding such confession only from "abnormals," it produces the adult, monogamous married couple as the norm. One of the many implications of this regime, scholars have pointed out, is that, over time, this epistemology came to be constitutive of and constituted by a homo/hetero split. As a result, it produces two and only two ontological possibilities for those who fall outside of so-called normal sexuality: one is out, or one is not (and hence is closeted).

Due to their affiliation with (colonial) modernity, its medical and psychiatric institutions, its expert knowledge and regimes of truth, sexual identification and outness (its requirement or any desire for it) are often discussed as signs of sexual imperialism, and their refusal is welcomed as a rejection of, or resistance to, the imperatives of colonial modernity. Scholars of queer of color critique have noted, for instance, that outness is not always available to, or desirable by, all queers,[28] positioning it at times as a white man's "drama."[29] Perhaps in the most widely cited account of Middle Eastern sexualities, Joseph Massad has critiqued not only outness but also what he saw as an increasing imposition of the larger sexual epistemology that informs it by international LGBT activism on (in his case) the Arab world and has argued that enforcement of the homo/hetero binary on desiring subjects only works to further heterosexualize the world.[30] I will return to Massad's argument in the concluding chapter, where I discuss in detail the role of this particular definition of modernity as well as cultural difference in queer studies. For now, however, I will simply interrogate the ways in which the promise of outness is complicated by Ahmet's story in ways that cannot be reduced to an imposing (Western) epistemology of the closet, on one hand, and authentic sexualities and desires untouched by, or resisting, Western imperialism, on the other.[31] In other words, I ask, how else can we understand contemporary queer epistemologies (and ontologies) marked by presumed "cultural difference" without reproducing the universal/particular binary?

This question is especially worth posing in the context of a persistent "reliance on the family as a primary locus of difference and inequality," particularly when discussing sexualities transnationally.[32] Heeding this warning, let us investigate queer critique of the family, the second key term in the *Independent*'s narrative. The genealogy of this scholarship could be summarized as follows: The initial theorization of the formation of autonomous, urban gay and lesbian subjectivity by breaking itself free from family bonds with the dissolution of the family as the primary economic unit has received at least three responses.[33] One body of work focused on the queer remaking of kinship and alternative families and homes; another underlined the white liberal individual norm in the "rejecting the family" model, echoing critics of white liberal feminism's call for women to break free from the family for liberation; and a final one put forth a structural critique of family as a neoliberal institution with a special focus on the legalization of gay marriage.[34]

I suggest that the tension between the second and the third bodies of work is illustrative of exactly the kind of risk brought up by Inderpal Grewal and Caren Kaplan: While family becomes an indisputable target of critique when discussing neoliberal families, gay marriage, and (presumed to be white) gays' and lesbians' desire for marriage, when the subjects who desire and orient themselves toward the family are people of color, the critical impulse is to focus on the historical denial of this formation to people of color by racial capitalism.[35] Of course there is no denying that the same liberal capitalist structures have produced different possibilities for differently racialized and classed people, in this case throughout US history, welcoming white subjects into the folds of the family and forcing people of color away from it. Historical context is not only welcome; it is in dire need in such analyses. The point I would like to make, however, is that when our critiques center on the United States and its particular history and, as a result, focus on particular understandings of whiteness as a force that has shaped subjects' proximity and distance from particular institutions, such as the family, we risk the danger of reifying, for instance, the relationship of people of color to the institution in question in our attempts to critique the Western liberal center by reducing it to whiteness. In other words, when we critique a rejection of the family for being white, are we not inevitably repeating the treatment of family as the locus of cultural difference? Are there no queers of color in America, or queers elsewhere in the world for that matter, who have complicated relationships to the sign and the institution of the family, including a plain rejection of it? And if they do, are they acting white?

The danger here lies within the search for particularity in order to reject universality, which results in certain subjects bearing the burden of particularity itself. Translation studies scholars warn us (see the introduction) that particularity is always complicit with universality.[36] I am not suggesting, of course, that the extremely insightful critique of universality of family by scholars such as Angela Davis, Patricia Hill Collins, or Jose Muñoz equals a suggestion of an alternative universal for women of color or queers of color.[37] I am simply proposing that while it is important to underline the whiteness of norms when that is the case, it is equally important to clarify that whiteness is *part* of a larger problem with universal claims about subversiveness, anti-normativity, or liberation. Finally, I suggest that there is a further potential danger in these critiques of the universal as white. Since most of this scholarship is produced in the United States and Western Europe, there is, at times, a slippage between US-based race critique, postcolonial critique, and transnational critique. Following Grewal and Kaplan's analysis of the export of US categories of gender *and* race through the US womanism's understanding of "woman of color,"[38] I suggest that queer studies be equally wary of exporting the particular US inflections of race in "queer of color" to other geographies.

Let us turn to some of the debates in the aftermath of Ahmet's death in order to reflect on what alternative approaches to outness and the family emerge when we move away from the universal/particular binary. On a July afternoon after the murder, a group of activists gathered on the terrace of the Lambdaistanbul office to discuss the protest to be staged. A Lambda volunteer reported to the rest of us that a couple of Ahmet's friends had given an interview to the daily *Sabah* earlier in the day at Lambdaistanbul's premises, where they had made such statements as "Ahmet should not have told his parents that he was gay." At the time, Lambdaistanbul did not have a rigid politics demanding that everyone who is gay must come out, and members were very careful not to photograph those who were not out to their families at their meetings and protests—even though, at the time, LGBT events and protests almost never made it to mainstream news.[39] Nevertheless, outness was imagined as an ideal that would be realized by anyone who wanted and felt safe to do so and ideally by every LGBT person one day. Thus, to many at that meeting, the statements made by Ahmet's friends sounded like disconcerting anti–coming out narratives.

Yet, a closer look at conversations that took place during the interview reveal how Ahmet's friends complicated the outness/closet binary: They identified as gay men/bears, did not believe in coming out, *and* led lives that refused to fold themselves into the heteronormative order their parents wished for them. When their parents brought up marriage, for instance, they responded with "it will happen if it is my *kısmet*" or pointed out examples they knew of unhappy marriages as reasons not to get married.[40] Hence, they did not engage in marriage refusal by coming out, but by situating marriage as a path leading to unhappiness for enough people that one should question it as a social good, or as a path simply not meant for, and, hence, not to be prescribed for everyone. While these statements were not made out of explicit political concerns and were positioned as *idare etmek* (managing the situation) by the men who made them, by destabilizing marriage as a social good that can be uniformly prescribed to subjects, Ahmet's friends were refusing not just the promise of happiness offered by the institution of marriage but also the promise of happiness offered by coming out.[41]

Hence, unlike Tom Boellstorff's Indonesian *gay* men who did not perceive their *gay*ness and cultural expectations for marriage as incompatible, Ahmet's friends did not see marriage and children as inevitable or understand the family as marking cultural difference. In other words, they rejected the family as an institution without a reliance on gay identity or a Western lifestyle. These kinds of rejections are especially meaningful at a time when the Turkish government seeks to situate the Turkish family as the marker of cultural difference in order to subject it to the same neoliberal transformations we see elsewhere. As the AKP encouraged familial responsibility in social care in accord with IMF-guided structural adjustment programs as well as EU integration, Erdoğan, then prime minister, simultaneously critiqued the "mentality which views living away from parents as modernity" and promoted the three-generational "strong Turkish family," which he contrasted with weak family ties in the West.[42] Cultural difference *and* superiority to an imagined West where allegedly the smelly corpses of elderly people are found in their homes days after their death mark governmental discourses about the Turkish family, while neoliberal policies that limit social welfare provisions enlist the family to stand in for government services.[43] Thus, rejection of the family in contemporary Turkey is more properly understood in the context of neoliberal Islam's attempts to fold subjects into conservative institutions and not as a desire for Western lifestyles.

Further, unlike Martin Manalansan's Filipino gay men, for whom gayness was something to be "felt" by others, including their families, and coming out was a white man's drama,[44] the way bears present often made it impossible for their families to "feel" anything without a speech act. The bear community's aesthetic valuation of hairy, larger, at times balding, and certainly older male bodies means that bear looks overlap with some of the fairly conventional tropes of Turkish heteromasculinity.[45] In other words, the bear aesthetics in Turkey often leaves no room for anything to be "felt" by one's family regarding gayness, as it is not predicated on subverting but rather embodying gender norms. So, unlike Manalansan's Filipino gay men, who did not feel they needed to come out to be felt as gay, Turkish bears would have to come out to make their gayness known. The discursive performances they preferred, however, were not those about who they were, but those that spoke to what marriage is as an institution, which I argue ultimately interrupts and transcends the homo/hetero binary. In short, bears' position vis-à-vis outness was not one where Westernized/global versus local were the operating terms, but a site where one navigated the hailing of the institutions of marriage and the family instead of the hailing of particular identificatory regimes.

Ahmet himself offered a complex narrative around questions of outness in a letter he wrote for the online bear magazine *Beargi* six months before his murder, which was widely cited in the Turkish news as proof for his family's crime. While he emphasized the Eastern Kurdish roots of both his parents as well as his mother's (Islamic) piety as reasons for their lack of understanding his sexuality and for why it might have been wiser not to have told them he was gay, his account did not evoke a narrative of backwardness and liberal progress. Ahmet's piece, "Don't Lie, Take Off Your Mask, and Be Proud," expressed, despite the resolute title, conflicting feelings around coming and being out and sounded cautious about "recommending" it: "The theoretical experiences I had gained from my friends told me that I would be telling the truth and feel proud. Yes, I am proud because I have gotten rid of lies. But know that you will be starting a difficult fight and always avoid telling them, if you think it will be hard for your family to understand you."[46] Situating a simple conception of outness equaling pride and joy as "theoretical," Ahmet, to whom the *Independent* refers as "the man who might be described as Turkey's gay poster boy," clearly complicated any out-and-proud rhetoric and ended his letter with the suggestion that readers avoid telling their parents if they believe their parents will have a hard time "understanding" them.[47] This gesture toward an epistemic break between families and selves cannot be accounted for by a simple rhetoric of homophobia, backward cultures, and violent families. While he claimed some pride and understood that telling the truth about his sexuality was important, Ahmet nevertheless voiced ambiguity about the disjuncture between theory and practice and was torn between feeling happy about no longer having to live with telling lies and the difficulties he was then experiencing as a result of coming out.[48] Nevertheless, the discrepancies between himself and his family and between theory (seemingly derived from the experiences of others) and his own practice were not uttered in ways to signal binaries as perpetuated by the *Independent*'s narrative but to mark epistemic and ontological *difference* that nevertheless cannot be reduced to cultural difference or questions of authenticity. Not having fulfilled its promise of happiness, outness as a gay social good occupied a more ambiguous place in this narrative than what would be found in media portrayals prescribing particular forms of being and living as a gay man.

The family narratives emerging from the news story of Ahmet's death were not confined to local conversations about outness to one's family or Ahmet's parents, however, but extended to transnational networks. Soon after Ahmet's death, his friends started a blog called *Ahmet Is My Family* featuring a YouTube tribute video in response to Ahmet's own family not acting like a "proper family" should, in life and death alike.[49] The clip featured bear-presenting, presumably gay, men from a range of countries around the globe, from the United States to Spain, Chile to Canada. Produced with sweet and sentimental background music, the video frames each man on his own, sitting at a café in France or standing on a beach in Spain, some inside their homes and others in parks or on the street. They look directly into the camera, pronounce their name and where they are from, and all conclude with the statement "And Ahmet is (part of) my family." The names, hometowns, and the words "Ahmet is my family" are uttered in English, French, and Spanish with some men speaking English with accents, suggesting their likely non-native speaker status. The visual display travels between the video recording of Ahmet's transnational family, a black-and-white drawing of Ahmet, and signs in English, Japanese, Spanish, German, Turkish, and French all of which read, "AHMET YILDIZ is my family." The various languages in both spoken and written form evoke an international family that embraces Ahmet, each speaker marked by national (and often colonial) languages. The national borders presumed to be marked by national languages are overcome in this gesture of translatability of the sentiments captured by the phrase "Ahmet is my family" and its many linguistic iterations.[50] Queer families are thus presented as a global phenomenon and queer kinship as a universal(izable) sentiment.

The universalization of the queer family also necessitates the universalization of a particular, liberal understanding of family. Toward the end of the clip, two other phrases are displayed in English only: "AHMET YILDIZ was a victim of a 'gay honor killing,'" followed by "AHMET YILDIZ—Missed by His Real Family." While this transnational embrace of Ahmet as a member of a family that loves and accepts him for who he is is well intentioned, the families we choose narrative framework employed in the video creates a distinction between the right kinds of families (marked as "real" families) and the wrong kinds of families, thereby hiding the fact that the family as an institution is home to all kinds of violence, ranging from domestic violence to incest. This is made possible by the private family's modernist historicity which assumes that families have become less violent as they have evolved from feudal to modern—similar to an understanding of the history of punishment as a quantitative shift to *more* humane and *less violent* practices, which has been critiqued by Foucault.[51]

The narrative of Ahmet's "real family" is partially accomplished by establishing the truth status of Ahmet's murder as a gay honor killing, both in the video and on the tribute site itself. Almost without exception conceptualized as violence by family members against women, the term *honor killing* has been critiqued as a framework that produces domestic violence against women in so-called third world countries as an Oriental pathology and that homogenizes and stigmatizes entire countries and cultures, especially those that are imagined to be marked by Islam.[52] It has also been criticized as a mechanism for outsourcing patriarchy from the United States and Western Europe to "backwards geographies" and thus establishing the first world as having outgrown patriarchy.[53] Nevertheless, honor killing continues to be not only evoked in Euro/US media to understand the Middle East and its patriarchal traditions or occasionally its expansions to Europe via immigrant communities. It also constitutes a concept heavily relied on by local feminists who are concerned with violence against women.[54]

I will turn to the national logic of honor killing that attributes this allegedly special form of violence to Kurdish families and their backward customs in the next section. I would like to note here that *gay honor killing* works as a narrative that contributes not only to a national but also to a transnational division of labor between what is considered to be the West versus the non-West, mapping family violence onto the non-West and producing the myth of the West as the location for stranger danger. As "honor killing" travels internationally to tell the story of what happens to, in this case, gay people in backward third world countries, it is used to discipline kinship structures into becoming neoliberal families where family is supposed to function as a safe haven and provide love, support, protection, and any other social services that citizens might need. This is exemplified in the Istanbul Governor's Office's initial refusal to provide protection to Ahmet when he had filed a complaint against threats he was receiving from his family and in the subsequent murder trial, at the end of which Ahmet's father was charged with the crime and found guilty. In other words, neoliberalism's shrinking of the social functions of the state and its crafting of the private family as the proper sphere of care and safety dictate when the state can and should withdraw from the site defined as the family as well as when it will intervene with its disciplinary functions.[55]

On the other hand, the use of honor killing situates Ahmet's murder as an Eastern (and as we will see in the next section, in some contexts Muslim) form of crime and hence provides a constitutive outside for Western homonormativity. In other words, through the employment of the phrase *honor killing*, family violence is relegated to the East to conserve both the Western family romance *and* the myth of stranger danger. As critics of neoliberalism in the United States, such as Gillian Harkins, have shown, during the late 1980s and early 1990s a discourse about incest proliferated in the United States, yet resulting legislation focused on pedophilia imagined as stranger molestation, thereby shifting the focus from harm to risk.[56] This production of stranger danger through the replacement of incest with pedophilia shifted both the responsibility for child sexual abuse from heterosexual fathers to gay male unknowns and criminalization from predominantly white households to strangers of color. Increased neoliberal demands for hate crime laws by LGBT activists, scholars contend, also reproduce the logic of stranger danger. Such theories about danger and crime are produced in a transnational context that relegates family crimes to Eastern "cultures of shame," supposedly distinguishing essential elements of the East versus the West as marked by shame versus guilt. In other words, US histories of neoliberalism and homonormativity unfold in a transnational world where family violence is displaced onto the so-called non-West. This works to veil the shaming practices that happen in US high school hallways and classrooms that lead to a lot of young queer people taking their own lives. Of course, the discourse of the West as the location of stranger danger also hides the domestic violence and abuse perpetrated in Western homes on both queer and non-queer bodies. Attention to transnational discourses such as these helps resituate the current discussions around neoliberalism and homonormativity in the West from being imagined in relationship to particular normativities produced within America, for instance, to considering *over and against which nations and bodies* such projects are built.

Islam and Multicultural Exclusions

Not surprisingly, when the "Ahmet is my family" video was posted on YouTube and gained wider circulation, it elicited responses that were informed by and, in return, reproduced its logic. Most viewers echoed the sentiments in the video by posting their own names and locations and claiming Ahmet as their family. Yet, several other voices emerged to state their sentiments about who, or what, they thought had killed Ahmet Yıldız. While such comments as "Islam is a peaceful and tolerant religion. /sarcasm" (by *thomaserossi*) crafted a direct link between Islam as *religion* and honor killings in general and the killing of a gay man in particular, others, such as "I feel bad for_the GLBT communties in muslim countries its just so bad over there. very sad" (by *gilbertblaze*), imagined Islam as a *national trait/culture*. Others were threatened by the geographic and political proximity of an Islamic/barbaric Turkey and configured Islam as tradition: "If turkey will be a EU member we gonna let Spain to feed them is that ok with you? want it or not turkey IS a muslim country. you cant change their traditions" (by *digital2222*). But either as religion, national trait, or tradition, Islam was imagined to be at the root of honor killings even though nothing in the tribute website or video indicated such a connection.

Islam is of course imagined not only as the root cause of gay honor killings but also of homophobia in general. In chapter 1 I discussed the use of LGBT rights as a litmus test for headscarf activists' sincerity in their claims to support human rights. While in the context of Muslim-majority Turkey a performance of Islamic *piety* (signaled by the veil) was what led to suspicions of lack of support for homosexual rights, in the transnational circulation of "Ahmet is my family" video, a country associated with Islam was enough to signal backwardness teeming with homophobic violence. In line with Jasbir Puar's analysis of homonationalism as a global order of "civilizations" that ranks nations according to their "gay friendliness" and imagines certain geographies as already fraught with "homophobia,"[57] these comments not only slid back and forth between freezing Islam as tradition, culture, or religion and equating all three, but they also extended the geography of homophobia beyond Turkish borders into its neighbors: The comment "Does anybody of you know. how many boys in IRAN forced for a sex change operation? does anybody of you know how many gays are killed in public there?" (by *vampyriyo*) clearly imagined the Middle East as a region marked by homophobia, where Turkey and Iran, despite numerous differences in their histories and current governments, are indistinguishable. Regularly performing an erasure of racism and xenophobia in its attempts to save brown gays and lesbians from their backward traditional cultures, this logic also invisibilizes those queers who do not fare well in seemingly homo-friendly nations—where privileges are based on race, ethnicity, class, and other categories.[58] In other words, critical scholarship on honor killings and homonationalism demonstrate that both systems operate with similar structures of ascendency of whiteness and a restructuring of life and value in neoliberal and Orientalist orders. As a result, those who live as surplus existence in modern societies are rendered as collateral damage of neoliberal capitalism, and others are annihilated in geographies deemed to be fraught with acts of terror as collateral damage of securitization. Further, the fight against homophobia works to justify imperial violence and occupation as morally righteous and even supportive of democracy.

Stopping our analysis here, however, would contribute to the erasure of the multicultural exclusions, racial nationalisms, and security logics perpetrated by Turkey's very own neoliberal Islamist government. In order to continue to unfold the story, I turn to the court case that was getting ready to move forward with a single witness, Ümmühan Darama, while transnational circuits were associating honor killings with Islam with few voices contesting it. As a woman who received Islamic education from an early age, Darama made a living partially through private group seminars she gave on living ethically according to Islam. She also had owned several businesses, the last one being the café in front of which Ahmet was shot. As previously noted, Darama herself was injured in the shooting, with a bullet hitting her in one heel. During our lengthy conversation, she told me about her suspicions that she might have been the target of the bullets. She had been married to her now-deceased ex-husband via Islamic matrimony, which, as has been noted, has no legal standing in Turkey except when conducted in tandem with a secular, official engagement. Since her husband's death, Darama had been trying to get her son to be awarded his share of the inheritance. While her husband had registered their son as officially his, Darama told me that the uncles who did not want her son to receive an inheritance had had the official relationship removed from the records. She did not know how much money was involved but had traveled to Switzerland to track down a bank account that she thought was linked to the will. She recounted that after she started the legal fight for her son's inheritance, her businesses began to be attacked. In fact, her café was shot at a few times a couple of weeks *after* Ahmet's death.[59] Darama took Ahmet's murder as a warning, as the shooting took place at night when no one was present, and closed the café because she was worried for her employees' well-being.

While she was confused about how her own fight for justice for her son might have coincided with Ahmet's death, she strongly believed that there was a link and that the court case might result in finally exposing and penalizing those who had been trying to harm her businesses and intimidate her into giving up her personal fight. While Ahmet's story, described as a gay honor killing, received international media attention and easily fit into the narratives of transnational justice movements and was able to mobilize them, other sexual others in Turkey, such as Muslim single mothers who only engage in Islamic matrimony, do not have any transnational or, for that matter, national movements that will support their search for justice.

Not recognized by the legitimizing institutions of the nation-state, *nor* by national and transnational feminist and queer movements, such figures as Ümmühan Darama are not part of queer identitarian movements that only recognize legible othering but not abjection. Ahmet's story becomes recognizable transnationally the moment he is named as a gay subject who was the target of easily identifiable violence. Darama, on the other hand, does not correspond to a recognizable subject position that is already established as a minority within a liberal and neoliberal framework, even under neoliberal Islam, and therefore lacks the potential to be folded into multicultural diversity projects. Neither is her continuous battle with state institutions and with the "invisible powers" she suspected were linked to her dead husband's male kin identified as violence. This is not to portray Darama as an opportunist given her stated self-interest in the case, and I hope I make clear the structural realities that make it impossible for her to utilize the kind of pressure that transnationally backed justice movements are able to exert. Further, Darama's desire to be a witness for Ahmet's case was informed not only by her own search for justice but also by her beliefs as a Muslim woman: "I am a teacher of religion. Homosexuality is haram," she had told the daily *Radikal*, the only Turkish paper that had featured a lengthy interview with her. When I asked her to elaborate she told me, "It is Allah the greatest who interrogates people; [mortal] subjects cannot punish. . . . Murder is the biggest sin."

She added, "Homosexuality is haram, but so is smoking" while chain-smoking throughout our three-and-a-half-hour conversation, which involved a brief interruption so that she could run to the store and buy another pack. She explained that the reason homosexuality was haram, just like smoking, was that it is harmful to the human body that, after all, we borrow from Allah.[60] She said, "But during my seminars, married couples also ask me about this, so what are you going to do?" Thus treating homosexuality as (anal) sex acts, which she understood to be harmful to the body but engaged in by many (just like smoking), Darama rendered the homo/hetero binary irrelevant to Ahmet's story and disrupted the epistemology of the closet. On the other hand, her fairly individualized understanding of religious duty and sin, which signaled a potential right to sin as well as the need for individual responsibility, troubled discourses of liberal tolerance.[61] Darama's comparison of homosexuality and smoking as haram—neither act more sinful than the other—echoes the discourse of the authors of Freedom for Everyone petition analyzed in chapter 1. Yet, differently from Darama, they actively emphasized the sinful nature of homosexual relations, especially when evoking the discourse of homosexuality as sin to counter the discourse of homosexuality as illness. Darama, on the other hand, had no such investment—her own smoking, even as she denounced it as haram, spoke to her acceptance of not necessarily haram but its individual nature. A sin was something between a subject and Allah—her understanding of Islam made no room for others evaluating one's relationship to God, including acts of halal and haram. This position also directly contradicts the AKP government's evoking of Islam in order to moralize and polarize the public, which I discuss in detail in chapter 4.

Perhaps it was also her position on religious authority that made her reject religious orders. Unprompted, she told me she found it worrisome that in Istanbul increasing numbers of citizens were choosing to follow the leaders of religious orders. Darama's understanding of Islamic piety worked to embolden her vis-à-vis any and all authority—I fear nothing but Allah, she proclaimed. This fearlessness was what enabled her to continue her struggle to attain her son's inheritance despite attacks and her continued involvement in Ahmet's court case despite police discouragement. In the interview she had given to *Radikal* she had mentioned that the police had asked her to stay out of this "dirty case." While I assumed this was a reference to Ahmet's gayness, I nevertheless decided to ask her about it during our interview. She recounted that the police had told her that Ahmet and his boyfriend were in the business of making pornographic video recordings and selling them in Europe. This turned out to be a reference to a video Ahmet was asked to submit as evidence of his gayness in order to qualify for exemption from military service.[62] At the time of our interview, Darama had no reason to doubt the porn sale in Europe story but nevertheless was unfazed by this suggestion, insisting that it was her duty as a Muslim to stand up against violence. Thus, in her case, Islamic ethics and duty meant not necessarily submission to authority, but a deeply engaged, ongoing critique of it.

Recent discussions of Islam and female piety have predominantly addressed submission to external authority and the challenges this religious requirement poses to liberal ideas about agency and resistance. Saba Mahmood's seminal *Politics of Piety* has forcefully intervened in feminist theory's assumptions that the only forms of engagement with norms available to subjects are submission and subversion and that agency resided only in the latter. Even as Mahmood recognized instances where women in the Egyptian *dawa* movement at times found themselves in the position of disobeying their husbands or other male authority figures in order to continue practicing Islamic ethics, her emphasis on *sabr* (patience; endurance) as an active engagement with difficulty makes a clear division between Islamic and secular engagements with the concept. In her account, secular liberal women understood patience as a form of pragmatism, a way to accept and deal with hardships, while pious women emphasized that this constituted a way of living one's pain piously.

The question of submission and modesty as defining features of female piety have been complicated by scholars who have asked: What of those contexts in which female submission and modesty are employed by state security forces in order to discourage political dissent and punish protesting female bodies?[63] Not only does this account overlook the question of Muslim female agency and social change, especially since we cannot possibly assume that all desire for social change to be liberal, but it also leaves out figures like Darama who understand their faith as a form of fearlessness vis-à-vis authority and as an invitation to question and challenge it. Darama's distaste for human authority and her suspect of religious orders is especially poignant under the neoliberal Islamist regime of the AKP, which continuously discourages and punishes dissent and demands boundless loyalty from its followers and obedience from all. Referred to as *biat* in Turkish, this authoritarian demand for allegiance has been targeted with criticism by most oppositional voices in the country. The particular danger of reproducing anthropological difference in this instance lies in imagining submission as authentic and disobedience as foreign to Islam, which is enabled by reducing demands for social change to a liberal impulse.

If "gay honor killing" is an archive that gains robustness, coherence, and consistency as it circulates transnationally, then Darama is a figure who haunts this archive. She disrupts not only the Islamophobia that sticks to honor killings as a backward and traditional form of crime but also the easy narratives of exclusion, violence, and justice that are evoked by the archive both in and outside of Turkey. The fact that Darama found herself excluded from state mechanisms of justice, familial networks, and social justice movements speaks to the unsustainability of binaries of the state versus the family *and* state mechanisms versus social justice movements. It also reveals the pervasive logics of not only homonationalism and Islamophobia but also the multicultural exclusions of neoliberal Islam in Turkey. Her story is a testimony to what we have to gain from moving beyond the possibilities of identitarian politics and from adopting an expansive vision of what forms of violence are being perpetrated on all kinds of citizen-subjects because their sexualities, intimacies, and kinship formations are left outside of the legitimizing institutions of, in this case, the neoliberal Islamist nation-state. It is also a reminder of different modalities of Islamic piety, not all of which are predicated on submission. Some clearly can imagine resistance to brutality and a rejection of blind loyalty to other subjects to follow from one's duty to act "with the fear of Allah."

Difference, Unincorporated

While it is common to encounter attributions of honor killings to Muslim cultures transnationally, the geographies of honor killings marking family violence and backwardness shift depending on where, and by whom, the scholarship and popular narratives on the topic are produced. Islam is not always claimed as the culprit, especially if the feminist humanitarian critique comes out of Muslim-majority countries or is produced by Muslim authors, among whom it is common knowledge that honor killings are denounced by Islamic religious authorities.[64] When produced in these geographies, or by those with diasporic connections to them, it is very frequently Kurds and

Kurdish feudal customs that are presented as responsible for honor killings.[65] For instance, the 2004 volume *Violence in the Name of Honour* speaks of "the gender war on women," universal patriarchy, and women's lack of feminist consciousness, tropes that have been deeply problematized by transnational feminist scholarship,[66] and names Iraqi Kurdistan as well as Kurdish communities in Europe as locations of honor killings.[67]

This bears similarities to wider Turkish scholarship on the topic, some of which is included in this volume. Honor killings in Turkish are in fact called *töre cinayetleri* (custom killings), situating the cause of violence in backward traditions and customs, which are imagined to be located in Turkey's Kurdish and feudal East. In cases of *töre cinayetleri* in Turkey, violence, commonly against women,[68] is presented as a matter of tradition, which lets the role of institutions, such as the law or the state's negligence in not funding women's shelters, fade into the background—a process Dicle Koğacıoğlu termed "tradition effect."[69] This process is facilitated especially by the discursive construction of tradition as native, simultaneously archaic and timeless, and institutions as modern, contemporary, and timely. It is also facilitated by the perception of these purportedly backward traditions as not authentically belonging to the *Turkish* nation, customs, and traditions. In other words, the *Independent*'s narrative of Turkey's internal clash of civilizations is also very much a national narrative about the Turkish state and the Kurdish feudal family, representing modernity and tradition, progress and backwardness, respectively.

In her critique of common descriptions of social and political processes in Eastern Turkey, Lale Yalçın-Heckmann underlines that in Turkish scholarship, "Eastern social structure" is often described as "'traditional,' 'unintegrated,' 'fragmented' and 'underdeveloped.'"[70] This inevitably begs the question of what this social system is supposed to be integrated into and gives away the Turkish state's historical assimilation policies regarding Kurds and other minorities. Yet as a project uneasy with itself, Turkishness has historically attempted both to erase and incorporate Kurds and has ultimately treated them as unincorporable *difference*. Custom/honor killings constitute one of the markers of this unincorporability, marking Kurdish citizens as inherently different. Every honor killing functions as a performative failure of the promise of incorporability and as proof of the presumed Kurdish *essence* that no amount of modernization can wash off. The unincorporability of Kurds, and the anxieties that follow from it, are also to be found in the social science descriptions of Kurdish tribal loyalty, often understood and described as a challenge to national loyalty to the Turkish state—both in its object of loyalty but also in its form, which is configured as irrational and traditional (as opposed to rational and modern).[71]

The Kurdish armed resistance that was organized by the PKK (Kurdistan Workers' Party) in the late 1970s and that turned into an ongoing, wider separatist armed conflict with Turkish Armed Forces beginning in 1984 have marked the Kurds' supposed failure of showing national loyalty not only in terms of their presumed feudal social organization but also in terms of their framing as terrorist subjects aiming to undo national unity. The armed conflict led to tens of thousands dead and decades of states of emergency, curfews, and forced migrations resulting from the military burning down villages for "aiding terrorism."[72] Following the capture and imprisonment of PKK leader Abdullah Öcalan, who called for a cease-fire (which led to fragmentation within the Kurdish liberation movement), and as a result of Turkey's admittance to the EU accession process, Turkey enacted several failed neoliberal inclusion projects, such as a Kurdish-language public television station and primary education conducted in the mother tongue. The period following Öcalan's capture cannot be recounted as a homogenous, well-intentioned peace process, however; in the mid-2000s, such events as the bombing of the Umut Bookstore in Şemdinli, which left one person dead and several injured, by figures who were revealed to be members of the Turkish gendarmerie's intelligence unit JİTEM, troubled the AKP government's narratives of neoliberal inclusion.

A renewed cease-fire beginning in 2013 ended in July 2015 following President Erdoğan's declaration annulling the Dolmabahçe agreement that had been collectively announced by ministers from the AKP government and the pro-Kurdish HDP's negotiation team. It is impossible not to draw links between Erdoğan's calling off the negotiations and the HDP's success in the June 2015 elections. Garnering an unprecedented 13 percent of the vote via a campaign that openly challenged Erdoğan's push for a presidential system, HDP not only became the first pro-Kurdish party to make it over the 10 percent threshold necessary to gain seats in the parliament, but the party also managed to end AKP's parliamentary majority, which was necessary in order to push the proposed presidential system through. Within a few months of the June 2015 elections, HDP rallies, a socialist youth delegation in Suruç on their way to bring aid to Kobane, and a Democracy, Peace, Labor rally in Ankara were all bombed. Some of these events have been linked to the Islamic State, but as many pointed out, the AKP government had been criticized for supporting Islamic State militants in their fight against Bashar Hafez al-Assad in Syria by allowing direct arms and ammunition aid as well as lax border control in southern Turkey. Using the so-called state of terror in the country, AKP was able to recover more votes than it had lost, and after a hung parliament, regained power in November 2015. Since then, the Kurdish southeast has experienced numerous military operations and twenty-four-hour curfews for weeks on end, as well as arrests and removal of mayors from their posts, especially in parts of Diyarbakır where Kurdish towns have declared autonomous zones in order to stand up to the increasing authoritarian oppression and violence perpetrated by the government. The military operations climaxed in July 2016 during the Turkish military's siege of Cizre (under curfew at the time), with the killing of 177 civilians, including 25 children in their homes. The endless detentions, arrests, and purging of Kurdish politicians, journalists, and intellectuals, as well as Turkish academics who have stood up against violence against Kurds, are still continuing.

When rethought in the context of the historical and ongoing war of the Turkish state against its Kurdish citizens, the exceptionalism of Ahmet's death, as well as that of any others recorded as honor killings, demand scrutiny. The framework of honor killing not only privileges sudden death as violence, it overlooks the many slow deaths that transpire at the hands of family members as well as other social institutions, which need to be a part of our thinking about violence. It also exceptionalizes the Kurdish gay life in the metropole as valuable while overlooking the historical divestments from Kurdish regions, forced migrations, mass arrests, jailings, purges, and Kurdish lives and deaths under indefinite curfews and military operations; proving the lack of value Kurdish life has had, and continues to have, in the Turkish Republic. *Töre* (custom) further provides a racializing script that produces honor killings as a Kurdish pathology and singles out sudden deaths (which are enacted by Kurdish bodies on Kurdish bodies) as newsworthy and real violence, adding to the neoliberal understanding of the family as a safe haven. The unacknowledged distribution of slow deaths among Kurds caused by the Turkish state for a long time marked such violence as less significant because it was seen as less murderous. The transnational mourning of Ahmet's murder because he was a gay man, as well as the national rhetoric blaming his death on Kurdish customs, work only to erase the many deaths and death-like conditions Ahmet could have experienced had he been living in what the Turkish state deemed as terroristic geographies of the Kurdish southeast. Similarly, the fact that Ahmet's body was not claimed for a week is of course worth mourning, but this fact cannot be understood separately from the thousands of Kurdish bodies rendered un-buryable and un-grievable due to their dismemberment or from being burned to the point of being unidentifiable.[73] During the siege of Cizre, Kurdish citizens were handed their dead in the form of hardly identifiable body parts in plastic bags, and the family of ten-year old Cemile Cizir Çağırga kept her corpse in an icebox for days with the hope of being able to give her a proper burial once the curfew was lifted. Banu Bargu refers to this war on dead bodies, this "dishonoring, disciplining, and punishment of the living through the utilization of the dead as postmortem objects and sites of violence" as "another necropolitics": "an entire ensemble of diverse practices that target the dead as a surrogate for, and means of, targeting the living."[74] In the context of the war on Kurdish bodies, insulating and valorizing the individual death of a Kurdish gay man invisibilizes and thus shores up the logic of the racial state.

Conclusion

My desire to complicate the story of Ahmet's murder and to show how exceptionalizing the death of a Kurdish gay man invisibilizes various other injustices is by no means to dismiss the tragedy that is Ahmet's death or to undermine the fight for justice by those who loved him. Yet it remains important and necessary to keep asking how the framework of honor killing sensationalizes and racializes particular forms of violence both nationally and transnationally and how circumscribing demands for justice with minoritarian frameworks leaves certain subjects altogether outside of intelligibility. It is also important to question the power of a prefigured honor killing framework to foreshadow who will be charged with murder.

While the question of who actually killed Ahmet is not the key question that guides my analysis, and while I find that an exclusive focus on this question in fact hides other, more pressing, questions about justice that we might want to ask, I will briefly visit the charges resulting from the lawsuit in order to reflect on the limits of juridical justice. Throughout the case, and in its aftermath, several people voiced questions about the murder as well as dissatisfaction with the court decision to charge Ahmet's father for the crime. For instance, Darama raised the question that the format of the murder did not really fit the profile of customary honor killings, as no one from the family had claimed responsibility for the murder. Most often, when a family kills a (usually female) member to supposedly cleanse family honor, the point is for a family member to publicly admit to it and turn themselves in, she pointed out. The fact that no one had come forth to claim Ahmet's murder as a purposeful act made it questionable whether this was an honor killing at all.

Further, there was the fact that two cars had simultaneously approached Ahmet's parked car. While one had blocked his exit, gunshots were fired from the other. Then both cars drove off simultaneously. Ahmet's boyfriend complained to the media, and during his interview with me, that the court kept failing to request registration information for one of the cars even though they knew of its existence. Plus, Ahmet's father was an old man with a prosthetic in one leg—how could he possibly have driven, shot at Ahmet, and escaped with such swiftness? And who had driven the other car? Ahmet's friend Şervan, who also had known his family a little, mentioned in our interview that Ahmet's father was a "weak" man and that he was not in charge when it came to family affairs. He said it was possible that the family might be behind Ahmet's murder but that he could not imagine his father wanting it. As the only son of his parents, Ahmet was a prized child.

I do not bring up these opinions to refocus the discussion on who the *real* murderer might be, but to point out that the juridical reflex of charging the father with a murder categorized as an honor killing is not only theoretically questionable but also an unsatisfactory response to those who followed the case hoping for justice. Despite these doubts, Ahmet's father was the only one charged with the murder. Yet, perhaps what ultimately finalized the reification of the framework of honor killing as *the* story of Ahmet's murder, and his father as *the* murderer, was the 2012 movie *Zenne* (English title: *The Zenne Dancer*), allegedly based on Ahmet's story. Debuting at the Antalya Golden Orange Film Festival in Turkey, and collecting several awards, including for "best national film" and "best debut film," *Zenne* went on to screenings at various Turkish and international film festivals. As suggested by its tagline, "truth sometimes kills" (*dürüstlük bazen öldürür*), the movie perpetuates Ahmet's murder as punishment for truth, equaling outness with honesty and the closet with the lack thereof. In the movie, many of the allegations gain the status of truth—Ahmet's father is depicted as the murderer, even though the movie also suggests that the real demand for it came from Ahmet's mother.

Told as the tragic story of a Turkish gay man, the narrative of the movie demonstrates how the framework of gay honor killing coalesces and upholds neoliberal narratives, presenting both the pursuit of happiness and violence as individual events. With no mention of structural violence perpetrated daily on Kurdish bodies by the Turkish state, the movie in fact depoliticizes a story it presents as political: politics are reduced to the right of minoritized and legible liberal subjects to individual happiness. It is not that the state does not make any appearance in the movie, however. The Turkish state is found guilty for forcing gay men to turn in visual proof of their gayness in order to be exempt from military service. No doubt such state and military practices deserve this critique, but this focus forgets Ahmet's Kurdishness vis-à-vis the state and the military and only remembers it vis-à-vis the family. Kurdishness is evoked to signal backwardness and traditionalism but not to expose racialized state violence. Perhaps as a result of its equation of Kurdishness with backwardness, the movie also collapses ethnicity and class—something Şervan brought up during our conversation as one of his critiques of the film. Ahmet's family was upper middle class—why were they depicted as working-class people with a modest home? The so-called backwardness of honor killings and of Ahmet's parents is thus amplified by Kurdish ethnicity, religiosity, *and* an invented lower-middle-class status. The *Independent*'s narrative and its many erasures are thus echoed in this Turkish production, shaping how Ahmet's story will be remembered nationally and internationally.

Yet Ahmet's story is full of actual details that interrupt neoliberal frameworks of minoritarian subjects and simple accounts of backward families. It allows us to ask questions as to what counts as justice, who benefits from existing structures of it, who feels satisfied with what they deliver, what lives are always already left out of these structures, and what deaths are rendered un-grievable. There are ways to tell Ahmet's story that do not rely on frameworks of honor killing, outness, and families of choice and that do not rely on alleged alternatives that end up reifying custom, tradition, locality, and cultural authenticity. There are ways to understand his story and imagine justice, compassion, and finding different ways of living meaningful and self-determined lives. While the details of Ahmet's murder might remain the same, envisioning other ways of understanding his life and death remain important, given that language, knowledge, and ways of thinking about the world travel more intensively than ever before and because we all live our lives in the light, and the shadows, of narratives that unfold within the context of intensifying transnational connectivity.

Three

Trans Terror, Deep Citizenship, and the Politics of Hate

In the winter of 2008, when I first started meeting up with trans sex workers in Ankara, the most pressing issue on their personal and activist agenda were the heavy fines they were receiving due to Kabahatler Kanunu (Law of Misdemeanors), which had been modified in 2005 under the AKP government.[1] Trans women recounted how in the past they would often endure police beatings while a plastic bag was pulled over their heads and then were dumped in large garbage disposal areas outside of the city.[2] During the time of our conversations, however, this treatment had been replaced by fines they received under the Law of Misdemeanors when simply walking in the streets, standing on a street corner, and even when sitting in a car parked by the curb. The Ankara-based queer activist organization Pembe Hayat (Pink Life) was trying to keep track of the fines trans women were receiving in Ankara and Istanbul in order to prepare a report and file a complaint. It seemed that it had become impossible for most trans women to be in public without being fined—some received multiple fines a day and struggled to pay them off.

This did not mean that older forms of physical violence against trans women had been simply replaced by economic violence; rather, the latter was superimposed onto the former. Alongside documenting the fines handed out by the police, trans sex workers were also starting a campaign demanding a hate crime law given the persistence of trans murders. In this chapter

I trace the travel of the concept of hate crimes to Turkey and investigate the demand by trans sex workers for a hate crime law. This social justice move may seem peculiar in the context I describe, since as I detail below, trans sex workers have historically been and continue to be prime targets of state and police violence and are therefore under no illusion regarding the protective potential of the law, law enforcement, or the state. Their demands for a hate crime law needs to be understood, I argue, not as a desire to be folded into respectable citizenship, but as a recognition of the structural and affective conditions of life under neoliberal capitalism. A rethinking of demands for hate crime laws is also necessary because *hate crime* functions as a cultural as well as juridical concept. Hate, as we will see, is theorized by these activists as the logic of distribution of uneven life chances by neoliberal capitalism, the state, and what I refer to as deep citizens, who I define as civilians who distribute violence following what they understand to be state ideologies. As a result, their demand for a hate crime law is informed by their refusal of life as defined by neoliberalism.

This theorization of hate emerges from trans women sex workers' intimate relationship with public space. The neoliberal transformations in Turkey since the 1980s, especially urban restructuring projects, have resulted in an increased securitization of inner-city spaces as well as changes in the police force. One of the important outcomes of these shifts has been the transfer of the discourse of terror from Kurdish rural regions to urban spaces, resulting in various groups being targeted with the logic of terrorism. It is through the discourse of *travesti terörü* (transvestite terror) found in news media coverage that trans women's relationship to the public was framed and their exclusion from public space justified. The deployment of terror as the logic of rendering subjects criminal, monstrous, and less than human extends today to a large part of the population.[3] Tens of thousands of academics, political figures, journalists, artists, lawyers, and judges in Turkey are tried with terrorism-related charges, and many events have been cancelled especially under the state of emergency declared following the coup attempt in the summer of 2016, including all LGBT-related events in Ankara (the capital city) due to security measures. I recount many of these more recent developments in the next chapter. In this chapter, I trace trans women sex workers' experiences that connect labor, precarity, urban development, and increased securitization in order to discuss the links between the logic of terror with that of hate. I will show that these changes have meant that both the police extortion practices and the dislocation of trans sex workers from public space have become individualized over time, an individualization against which trans sex workers organized collectively. I will then turn to a discussion of trans activists' interpretation of hate and life under neoliberal Islam in order to reflect on what lies behind such demands as hate crime laws. As we will see, far from constituting local authenticity or an essential cultural difference, trans sex workers' analyses provide us with important tools with which to think about conditions of life under neoliberalism and securitization everywhere, including the question of the incorporation of difference itself.

Through this story I argue that we need to rethink the presumed figure of the demander of hate crime laws, which in existing literature is often theorized as a gay or lesbian subject with class and race privileges asking for police protection from criminal others precisely because they imagine themselves as subjects of protection and not targets of police violence.[4] These, according to queer and trans studies scholarship, are homonormative figures who demand inclusion into the neoliberal ranks of respectability and as a result contribute to the criminalization of poor people of color and to the expansion of the prison-industrial complex. I recognize that the parameters of these analyses are primarily confined to the contexts of the United States and secondarily to those of Western Europe. Yet the task here is not to rely on cultural difference in attempts to decenter the United States or Western Europe and to show how these theories fail to account for the activism of trans sex workers in Turkey. Instead of understanding the travel of hate crime law demands to the context of contemporary Turkey as a mimicry of Western LGBT politics *or* seeking radical alterity in the subjects that speak it, a critical translation approach demands that we see the significant parallels between these contexts, including the ways in which neoliberal urban restructuring and increasing authoritarian securitization unfolds in each. Therefore, my argument, while grounded in the particularities of Turkey, extends beyond them to suggest that the voices of trans women activists to be found in these pages make a case for listening with curiosity to similar demands made elsewhere instead of assuming that each call for a hate crime law uncritically reproduces the logic of neoliberal inclusion.

Further, understanding hate crime not just as a juridical but also as a cultural concept necessitates that we attend to the structures of feeling at work in a particular political moment. It is precisely because of their experiences of hate and terror that trans women sex workers evoke "hate crime" in order to make sense of the structures they inhabit. The times in which their demands were made also feature law taking on particular meanings, since at present lawyers and judges constitute a politically targeted group in Turkey alongside human rights activists, educators, academics, and journalists, with more than four thousand judges and lawyers sacked, jailed, or both in the summer of 2018.[5] Feminist legal activism where feminist lawyers and NGOs become legal advocates for cases of violence against women and of violence against queer and trans subjects continues to be a strong tradition in the country.[6] Almost all LGBT activist organizations have volunteer lawyers supporting them in addition to an official lawyer who are increasingly central to social justice work with the rising rates of jailed activists and of the banning of gatherings and events (which I will speak more about in chapter 4). Law itself, in other words, is experienced as a political battlefield in Turkey, and most legal battles being fought are far from being projects of liberal inclusion or so-called equality—they are rather about social, political, and economic survival. While I do not focus on trans/feminist legal activism in this chapter, and understand transfeminine sex workers' demands for a hate crime law as a response to a culture of hate, I find it necessary to underline this context and caution against universalizing the functions of law in our attempts to critique the universalisms it produces.[7]

Law and the Politics of Public Space

The 2005 Law of Misdemeanors was of course neither the beginning of trans women's issues with the police nor the first legislation of various subjects' access and relationship to public space. In fact, centralization of the police force citing public order issues dates back to the Ottoman modernization period, or Tanzimat, and was key to "the process of the centralization/modernization of the state."[8] Further, the police force was designed, in the Ottoman Empire and elsewhere, to protect propertied classes in the density of urban space.[9] Mark David Wyers maintains that the regulation of sex work and brothels has always been a classed matter in the late Ottoman Empire and early Turkish Republic.[10] The historical attempts to contain sex work within the confines of brothels in order to secure the public space for the virtuous inevitably meant that "the constant battle waged by the morals police against clandestine prostitution represented, in part, the struggle to define space."[11]

The centrality of the police force in general, and its role in defining public space in particular, intensified around the globe during the neoliberal era, especially starting in the 1990s with the targeting of various minorities and revolutionary groups.[12] In the case of Turkey, the way in which law enforcement attained growing powers has deep ties to the post-1980 political rule that linked the (neo)liberalization to the Islamicization of the nation in the war against communism. In the introduction I discussed that the proposal of Islam, and, more specifically, what was referred to as *Türk-İslam sentezi* (Turkish-Islamic synthesis), as a remedy for healing political rifts in the country also led to the relaxing of the activities of religious orders and increasing the number of İmam Hatip (imam training) schools in the nation. While on the surface this remedy was intended to stop the divisions between communists and the fascist ultra-Right, it was accomplished in conjunction with the US war against the communist threat and ultimately led to the crushing of the Left in Turkey. The formula of Turkish-Islamic synthesis also swung Islam to the right, foreclosing Left definitions and approaches to Islam.[13] It was in this climate of promotion of a Turkish-Islamic synthesis that the cleric Fethullah Gülen emerged as a prominent figure.[14] Initially a member of the Nurcu religious sect and founder of the Erzurum chapter of the Association for the Fight against Communism (Komünizmle Mücadele Derneği), Gülen rapidly developed his own following. His "houses of light" (*ışık evleri*), informal dormitory-style homes where young men were hosted and where his sermons were played for guests, would later become key sites where student-followers would be encouraged to join the police schools and police academy and then to invite fellow students, especially those attending school away from home, to spend their weekends in houses of light.[15] Regulations that in the 1990s relaxed the qualifications for application to police schools paved the way for what essentially turned into a houses-of-light-to-police-academy pipeline.[16]

Given the historical ties between anti-communism, right-wing Sunnism, and the police force, it should not come as a surprise to see in the 1990s the police specifically target Muslim minority Alevi radical Left neighborhoods under the guise of fighting against "Left terrorism."[17] During this state of emergency period, southeast Turkey's regional mayor Hayri Kozakoğlu, who had fought against the armed Kurdish Workers' Party (PKK) in rural southeastern Turkey, had just been appointed to Istanbul in order to start pilot programs in neighborhoods that were marked as locations of urban leftist terrorism. Also during this same period, militarized police forces, such as Çevik Kuvvetler (Riot Police) and Özel Harekat Timi (Special Operations Team), were formed, which set up barricades and checkpoints surrounding the Alevi neighborhoods 1 Mayıs, Gazi, Armutlu, Okmeydanı, and Gülsuyu.[18] The discourse of *varoş* (ghetto) that emerged during this time and that presented the political radicalism of these neighborhoods as class-cultural differences further alienated middle-class citizens of Istanbul from what was presented as dangerous and heavily militarized and policed areas of the city.[19] Therefore, the policing of poor and radical-Left Alevi-majority neighborhoods was not an attack on a blanket urban poverty as much as it was the targeting of the revolutionary Left within the poor and working classes.[20] During the same years these neighborhoods were targeted, other poor areas of Istanbul that housed squatter homes were approached not with criminalization, but with the municipality and the government's desire to mobilize them as a voter base. Newly arriving immigrants often built squatter homes illegally on public land and in close proximity to wealthy gated communities. Municipalities issued pardons and distributed titles for the land in exchange for political loyalty at the ballot box. In other words, poverty that was incorporable as voter base was governed differently from poverty that was radicalized and therefore not worth government investment.[21]

The 1990s also saw the first organized attacks on the neighborhoods of trans sex workers and the collective forced displacement of trans women from their homes. The first well-known case of this took place during the United Nations Habitat II meetings in Istanbul in 1996.[22] As Taksim Square, the promenade İstiklal, and the surrounding side streets were experiencing a significant makeover to render the area more presentable to international visitors, street kids and stray dogs were removed from the vicinity by the police. Simultaneously, a more violent gentrification project targeted Ülker Sokak (Ülker Street), where a number of trans women lived and worked. Their apartments were besieged, their windows and doors broken, and the women were threatened and ultimately physically assaulted by those deemed to be *mahalle sakinleri* (ordinary inhabitants of the neighborhood).[23] Ülker Street constitutes one of the early moments of collective displacement of an undesired minority for the purpose of rent-seeking under the rubric of urban renewal. Pınar Selek's detailed ethnographic account of the incidents documents the role played by various entities, including the police, the Association for the Beautification of Beyoğlu and Ayaspaşa, the neighborhood's "ordinary inhabitants," and nationalist youth groups who joined the attacks against trans women until they finally left their homes and fled the neighborhood.[24] The police involvement in this incident is reported to be fairly direct: While some trans women were under the impression that the police officers were paid to dislocate them by the owners of large nightclubs in the Beyoğlu district that were losing significant income to Ülker Street, they also mentioned the officer in charge, Hortum Süleyman (Süleyman the Hose), as a figure who had made it his personal mission to clean Beyoğlu of trans women. Officer Süleyman had been appointed as the superintendent of the Beyoğlu police squad in the early 1990s and earned his nickname during this initial period by systematically beating trans women with a hose at the police station. He recounts in his interview with Selek having been previously (and according to himself, unfairly) discharged from the region and eventually having been reinstated during the Habitat II period.[25] It was under his guidance that police officers broke windows and doors of trans women's homes, destroyed their belongings, and burned down some of the apartments by throwing Molotov cocktails.

During this same period, the go-to narrative for media when reporting on trans sex workers was *travesti terörü* (transvestite terror), where third-page news would present trans women as irrationally violent, allegedly terrorizing innocent male bodies with pocketknives and switchblades as they roamed freeways for sex work. The logic of the irrecoverable monstrosity of trans women was echoed in the police treatment they received as well as the growing number of trans murder cases, where perpetrators often received reduced sentences by claiming to have been provoked by the deceased. Perversely featuring the murderers' testimonies as evidence for trans women's alleged terrorism aimed at the (male) national public, media reports on these cases further reified the monstrosity of the trans women's bodies and contributed to the "trans terror" archives, citing testimonies in which trans women allegedly attacked the murderers physically, insulted their manhood, and offered them reverse/perverse relations (*ters ilişki*) as legitimate reasons for a reduction in sentence.[26] In other words, in the 1990s as the Turkish state claimed to be fighting Kurdish terror in the rural east and southeast, a militarized police force was being forged to fight alleged leftist terror and transvestite terror in the urban west. It was remarkable, as trans women noted, to watch police officers who had been so viciously violent in the past handing out citations in the 2000s.

It would be easy to regard the Law of Misdemeanors as a drastic historical change whereby police extortion replaced brute state violence. Yet, extortion by the police had a long history for trans women, as Mother Hülya reminisced about sex work in the 1960s and 1970s. "Back then, we did not even endure nosebleed. Police squads would arrive at Abanoz [Street], they would take whatever they would behind closed doors, and then would leave."[27] One would be hard-pressed not to see the clear differences between the old extortion system and Kabahatler Kanunu, however: First, whereas in the old system Mother Hülya referred to police had informal dealings with the owners and managers of brothels, in the case of Kabahatler Kanunu, each individual trans woman, presumed to be a sex worker, was targeted—in other words, extortion was *individualized*. As an extension of this, sex work was respatialized/remapped from the brothel onto the bodies of trans women.

Second, the law worked to *codify extortion* and positioned the state as the direct beneficiary. And third, Kabahatler Kanunu ultimately was employed by law enforcement toward banishing trans women from the public sphere altogether. Therefore, the Law of Misdemeanors is best understood as part of a larger system that marked trans sex workers' bodies simultaneously as surplus existence *and* extractable labor.[28] What did the Law of Misdemeanors legislate against exactly, and under what pretense did it target trans women?

Under this legislation offenses that threatened *toplum düzeni* (social order), *genel ahlak* (general morality), *genel sağlık* (general health), *çevre* (environment), and *ekonomik düzen* (economic order) were codified and "protected."[29] Ambiguous phrases in various articles in the Turkish penal code, such as "social order" and "general morality," were nothing new and historically had given the police extreme freedom to discipline citizens through claims that they disrupted them.[30] For instance, the ambiguity of "general morality" in the context of state-regulated sex work had given Turkish police the freedom to investigate any cis- and heterosexual-presenting women suspected of being engaged in *vesikasız* (unregistered) sex work.[31] Yet, in the case of trans sex workers, the excuse of "potential illegitimate prostitution" was not employed to discipline them into respectable citizenship. Since their existence was always already affiliated with sex work, unlike cis women, trans women did not need to be caught sharing a hotel room with someone who was not an official spouse or to be walking alone at night to be assumed to be a sex worker. And because they were not considered recoupable in terms of national morality, trans sex workers—viewed differently from "individuals to be corrected"—were treated as being akin to human monsters who could not possibly be disciplined, corrected, and folded into respectability.[32] In other words, the monstrosity of trans women's bodies, which was reified in perpetual news of so-called transvestite terror, was also affirmed by the police conduct toward them.

Yet, while not recoverable into proper respectability and national belonging, trans women nevertheless occupied a peculiar space of simultaneous disposability and extractability, reminding us that these two conditions do not need to be mutually exclusive. On one hand, they were surplus existence and were never meant to enter the labor force: their exclusion from institutions of education and respectable as well as disreputable jobs (such as licensed sex work) spoke to such marginalization.[33] They were also easily disposable by the police and vigilante civilians, as experienced in frequent trans murders as well as organized attacks on their neighborhoods, for which ordinary citizens seemed to be readily available. At the same time, when they found access to work and income, the law and the state appeared as agents of extraction *while* marking their labor and their public existence as illegal. While the state refused to recognize their labor *and* the conditions under which they were made to labor, the Law of Misdemeanors managed to extract value from trans women while making their work conditions increasingly impossible.[34]

Among the offenses coded and criminalized in the Law of Misdemeanors, along with soliciting, drunkenness, littering, smoking, and carrying guns, the items *işgal* (occupying) and *rahatsız etme* (disturbing) are especially noteworthy as they are repeatedly used in fining trans sex workers. The item *işgal* refers to unlawful occupation of land and thus implies the lack of belonging of those engaged in the occupation.[35] The logic of işgal produces the subjects it exiles as outsiders and unlawful occupants. The ability to define public space as unlawfully occupiable gives free reign to police officers to interpret and therefore *make* the law as they decide whom to fine and whom to treat as regular citizens walking or standing on sidewalks. Therefore, the exercise of the law works simultaneously as a codified extortion mechanism, as indicated by trans women's accounts of police officers who smile and say, "You know how to make the money to pay for this," and contradictorily as a method of turning the entire city into a prostitution-free and trans-free zone.

Thus, I join scholars who have emphasized the interpretive powers of the police as well as selective enforcement of laws especially when targeting the disenfranchised.[36] While not designating any particular area of urban space as a prostitution-free zone, the Law of Misdemeanors turns the entire city into a space of exclusion and gives the police definitional powers to determine which subjects are lawful in public space and which are not.[37] There is nothing in the law of offenses that *categorically* renders particular subjects unlawful and excluded.[38] Thus, while it is important to pay attention to the categorical exclusions we can directly read off the laws, I suggest we also pay attention to what the state at times refuses to openly criminalize.[39] Kabahatler Kanunu illustrates that looking at direct and categorical criminalization (of sex work or transfemininity) will help us uncover only one level of state regulation of those who are rendered sexually abject and excluded from proper citizenship and belonging in the nation.

The respatialization of the brothel and the reification of the disreputable, the undesirable, and the abject in the body of the trans woman (always presumed to be a sex worker) continued with gentrification projects in the neighborhoods of Eryaman (Ankara) in 2006 and of Avcılar (Istanbul) in 2012. I will speak to the changing nature of the police involvement in those cases in more detail below, but in both cases it was obvious to trans women that their displacement was tied to urban renewal projects and rent-seeking. Ten years after the Ülker Street incident, in 2006 in Eryaman, trans women suddenly began to be attacked by civilians, on the streets and in their homes, shot at, cruelly beaten, and their properties seized.[40] As a result, many trans women escaped either to the inner city or left Ankara altogether, some leaving their homes and almost all leaving their belongings behind. Trans women speculated that the thugs who attacked them were hired by the Etimesgut mayor's office to assist the gentrification of Eryaman and that the police were told to keep quiet. In the words of "A":

> Money talks. The police always take bribes from travestis. "Don't make a fuss, do your work, but also see me because I let you do your work," says the police.[41] But this time orders are from a higher place. The order is from [Ankara mayor] Melih Gökçek, even higher, from the Ministry of the Internal Affairs they say.[42] Melih Gökçek apparently said years ago "We threw them to Eryaman from inner city; they will not be causing any disorder in the city anymore." But Eryaman has started to become part of the inner city, there are five thousands apartments, Kontaş Canberk Construction Company is building luxury condos on the same street where the *travestis* walk [çarka çıkmak]. People are going to pay for those luxury buildings, [but] when they take a stroll in the evening and see *travestis* around, or hear that that is where the *travestis* walk the street, they won't buy those apartments. There is Ministry of the Internal Affairs, Etimesgut Mayorship, the construction company, the police involved in this. It is a very organized cleansing operation.[43]

Another six years later, in 2012, a group of trans women who had homes in the Meis housing development in Avcılar were targeted by several civilians living in the same complex. What started as "marches against prostitution" turned into violent attacks on trans women's homes and setting parts of the housing complex on fire, as a result of which police padlocked seven homes despite the lack of any evidence of illegal activities.[44] Soon thereafter, one of the trans women who had been left homeless was murdered. Most of the women ended up selling their homes for under-market prices and leaving Meis: Several news reports by trans women or trans-friendly journalists indicated that the real estate market in Avcılar, which had taken a hit after the 1999 earthquake, was picking up again due to its prime location by the sea and its proximity to the new public transportation system Metrobüs. As the area was regaining its marketability to the middle and upper classes, trans women who had become homeowners when the area was undesirable suddenly found themselves in the way of projected real estate values.[45]

As scholars have noted, the containment of so-called bad publics becomes especially important when cities try to package and market various areas to respectable middle classes.[46] At the same time, the value of bodies marked as surplus existence is precisely their valuelessness, signaling areas of investability in times of speculative finance.[47] In the case of urban trans women in Turkey, the simultaneous displacement that I recounted via the Ülker Street, Eryaman, and Avcılar incidents *and* the deployment of extraction via the Law of Misdemeanors speaks to multiple layers of neoliberal state violence that do not necessarily have to neatly slot bodies into categories of extractable labor and surplus existence. Trans women's bodies continue to mark the location of the undesirables, both in terms of alleged perversion and criminality and also as an embodied obstacle to urban renewal projects *while* their laboring bodies are seen as sites of extraction.

Kabahatler Kanunu is symptomatic of the growing powers allocated to the police as well as the rapidly disappearing public spaces in Turkey, which historically were always ethnically, religiously, and nationally coded. The privatization of public goods starting in the 1980s especially accelerated during the consecutive AKP governments. Transfeminine sex workers' experience of the individualization of life, debt, and survival under neoliberalism is echoed among many other subjects who are targeted by urban renewal and the ensuing dispossession it causes. For instance, one of the AKP's large-scale undertakings has been the transformation of slum neighborhoods via Housing Development Administration (TOKİ) projects. TOKİ, which defines its mission as "building the Turkey of the future," operates under the prime minister's office and has become the official urban transformation arm of the government. The replacement of slum neighborhoods with TOKİ housing structures was presented to the public as state benevolence—a means of helping people become homeowners with access to proper titles and infrastructure that most *gecekondu* (squatter) neighborhoods lacked. However, the project resulted in many older inhabitants taking on cumbersome mortgages that they struggled, and at times failed, to pay off. Old squatter inhabitants found themselves having to participate in the economy in new ways, such as having to rely on purchased foods from grocery stores, making their lives more costly compared to when they were able to grow some of their own vegetables in their gardens or make their own bread in outdoor bread ovens.[48] They also reminisced how their old dwellings allowed them to have a much more communal life where they could throw chairs in front of their simple homes to chat with neighbors and shared the food they grew. In the new TOKİ apartment complexes, systems of solidarity and sharing of resources were replaced by individual apartments, individual expenses, and worries about individual debts.

As an extension of the same individualization of life that neoliberalism fosters, Kabahatler Kanunu also performs an individualization of punishment and, therefore, of crime. While trans women from these neighborhoods were targeted for displacement as collectivities, to which they had resisted in solidarity, the fines they were receiving for occupying public space targeted them individually and thus in theory were harder to resist. Pembe Hayat (Pink Life) worked precisely against this neoliberal individualization of crime, of debt, of violence, and, therefore, of life. Their efforts to document the hefty volume of fines that trans women were being handed under Kabahatler Kanunu, as well as all other forms of police and state violence, resisted such individualization. Pembe Hayat, often simply referred to as *dernek* (the association) by trans women, was a place to organize against the conditions under which they were made to live, a place to seek legal support against arbitrary detentions and to form a collectivity in the face of the individualization of life. Trans women had already lived and survived in collectivities and had habits of checking in on each other almost daily, paying home visits, and taking care of each other when someone became ill or was incarcerated. The association was in many ways simply a politicized extension of these collective lives.

It was in the context of this perpetual violence at the hands of the police, the state, and its extractive and criminalizing systems that trans women started a campaign to demand that a hate crime law be enacted in Turkey. Below I first discuss the conditions of street-based sex work that rendered trans women interdependent, producing solidarities and tensions around questions of labor, consumption, and life. I then turn to trans women's understanding of hate in order to make sense of this demand, which extends beyond frames dictated by liberal subjectivity, juridical humanity, and neoliberal respectability. Situating this discussion in the context of the changing dynamics of the distribution of violence in contemporary Turkey, I will show that analyzing the division of labor between law enforcement and the subjects I call "deep citizens" in the violence perpetuated against trans sex workers is not only useful for gaining insight into their structural understanding of hate but also valuable in making sense of the increasing deployment of marginality onto larger publics under neoliberal Islam.

Public Space, Sex Work, and *Gacı* Ontology

Privatization of public space under neoliberalism had a direct impact on trans sex workers' lives, as their livelihood was made to depend on public spaces. Several historical transformations had contributed to trans women finding themselves with little to no alternative to street-based sex work for survival, with the 1980 military coup emerging as the central turning point in the accounts of older trans women with whom I spoke.[49] This was not only due to neoliberal measures that would be introduced soon after and slowly change urban public spaces and sex workers' access to them. It was also because during the postcoup junta government all trans entertainers were banned from taking the stage and because the glorious days of the casinos and nightclubs where older trans women recalled performing regularly were over—not only in urban centers such as Istanbul or Ankara but all over the country, including Mersin, Adana, Antep, İskenderun, Antalya, and Samsun.[50] The legislation banning their access to stage performance was worded as "barring men from performing in women's attire"—a first in the nation, since living or performing as a cross-dressing or trans person had never been outlawed in Turkey. Many trans women and gay men faced demeaning treatments, including having their hair shaved off, and were exiled from Istanbul.[51] The most widely known case of the ban is that of Turkey's trans diva Bülent Ersoy, who had to spend several years living in Europe during the stage ban, only to return to Turkey during Turgut Özal's liberal government that granted her amnesty due to her exceptional voice.[52] The liberal exceptionalism of Ersoy's case did not lead to a reviving of 1970s nightlife or the relaxation of regulations around trans women's access to public space, however.[53] This initial ban, as well as crackdowns on brothels and homes that only intensified with increasing privatization and gentrification of urban spaces, led to trans women sex workers losing their usual workspaces, which had historically provided community and a certain level of safety.

The old venues had not only provided legitimate spaces of work to trans performers. They had also made room for a capacious understanding of entertainment, where sex work might or might not be part of what performers offered. This moment of cracking down on trans performers should be understood as part of a longer history of separating entertainment and sex work in the republic and the containment of clandestine prostitution in a system that is based on regulation.[54] Wyers documents that in the early years of the republic eugenicist concerns, combined with "urban vice" discourses of policing and a desire to set the respectable citizenry and virtuous women apart from the debased, immoral prostitutes, resulted in heavy regulations of sex work and of brothels as its "proper location."[55] The alleged containment of sex work in the space of the state-authorized brothels produced clandestine prostitution as something that blurred the neatly arranged spaces of the city into respectable zones and areas of vice and, thus, as a problem to contend with.[56] Therefore, rather than the originary moment of the distinction between entertainment and sex work, I suggest that the trans stage ban of the 1980s, through the folding of Bülent Ersoy, one single trans woman, into respectable singer status due to her exceptional talents, deployed two clear-cut and mutually exclusive categories, talented stage-performer and sex worker. This distinction as a result categorically cast all trans women, save for one exceptional singer, offstage, into disreputable and presumably unskilled sex work.

In addition to having lost historically available work spaces, trans women continued experiencing other forms of exclusion, which led to high levels of economic precarity and street-based sex work. Being systematically left out of access to institutions of higher education and the formal economy, and often finding that they needed to leave their family homes in order to lead gender-affirming lives, trans women found little to no way to financially support themselves or afford the various costs of transition. It is not only the purportedly respectable jobs of the formal economy that are unavailable to them but oftentimes also the formal sex work economy.[57] While sex work is not criminalized in Turkey,[58] it is highly regulated by the state.[59] Brothels operate during the day, and licensed sex workers often complain about the low pay and high fees as well as the inability to choose clients.[60] These are enough reason to reject state-run brothels as proper sources of income, but many trans women also face the structural problem that sex work legislation demands that all sex workers be officially assigned the status of women. Some trans women do fulfill all of the government mandates necessary to get medical and psychiatric approval to qualify for an official sex change on their national identity cards, including undergoing sex-affirming surgery and obtaining proof of infertility.[61] However, many trans women do not follow the prescribed route to medically and thus governmentally sanctioned transness and thus do not qualify to receive state-approved woman status.[62]

Definitionally excluded from government-regulated sex work, most trans women joined others in the sphere of informal (*vesikasız*) sex work.[63] Their practice took the form of *çarka çıkmak* (to walk the streets; in queer slang, *lubunca*), which was perhaps the most dangerous, yet seemingly the only possible, method available to trans women.[64] Oftentimes *çark* (streetwalking) was combined with informal brothels run by "mothers"—older trans women took in younger trans women and trained them not only as sex workers but also in the ways of becoming *gacı* (queer slang for trans woman).[65] In other words, sex work, and in particular street-based sex work, and being a trans woman were intimately linked in the imaginaries and self-understandings of many trans women I have met, to the extent that it seemed to define some of the ontological conditions of being gacı.

The link between trans womanhood and street-based sex work was reinforced also by the fact that many transfeminine people sought other trans women for support and community during the early stages of living a public trans life, especially in urban settings. Networks of what were referred to as mother-daughter relationships provided younger trans women—assumed to be "in formation" and referred to as *gacıvari* (gacı-like)[66]—with the know-how and help for transition from older trans women. This training usually happened in the context of younger trans women working as domestic helpers (*domez* in queer slang) in more established trans women's homes in exchange for accommodation. The women who hosted them knew how to access hormones, where to go for laser hair removal, for shopping, or to get their hair done. As various procedures of transitioning were costly, more experienced trans women frequently provided financial help also by setting up the younger domez with paying customers for sex, at times letting them take on some of their own clients. Thus, the initiation to trans womanhood frequently went hand in hand with the initiation to sex work in urban Turkey, which represented the beginning of financial independence for younger trans women. Many trans sex workers continued working for a mother in informal brothels referred to as *koli* houses.[67]

Koli houses were important institutions that offered a sense of collectivity and socialization into trans womanhood. They were also an important component of street-based sex work. For one, they provided a safe space from which to work, especially since most trans women could not easily meet clients at hotels. This became apparent to me one afternoon as I watched Ayşin negotiate with her clients on the phone while sitting on the sofa in Esra's living room. Ayşin was the only cis woman who was part of the trans sex worker group I spent time with. A good friend of the group, she had known a number of the trans women for many years and had been lovers with a couple of them at different points throughout that time. When on the phone with clients, she was seductive yet firm: She demanded that they reserve a hotel room ahead of time and let her know the name of the hotel, the room number, and the name on the reservation. She did not entertain occasional offers to have sex in the car—I heard her tell a client off, clarifying that she did not buy his attempt to avoid paying for a hotel room as a "car fantasy." When I asked Esra why she or other trans women did not ask clients to reserve a hotel room instead of taking them back to the koli house, she explained that trans women simply were not granted access to hotels.[68] This was certainly due to high levels of transphobia but also to the fact that sex worker operated as a master status for trans women. As mentioned previously, media representations of trans women, especially in the 1990s and continuing in the 2000s, often portrayed them as sex workers who roamed the freeways looking for clients and as dangerous and violent subjects who were terrorizing the national (male) body with headlines referring to so-called *travesti terörü* (transvestite terror). The equation of trans women with sex work also manifested itself, for instance, in moments where trans women were approached for sex in the grocery or retail stores they frequented.

In other words, upon attempting to enter a hotel, trans women would be assumed to be prostitutes no matter the purpose of their visit, and their embodied existence within the space of the hotel would suggest to other clients that this was a disreputable establishment frequented for purposes of sex work. Even if trans women were able to "pass" enough to enter a hotel (meaning they were not read as trans and thus as sex workers), they never felt safe and could not rely on being protected by the hotel staff if anything went wrong or if police had to be called in.[69] In response to my question Esra asked: "How can I know that when a man calls me to [meet him in] a hotel that there will not turn out to be four, five men there to fuck me?," thereby summing up the distinction between trans and non-trans sex work. While this same possibility certainly existed for non-trans women who engaged in sex work, as a cis woman Ayşin not only felt more comfortable walking into a hotel without the risk of being turned away, she also felt that in case she needed to call for help the hotel staff would likely provide it. In the absence of alternatives, koli houses combined with çark constituted the only safer system for trans women to engage in sex work. Their dependency on public space for work and survival also infused their lives with various forms of policing and harassment, which I will discuss in the next section. Further, çark informed what I refer to as gacı ontology in important ways.[70] This was both because çark introduced a particular temporality to trans women's lives, which they experienced as contradicting other, conventional lives, and also because street-based sex work crafted links between their livelihood and safety in ways that rendered their lives deeply interdependent. These linkages and difficulties became clear one night during one of my visits to Ankara.

Ferat, a gay male friend and my companion on all the visits to Ankara, and I were sitting in Mother Ezgi's living room, waiting for Esra, Ayşin, Neslihan, and Pelin, who were out working the street. When they left, they were all in good spirits after a lengthy, fun evening of getting dressed, made up, and having their hair done.[71] All four women returned around half past midnight, a bit disheveled, disoriented, and Esra fuming with anger. They had run into Elif in Hoşdere, their first spot to pick up clients. Elif was a gacı they all knew well and whom I had met during previous visits when she and Esra used to work together. Trans women who did street-based sex work often employed a buddy system, working in pairs with a car. When one of the women picked up a client, she would ride in the passenger seat of the client's car back to the koli house, followed by her partner driving their car.[72] This way, the chances of being kidnapped, driven to the middle of nowhere, and being violated or murdered were reduced. This system also ensured that no one was taken into custody without the others' knowledge. While it increased their safety, it also created interdependencies between the women, which at times were stressful and challenging.

Elif was alone that night, and her arrival signaled trouble to other gacıs. She was often critiqued for being too materialistic—for instance, she was said to have saved up and purchased three apartments, something no other trans woman had accomplished. Further, Elif was known to settle for low prices—something other gacıs interpreted as a sign of her greed and as a selfish act that forced them to lower their own prices too. Esra said that in the past she would not have worked for less than 100 to 150 YTL,[73] but Elif was willing to work for as low as 20 to 30 YTL. And, indeed, that night Elif had settled for 20 YTL with a client who had asked for his money back as soon as they were done. Elif had rightfully refused—extortion was extremely familiar to trans women, and when confronted with a similar incident, almost without exception they surrendered the money. When Elif resisted, the man pulled out a shotgun and started chasing her down the street. The women recounted that despite their anger and disbelief that Elif was risking her life for such a small sum, they had run to help her and tried to convince her to give back the money to prevent the conflict from escalating. Esra seemed especially furious that Elif was willing to risk her own life, as well as theirs, for such a small sum.

There was no one in the room who did not agree that Elif's behavior was completely unreasonable. This incident was interpreted in the context of her other materialistic or, as trans women referred to it, *kapitalist* behaviors, such as hooking up with a staff member at a hotel they had collectively visited for a hot springs vacation in Mother Ezgi's hometown, which she had arranged thanks to her personal connections to the hotel director. The weekend ended up being ruined for trans women who had wanted a vacation *from* sex work as well as from being approached as a sex worker. Trans women's immediate affiliation with sex work meant that to undo that equivalence they could not risk a single exception. What they recounted as Elif's ambition for money had ruined their trip, as the hotel staff's behavior toward all of them immediately shifted from treating them as clients to approaching them as potential sex workers. Nalan smiled, as she described Elif: "How do you say? [She is a] Capitalist. I'd just call her dishonorable [şerefsiz], but you'd call her a capitalist."

Elif's capitalist behaviors included a range of acts, not all of which one could easily call rational, such as drastically lowering her prices for services in the face of no obvious need to do so.[74] Most readers also would not consider Elif's calculus between her own life and a few dollars as rational, especially since she was not in desperate need of such a small sum. Trans women's interpretation of her materialism as capitalist underlined the irrationality they attributed to capitalism, but more importantly, it emphasized their dislike of her competitive behavior. They did not simply complain about her competitiveness when it came to material things; they also criticized it when it came to such issues as her need to feel desirable by men and to be preferred over other women. For instance, she had tried to seduce other gacıs' husbands (and at times succeeded). In other words, all competitive behavior was looked down on by these women, and their everyday existence, their labor organizing, and their trans justice activism constituted a struggle against such individualistic, aggressive behavior. This was evident in the koli house system, with older trans women taking in younger ones, as well as in the buddy system they employed when working. It was also clear in the formal and informal ways that they looked out for each other. Ayşin told me that they rarely went a day without giving each other a call to ensure everyone's safety and well-being. One of the reasons they all preferred living in Ankara over Istanbul was that as a smaller city it made it easier to remain in close contact and to visit each other frequently.[75]

Pembe Hayat (Pink Life), which had initially started out as a *transseksüel* and *travesti* organization and then had evolved into a trans-led umbrella LGBTT association, exemplified the formal expression of trans women's investment in a *collectivist* liberation project. Whenever trans women were taken into custody, representatives of the association as well as their lawyer quickly showed up at the police station to ensure the detainee's safety and to debate the charges. Whenever trans women endured violence at the hands of the police or civilians, association members encouraged and helped them file reports. Pembe Hayat prepared its own reports on various forms of violence against trans women, including the fines handed out to them by the police under the Law of Misdemeanors. Pembe Hayat activists worked closely with Kırmızı Şemsiye (Red Umbrella), which focused on health and human rights concerns of sex workers, and both groups carried banners at marches that declared their desire for "a world without bosses and without pimps."[76] Putting the emphasis on the exploitation of labor and not on sex work itself, and refusing to distinguish between bosses and pimps, trans activists' critique of capitalism was evident in both the content of their political organizing and the format of their lives. Elif's competitive and individualistic behavior, summarized as capitalist, was an affront to the collective spirit they all worked hard to cultivate as activists.[77]

On the other hand, trans sex workers' critique of Elif's capitalism was complicated by their own relationship to consumption: Every trans woman I met enjoyed indulging in various pleasures. In fact, two of the earliest lubunca terms I learned were *habbe* (food) and *güllüm* (partying; having a good time), both of which gacıs spoke of as central to a trans woman's existence. Such indulgences are considered to be ontological conditions of *gacılık* (being *gacı*), yet they also constitute substantial expenses. In addition, most trans women spent a significant sum of their hard-earned money on younger handsome men, whose company they sought (*cicilik*; in queer slang, *lubunca*). While this was sometimes criticized among trans women, especially when they felt that a gacı was spending everything she earned on cicilik, the comments did not entail a moral judgment on indulgence but rather a concern about a fellow trans woman risking her financial safety for men. What was unacceptable, in other words, was not that Elif enjoyed earning money or relished material things, but that she saved up, purchased real estate, and invested her money in a system that perpetually failed trans women.[78] Most trans women left for çark at night, not knowing whether they would make it back home alive in the morning. Elif's investment in a future, which they were categorically denied, or at least could not rely on, seemed both strange and an ontological disavowal of gacılık.

Yet, as strange as Elif's behavior may have seemed to these trans women, they were critical of Esra as well. "What kind of *lubunya* is this?" asked Mother Ezgi laughing.[79] "A lubunya works at night and sleeps during the day. This one gets up at 9 in the morning and runs to association meetings." While Esra successfully managed to get many of the trans sex workers involved in some capacity in Pembe Hayat—including convincing their "pimp" Mother Ezgi to carry the banner demanding a world without bosses and pimps—a number of them nonetheless perceived Esra's behavior as another form of denial of being lubunya. It was not solely Esra's commitment to the association that conflicted with the lubunya temporality of working at night and sleeping during the day but also her occasional critique of what she perceived as unnecessary consumption. The same night of the Elif crisis, as we were sitting around chatting in Mother Ezgi's living room, Neslihan brought up her plans to stop by the car dealer the next day to check out a new car. Since they were a larger group working for Mother Ezgi now, Neslihan thought they could use another car to go out to work. Esra objected immediately—a new car simply meant more debt. "I'll work and pay it off," Neslihan resisted, but Esra would not cave. Debt meant that they would lose certain freedoms around what work to accept and what work to refuse. "Forget about that car; that car will not be purchased. You are still paying the installments of this car. How do you dare go into that debt? You will end up having to sleep with ludicrous [abuk sabuk] men to pay it off." As they now worked together as a team, they all had a say in expenses—the interdependence of collective labor also meant that disagreements on how work-expenses would be allocated/worked out had to be resolved cooperatively.

Thus, Esra was against materially investing in a future, but she was also against being (rendered) indebted to it and, therefore, being tied to a future of infinite labor. While Esra's position on precarity aligned with other trans sex workers when it came to what they understood as their bare life and the (non)value of money in the face of life-threatening danger, she departed from at least some of them in her analysis of financial precarity as part of the other vulnerabilities they experienced and as the very shape of existence. This was because neoliberal life links particular comforts and pleasures to credit and debt. Although the issue of credit and debt clearly is not a problem unique to trans sex workers, because they experienced indulgence—gullüm—as an ontological condition of gacılık, Esra's critique of debt, along with what they perceived as her refusal to follow gacı temporality, was at times experienced as her rejection of being gacı. Yet Esra's point was not completely lost on others because their labor was so intimately linked with chances of physical survival. Therefore, not having control over their labor due to concerns about debt meant risking their very bare life. Despite the ongoing tease of Esra's un-lubunya-like behavior, most of them organized under Pink Life to change for the better the conditions under which they labored and lived. Esra's understanding of precarity that tied financial debt to labor conditions and to violence was apparent also in her discussion of hate crime laws, to which I turn below after first contextualizing the changing dynamics between police and vigilante violence in the country.

Deep State and Deep Citizens

The relationship with increasing debt, labor conditions, and rising vulnerability is true for most people living under neoliberal capitalism of course, but it particularly crystallized in trans sex workers' experiences. This was because their debt rendered them both unable to choose clients and more dependent on access to public space, which meant being at the mercy of heightened police and vigilante violence. At the beginning of this chapter I discussed the shift in police violence from physical beatings to fines under the Law of Misdemeanors. Neither a historical decrease in physical violence experienced by trans women nor an increase in the seeming humanity of the Turkish police, this shift indicates a transformation in the administration of physical violence: On one hand, the police force has started to target a growing public of purported terrorists, a group now including anyone critical of the government, ranging from the Islamist liberal Right to the secular liberal or radical Left, to feminists and Kurds and queer activists (which I address in greater detail in chapter 4). This turn points to a deployment of marginality in the nation instead of a concentration of it at the lower echelons of society, which partially works through the deployment of the language of terrorism—a shift from the logics of Kurdish, leftist, and *travesti* terror that exclusively attached terror to the bodies of the marginalized to tens of thousands facing terrorism-related charges in the nation. As the police force turned toward administering violence against this growing body of alleged terrorists, physical violence against trans women has come to be administered increasingly by civilians and vigilante groups, accompanied by police inaction. Therefore, rather than experiencing a replacement of physical violence with economic violence through fines under Law of Misdemeanors, trans women continued to face physical violence but increasingly by civilians I refer to as *deep citizens*. This, I argue, had important implications for how trans women experienced and understood hate as a structural condition of life under neoliberalism, and it helps us make sense of their demands for a hate crime law. As I will discuss, since deep citizen violence has historically targeted various minorities and has spread through the larger national body over the past decade, trans women's theorization of hate has larger relevance for all who are struggling to survive under conditions of intensified neoliberalism and securitization.

One of the important differences between the Ülker Street incident of 1996 and the Eryaman and Avcılar cases of 2006 and 2012 was that in the later displacement of trans women from their neighborhoods the police were no longer direct perpetrators of the violent attacks but indirect actors by allowing such beatings to occur by standing by and not responding to the trans women's calls for help—in brief, by *not* enforcing the law.[80] Trans women who lived through the brutal attacks in Eryaman in 2006 reported that some assaults happened as the police stood by and watched and that at other times police took hours to arrive at the scene after the trans women called to report that they were trapped in their homes and afraid to leave because thugs were threatening them outside. Esma recounted: "A friend of ours spoke with one of the policemen at Eryaman Station, someone of a higher rank. This is what the police said, the police with a high rank guaranteed, 'Do not work in Eryaman, do not prostitute in Eryaman, you will continue your daily lives, you will not be attacked, your homes will not be raided.'"[81] Proving both that higher-ranking law enforcement personnel knew about the ongoing violence as well as their (at least perceived) control over the vigilante violence, this comment demands that we think about the distinct yet intertwined functions of these two entities.

In order to unpack this formation, whereby police violence is supplemented by police inaction during vigilante violence, I turn to the concept of *derin devlet* (deep state), which entered Turkish popular discourse most notably in 1996 following a car accident in Susurluk.[82] The collision between a Mercedes Benz and a truck on November 3 resulted in the deaths of three of the four people riding in the car and revealed deep connections between the police, organized crime, and the government, leading the media and the public to refer to these relationships as the "deep state."[83] This was not the first moment in the history of the republic where state actors were suspected of engaging in extrajuridical and illegitimate affairs and where "patriotic volunteers" were relied on to do the state's work.[84] Yet it was an important historic moment due to then prime minister Tansu Çiller's infamous public justification of organized and vigilante crime on behalf of the state: "Both those who shoot a bullet on behalf of the state, as well as those who are hit by one, are honorable." *Devlet için*, which translates both as "for the state" and "on behalf of the state," blurs the distinction between the two, rendering irrelevant whether actual orders were given to those who act.[85] The deep state thus invites purportedly honorable actors who internalize state ideologies to join the state's military and police functions. I call these citizens authorized by the deep state to shoot a bullet on its behalf *deep citizens*.[86]

Deep citizen violence is not unique to trans women's experiences, and Turkish history is marked by organized vigilante violence historically targeted at religious and ethnic minorities and, at times, also the Turkish Left.[87] During the infamous incidents of September 6–7, 1955, under the populist right-wing leader Adnan Menderes (whom Erdoğan often cites as an important historical role model), the businesses of Greek Orthodox, Jewish, and Armenian minorities in Istanbul and İzmir were ransacked for two days by civilians, which led to a mass exodus of the Greek Orthodox community from Turkey.[88] Almost four decades later, on July 2, 1993, a group of thirty-three majority Alevite writers, poets, journalists, and intellectuals who had gathered for the Pir Sultan Abdal celebrations in the Madımak Hotel in Sivas were burned alive in a hotel room by a mob of thousands, and more than fifty others were injured in attempting to escape. While the September 6–7 incidents were blamed on communists at the time, the head of the Special Forces Command (Özel Kuvvetler Komutanlığı) proudly claimed in a later interview that the events had been organized by his office.[89] And though many of those involved in the Madımak massacre received high sentences, the majority of those charges were dropped and their sentences reduced during the appeal process. Most of the defense lawyers of those charged for the attacks later became Welfare Party and AKP deputies, ministers, and lawyers.[90] Both of these incidents were marked by police inaction, and reports of the September 6–7 events later revealed that the police had been given orders not to leave their stations. While official records would invite us to think of these events as exceptional historical moments due to their scale, I suggest that we conceptualize them on a continuum with the Ülker Street, Eryaman, and Avcılar events, which are easily invisibilized in the national collective memory.

The concept of deep citizenship allows us to link these various forms of civilian violence in the history of the republic that aimed at bringing in line those who were positioned as threats to national or religious unity and as undesirables, whether religious, ethnic, sexual, or gendered others. Since the police force has historically aimed at establishing "public order,"[91] deep citizen violence emerges as a supplementary form of policing. This form of violence has been historically employed by various Turkish governments—the Menderes government, for instance, is argued to have been directly behind the attacks against minority businesses during the September 6–7 events. According to witnesses two weeks prior to the attacks, troops carrying lists of minority homes and businesses in Istanbul were roaming around and marking the buildings. I argue that several changes have taken place over the past two decades and have intensified under the AKP's neoliberal Islam: For one, the expansion of marginality within the nation, by which the previously respectable have been folded into the ranks of the suspect, the undesirable, and the terrorist, has resulted in making it difficult for the state to locate its targets. A non-Sunni name, an address affiliated with a minority neighborhood, or a gender-deviant outfit are no longer enough to detect the new targets of the Turkish state. Therefore, the police force now is increasingly in charge of policing the larger national body, and vigilante violence has taken over from the police to target those it can profile.

When I argue that the police now target the larger national body and deep citizens aim at identifiable minoritized publics, I do not mean to suggest that deep citizen violence is limited to those who can be profiled only in traditional ways. The period since 2008 has witnessed a proliferation of deep citizen violence now also targeting subjects who previously would have been deemed respectable but are newly profiled, for instance, as alcohol consumers. This was exemplified in a number of assaults by what is colloquially referred as "the calm people of the neighborhood" targeting attendees of art gallery openings in the Tophane district of Istanbul. The first recorded attack happened in September 2010—while a crowd had spread out on the sidewalk in front of the small gallery space enjoying beers offered by the exhibit, they were attacked by a group of men who were carrying sticks and bats.[92] While the attacks were downplayed by the mayor, the incident was portrayed by some as resulting from the tension between the inhabitants of the neighborhood and the newly established galleries that invited young men and women to drink alcohol in the streets. Yet this event cannot be understood separately from then prime minister Erdoğan's frequent criticism of alcohol consumption and from the ongoing state-led urban renewal projects. The same logic that motivates deep citizens to expel trans sex workers from their neighborhoods also propels them to assault beer-drinking youth in Istanbul now encouraged by a president who associates alcohol consumption with lack of piety *and* national betrayal as seen in his response to Gezi Park protesters. The arguments put forth at the time by some analysts that perceived the Tophane attacks as subaltern uprisings against bourgeois gentrification are indicative of the dangers of romanticizing the rising up of the people. Problems with gentrification and urban renewal are undoubtedly among the most significant issues of urban poverty and neoliberal inequality, but we need to continuously ask—remembering Ülker Street, Eryaman, and Avcılar—which projects of gentrification are encouraged by the state and which ones are allowed to be resisted.

The new profiling mechanisms under Turkey's neoliberal Islam now include public drinking but also private drinking during Ramadan: Indeed, the 2010 incident was followed by others, including in 2016 attacks on a listening party at a record store by a group who brutally beat up some of the attendees for drinking beer during Ramadan. The logic of Ramadan has also been evoked by the Istanbul Governor's Office for several years in a row to ban the trans pride and the LGBTİ+ pride marches, supposedly due to considerations of the public's religious sensitivities. Marrying a particular Sunni Islamic morality regime with neoliberal values, the Turkish government *produces* deep citizens with certain societal or religious sensitivities who are ready to be provoked or incited to violence while appearing to simply recognize existing sensitivities.[93] Finally, a recent statutory decree signed by President Erdoğan under the state of emergency in December 2017 declared that no legal, administrative, financial, or criminal responsibility will be borne by those citizens who acted to defeat the coup attempt and terror acts of July 15, 2016, as well any who acted against the continuation of those events *whether they carry an official title or act in official capacity or not.*[94] Not only officially acknowledging but also codifying the logic of deep citizenship, the Erdoğan rule fosters deep citizen violence by positioning *all* violence against the new terrorists of the nation as on behalf of the state, reproducing hate as the affective structure of neoliberal Islam.

What did it mean for trans sex worker activists, who had endured different forms of state, police, and deep citizen violence and had no trust in these institutions, to demand a hate crime law of the government? I now turn to the answers provided by trans activists to this question in order to think about survival and activism during neoliberal times.

On Hopeless Activism, Life, and the Politics of Hate

When I asked Esra, one of the founders of Pembe Hayat (Pink Life) to tell me about the organization's demand for a hate crime legislation, she responded: "In this country, all kinds of different people are oppressed by, not different kinds of hate, but the same hate. Those wearing headscarves, pious ones, trans people." She then proceeded to explain that the problem was that people experienced their oppression and therefore their interests as distinct from each other. This, she believed, manifested itself in how people elected representatives as well as in how they conducted their own political organizing. "I would not elect a representative simply because they advocate LGBT rights, without knowing what they think of animal rights, or environmental rights," she added. "People think: as long as you are my kind, it's OK [*benden olsun da nasıl olursa olsun*]. People are forced to make choices according to their own kind [*insanlar kendi türüne göre seçim yapmak zorunda bırakılıyor*]." She then added: "Not accepting difference and hating each other are things shaped by power."

Within the span of a couple of minutes, Esra both critiqued difference, the production of different kinds of people (*tür*), and the resulting perception of divided interests *and* also voiced a desire for the acceptance of the differences she had just dismantled. Her logic recognized that power both articulates differences that we need to be weary of, and produces hate for the very differences it creates. Later in the conversation, she said, "LGBTs are *different* [from each other] *like all other people*. They don't all think alike. . . . Being LGBT is not a quality that sets us apart from anything else. We can also be murderers, we can also be robbers, because we are human."[95] Difference is evoked here as akin to a human condition but not necessarily as an adequate system of categorizing and organizing human experience. Difference within LGBT subjects made them *like* others. As a committed trans activist, Esra did not need her activism to craft an ideal LGBT subject who deserved rights and dignity via a politics of respectability. Neither did she need LGBT to be a distinct "special interest group" represented by someone who specifically advocated for LGBT rights.[96]

Hate, the hate we all experience, functions here as a structural element of lives rendered precarious—precarity and vulnerability produce hate and are in returned perpetuated by it. Hate is not imagined as embodied in individual haters.[97] Hate cannot be categorized into "hate of the pious," "hate of trans people," or "hate of Kurds," according to Esra; resisting the separation of hate goes hand in hand with resisting the separation of its justification into "Kurdish terror," "Left terror," or "transvestite terror." We are oppressed by the same hate. This is not an entirely universalizing gesture, however, as Esra continuously recognized differences produced and maintained as meaningful. The hate experienced by those with headscarves or pious people is the same hate experienced by trans people, as Esra uttered all those subjects in one breath. "For instance, the suffering you cause me, its reflection hurts you, too."

In *Death beyond Disavowal*, Grace Hong defines difference as "a cultural and epistemological practice that holds in suspension (without requiring resolution) contradictory, mutually exclusive, and negating impulses. 'Difference' names an epistemological position, ontological condition, and political strategy that reckon with the shift in the technologies of power that we might as well call 'neoliberal.'"[98] It is this impossibility that Esra's words capture when she reflects on how hate operates. Her shuttling back and forth between asking for recognition of categorical differences, undoing those same categorical differences ("LGBT people are different [from each other] like everyone else"), and undermining them as faulty, insufficient, misleading, and, most importantly, produced by power (*iktidar*) speaks to the radical rethinking of self and community that Hong theorizes—a radical rethinking "that brings together and holds in suspension the conflicting goals of the preservation or the protection of the political subjects *and* the recognition of the others at whose expense that subject is protected."[99]

Esra's narrative also held in tension something that we might recognize as humanism and a decentering of the human through her continued mention of animals and the environment as subjects of rights. She centered herself as someone who would benefit from LGBT rights and hastily mentioned that she would not vote for a representative who only advocates for LGBT rights. She also shuttled back and forth between an investment in life and a divestment from hope. During our second interview, five years after we had first met, she declared, "I am an activist who has lost hope [*umudunu yitirmiş bir aktivistim*]. I don't believe anything is possible in this country [*bu ülkede birşey olacağını düşünmüyorum*]. I wake up eight times a night. Every home visit, I hear things like 'Be careful, they might be tapping your phone.' We live in fear of the state. . . . If this is our condition in this country, there is nothing left to hope. . . . The only thing I hope for is: 'When will something happen to me?—I hope nothing does.'"

"Are we really living?" she continued. "I am genuinely curious about this. I don't think we are living. We *think* we are—as we think about electricity and water bills, about rent, without doing things we would [actually] want to, worrying about the next month or the next day, about what we will eat the next day, or worrying whether we will starve. We don't live. We serve states. We serve those who govern [*başımızdakilere*], those parliamentarians, those ministers, those who form power, those arm traders, those who exploit us." A life experienced as so deeply precarious, infused with worries about shelter, food, and the bills that come with it, which if not paid ultimately render one homeless and starving, is the life we are offered under neoliberalism: a life that renders the life/death binary useless. Esra also objected to life as a limited existence with its contours drawn to serve governments, arm traders, politicians, and exploiters.

"And then we are fooled with thankfulness [*şükür*]." Esra refused bare life as something to be thankful for. Her activism without hope stemmed from the very fact of not properly living, which was a form of life in fear of losing bare life. The precarities that were produced under neoliberalism, under authoritarianism, under a deepening Sunni moralism, and violence distributed through the state and its deep citizens distracted us from the very fact that what we were offered as life might be something we not only refuse to be thankful for but also a form of existence we refuse to endure.

Then Esra turned her analysis on me, pointing out the precarities she had heard me utter over the years: "You, too, you are always saying, 'Hopefully I can finish my thesis, I hope I can get a job, I hope I can write this book . . . ,' all fears about a future you might not even want." Cleary the precarities in my life at those various moments she had met me were real, and equally clearly were they by no means comparable to the insecurities Esra and all the other trans women I know experienced on a daily basis. For them, whether they would make it back home alive was a question they asked themselves every night as they went out to walk the streets. But that is bare life, which Esra refused to be reduced to. A life that consisted of worrying about bills and debt and unemployment and immanent homelessness or starvation was no life at all. The hope "I hope nothing happens to me" was nothing but hopelessness.

Yet, as "hopeless activists," Esra and other volunteers of Pembe Hayat woke up every day and kept fighting for a life otherwise—a life where public space belonged to them and everyone else, a life not determined by bills to worry about, a life without hate. Hope has been a bad object of queer studies, critiqued as a sign of attachment to futures, institutions, and structures that work against queers as well as other bodies who have been left out of those structures.[100] The tension between queer negativity's conceptualization of hope as uncritical and normative and queer desires for change finds a potential resolution in Esra's words: The social worlds that trans activists inhabited left no room for hope (except for the hope to stay alive, which Esra refused as a meaningful wish), yet one did not need hope and the normative investments it required to continue working to change the world.

Trans women's demand for a hate crime law stemmed from their desire to make the Turkish government accept hate as a structural element of oppressive systems—a radically different wish from a desire for respectability by those who imagine themselves as subjects of protection by law and law enforcement.[101] In fact, trans women's long-standing fear and suspicion of police has extended to most LGBT subjects and many other non-queer and non-trans citizens who are critical of the government, which I will speak to in more detail in the next chapter. Thousands chant together during the annual pride march, "Polis, fuhuş yap, onurlu yaşa" (Police, do sex work, live honorably), subverting the state's respectability politics and inviting police officers to a different life.[102] We might all be burdened by bills to pay and rendered precarious through neoliberal systems, the chant recognizes, but here we are refusing to struggle with those precarities in ways that render others further vulnerable to state violence. So can you. Clearly distinguishing between respectability and dignity, the slogan maintains that serving the state for pay might seem to be a respectable position, but living through neoliberal precarities without hurting and rendering vulnerable others is the dignified way to live.

While trans sex workers continued living at the height of precarities produced by a system that distributes wealth upward, heightens vulnerability, and individualizes survival and suffering, as they experienced shifting forms of police organizing and varying kinds of state and deep citizen violence first-hand and up close, and as they mourned their friends lost to trans murders, their demand for criminalization of hate stemmed from their deep analyses of how violence and oppression are fostered and perpetuated in Turkish society. It might be true that every hate crime requires a hating criminal, but trans sex workers already understood the state and its various extensions, including law and law enforcement, as the singular most important structure of hate. Trans Cinayetleri Politiktir (Trans murders are political) is a long-standing slogan of the trans as well as larger queer movements in Turkey, which historically had refused the rendering of such violence to individualized crimes, decentered the individual perpetrator, and understood hate and killing as structural. In other words, they imagined hate crime "as a way of making visible the effects of hate, by *listening to the affective life of injustice*, rather than establishing the truth of law."[103] Perhaps it was their *collective* survival as a condition of gacılık, or their forced daily dealings with state apparatuses, or their heightened vulnerability to violence due to their labor conditions that made their analyses so insightful and their organizing so relentless though hopeless. Perhaps it was all of these. Refusing both being reduced to bare life and the neoliberal biopolitical life understood as "life as long as it serves (structures of) power," their activism against hate involved imagining a different kind of life altogether for all, away from state terror as well as neoliberal precarities.

Four

Critique and Commons
under Neoliberal Islam

In a scene from Rüzgar Buşki's documentary *#direnayol* (#re-sistayol) chronicling the pride week following the Gezi Park uprisings in 2013, trans activist Şevval recounts the significance of the LGBT *Blok* (LGBT bloc) stationed at the park throughout the protests.[1] Standing on a side street off İstiklal, the large pedestrian road leading to Taksim Square, she explains how all LGBT activists from different groups left their "association identities" behind thanks to LGBT *Blok* in order to gather and focus on what needed to be done during Gezi. On this crowded street, people enter the frame behind her: with different gender presentations, a number of them in costume, others carrying rainbow flags; a cis-and-straight-presenting couple can be seen to the side; and someone has a sign that reads "Direniyoruz Ayol" (We are resisting *ayol*), with that beautiful untranslatable formulation *ayol* adding a limp-wristed affect to the utterance. Şevval continues: "I think an amazing fusion happened. People who are not in our political activist circles also joined. Istanbul is a large city, a city of twenty million. There were lots of others, people who do not know activism and politics. We took some steps, they took some steps, and there was an amazing unison. And I think they, too, have joined the movement now, and they will walk with us." If the significance of LGBT *Blok* was to gather activists who might otherwise have differing, and even conflicting, political positions, the larger effect of Gezi was to bring together those with prior political affiliations and experiences and those who "don't know politics."

Şevval's amazement at these "apolitical subjects" joining political activists in rising up against a neoliberal and authoritarian regime gets at the heart of the question that animates this chapter: Who is the proper subject of politics? I am interested in this query in regard to queer politics in particular, as well as progressive politics more generally, under neoliberalism. While most queer studies scholars in the United States have been concerned with the co-optation of radical queer initiatives by neoliberal values and logics, other classed issues arise even in organizations that are vocal in their critiques of neoliberal capitalism. This is because at a time when voicing political statements is gaining increasing importance, so is the emphasis on the proper voice, the precise vocabulary, and the correct statement—all of which have deep ties to cultural capital. I witnessed this in earlier phases of my research with queer activists criticizing as apolitical those queers who did not master particular knowledges of gender and sexuality, such as understanding sexuality as an orientation or perceiving particular gender performances as reproductive of the norm.

My aim here is not to repeat tired critiques of political correctness, many of which I have my disagreements with, and neither am I interested in claiming particular political statements or sentiments to be Western and therefore not indigenous to Turkish sexual liberation politics. Instead, I ask: Who has access to such language? Who is left out of proper political subjectivity as a result? And how is political subjectivity classed in ways that are counterproductive to progressive politics? These questions are important not only because they show the significance of cultural capital to claiming proper political subjectivity and the exclusionary design of much of progressive politics. They are also crucial to wrestle with because under conditions of neoliberalism and right-wing populism they speak to a key problem faced by progressive political causes. Right-wing populism owes at least some of its popularity to positioning the Left as elitist and self-righteous in their weltanschauung and their demands while locating itself in line with the people, their realities, and their needs.[2] Left elitism is certainly not a fabrication of the Right, and I will reflect below particularly on the role critique plays in what is perceived, at least for some queers, as Left politics' exclusionary and alienating nature. This is not to altogether dismiss critique as a political strategy or even a disposition, but to draw attention to the impasses it can pose to building a commons. I suggest that instead of simply accepting critique as a queer or progressive good, we might do better attending to the moments of its failure to speak to the very subjects it seeks to hail.

A further challenge to the kind of progressive politics that is overtly reliant on critique, on the spirit of anti-ness (antifa, anti-capitalist, anti-racist, anti-sexist), and on a somewhat nebulous concept of resistance, is the fact that we live in a politically disenchanted world. Neoliberalism has not only *disenchanted* politics by allegedly moving it beyond ideology and turning it into a technocratic endeavor, supplying us with businessmen-cum-politicians, but it has also provided the circumstances for the right wing to *re-enchant* the world with fascist nationalism and conservative forms of religion. These are the ways in which many people are finding meaning, purpose, and even community these days. Critique, and often jaded critique bordering on cynicism, on the other hand, does not work to re-enchant the world. So, what do progressive movements have to offer in its stead?

This chapter tells two stories: one of critique and the other one of commons. The first story focuses on the relationship of queer activists to a queer bar crowd and exemplifies the limits of critique, while the second story, of the Gezi Park protests and the socialities it enabled for queer and non-queer crowds, demonstrates the re-enchanting promise of the commons. Following Silvia Federici, I understand "commons" to consist of sociabilities and models of coexistence that work with a spirit toward deprivatization of common wealth and "the creation of forms of reproduction built on self-management, collective labor, and collective decision-making."[3] In the first instance, we will see that their abstracted understanding of neoliberal capital led queer activists to overlook other forms of class distinctions. As a result, when politics was presented as a critical disposition requiring certain forms of language and knowledge, queers who were deemed as apolitical because they did not meet those standards felt alienated from politics. In the second instance, the Gezi protests, it was largely youth who to that point had considered themselves apolitical who were the protagonists of the largest public demonstration in the history of the republic. The protests illustrated a challenge to neoliberalism, its projects of privatization and material dispossession of the people, as well as its respectability politics. If it was due to AKP's deployment of marginality that many subjects found themselves in symbolic kinship with each other, it was their physical copresence that enabled what protesters referred to as the "Gezi spirit." It was the utopian coexistence and lived interdependence with "strangers" that many recounted as the euphoric, magical time that was Gezi.[4]

Similar to trans sex workers' rejection of both neoliberal life as defined by worries about bills and of being reduced to bare life discussed in chapter 3, the commons and intersectional solidarity politics that emerged during the Gezi protests refused the government's urban redevelopment projects as well as its definitions of morality and piety. All these new forms of protest, resistance, and solidarity are telling of the limits of neoliberal Islam but also of neoliberalism at large. It is in these collective refusals of economically responsible, reproductive, and morally upright citizenship and in turning to each other for collective mutual caretaking where the potential to redefine life altogether lies. But these redefinitions also require new languages—vernaculars that do not rely on either cultural capital or cultural authenticity and that do not conceptualize activism as righting wrongs or critique as admonishment. Perhaps it is time for queer activism to rethink its relationship to critique and language in order to work toward a commons where there will be collective and lived redefinitions of critical languages that will not require literacy in formal queer and sexuality studies knowledge.

Queer studies never set out to produce knowledge that would proceed to become a metaphoric gatekeeper, but unintended outcomes are still worth contemplating.[5] Since the field has come to command considerable cultural capital, we may want to take stock of its travels outside of the academy and around the world and reflect on how knowledge that is empowering for some can work to estrange others from what they perceive as politics itself. I suggest that the forms of commoning that Gezi enabled constitute a call to rethink the relationship between knowledge, critique, and politics under neoliberalism and contain cues for how to re-enchant progressive politics.

The Limits of Critique

Homonormativity and the Question of Class

When I first started researching queer movements in contemporary urban Turkey in the summer of 2008, the primary LGBT activist group in Istanbul looked like a dreamy example of queer intersectionality: Lambdaistanbul was an anti-militaristic, anti-sexist, anti-racist, anti-capitalist, anti-hierarchical volunteer-based LGBT solidarity association, as members repeated at meetings, on their websites, and during interviews. They not only engaged with social justice issues around sexuality but also understood the fight against misogyny, the oppression of ethnic minorities, the power of neoliberal capital, and the increasing militarization of the world to be critical to sexual liberation. In fact, Lambda had a number of Kurdish members at the time, and starting around 2009 they prepared signs in Kurdish and Armenian in addition to Turkish for the annual pride march. They participated at demonstrations organized by feminist and anarchist groups as well as in the sizable march that took place on May 1, Workers' Day.[6] Eren, who had been working with the organization as a volunteer for two years after having lived in the United States for a while, was ecstatic about the group: Unlike US LGBT movements that had become deeply commercialized over time, with pride parades reduced to everyone getting drunk under corporate sponsorship, the Istanbul pride march was a deeply political one that demanded queer liberation for all, with slogans critiquing the mandatory military conscription mixed with those against trans murders.

An awareness of the asymmetrical position of Turkey vis-à-vis Western powers, as well as global capitalism's role in world politics, permeated decision-making mechanisms of Lambdaistanbul: During a panel at the 2008 pride week I found out that Lambda had initially rejected financial support from an organization that worked closely with the Netherlands Ministry of Culture because their funding requirements were void of an understanding of the needs of Turkey's LGBT movement. In a similar spirit, I witnessed a forty-five-minute discussion during the 2008 pride week evaluation meeting, where members of Lambdaistanbul engaged in a heated debate about returning a five thousand–dollar donation that was made to the group by a rather well-known international nonprofit funding body for the arts and education. Some members had concerns about the political clout the founder of the organization might have asserted in regime changes in Eastern European countries, and most others agreed that Lambdaistanbul should not accept money from organizations that could easily be money-laundering mechanisms for global antidemocratic political manipulations. After a long-winded debate over whether there was such a thing as clean money, volunteers decided to return what was a significant sum for an association that often struggled to pay monthly rent and bills.

There were a number of reasons for Lambdaistanbul volunteers' heightened critical sense of neoliberal capital and the global political economy at large. For one, a number of them had been involved in Left feminist or socialist organizations prior to joining Lambdaistanbul. The group itself had been initially formed by trans sex workers, some of whom identified as communists or socialists.[7] A large group of trans women, including some of the founding members, had left Lambdaistanbul a couple of years before I started my fieldwork to form a different association that centered on needs as determined by trans activists.[8] Yet their socialist principles had for years shaped the politics of the group, including its collective memory. In fact, the earliest formation of the current pride march had taken place on May 1, when a handful of LGBT activists had joined the Workers' Day march carrying their rainbow flag. A Lambdaistanbul member who was a conscientious objector to the mandatory military conscription, and who had been imprisoned for his political position, had introduced anti-militarism as an important principle for the group.

In other words, Lambdaistanbul looked nothing like the LGBT organizations that have been critiqued for queer liberalism. US critics of homonormativity in particular have discussed how progressive movements have become increasingly infiltrated with the values, logic, and vocabulary of neoliberalism. This has resulted in a particular mainstreaming of LGBT politics with an emphasis on privacy, domesticity, and individual freedom and with such political projects as legalization of gay marriage; inclusion of gay, lesbian, and trans subjects in the military; and hate crime legislation.[9] Radical intersectional and multidimensional politics are increasingly reduced to various forms of single-issue identity movements and domesticated through neoliberal multiculturalism and diversity projects in which diversity matters only as long as it is predictable, marketable, and profitable.[10]

Homonormativity does not capture all aspects of class, however, as neoliberalism does not capture all aspects of capitalism. This became especially clear in Lambdaistanbul volunteers' relationship to the women-only club Kadınca—a space that was mostly, but not exclusively, frequented by queer women.[11] I often heard activists complain about the bar crowd, strongly disapproving of the infamous bar fights that seemed to be a staple at Kadınca and referring to the actions of its clients as "reproducing cultural practices of manhood." In fact, one of the early mentions of the club I had heard among the activists was in the context of a complaint about a fight that had taken place during one of the 2008 pride week parties. Some of the activists were suggesting that Kadınca should no longer be considered as a potential venue for pride parties. I was personally warned not to go to the club because of the fights and perhaps even more so because of what they perceived to be the sexually aggressive (female) masculinity of the clientele.

A further criticism I often heard from activist women was about the apoliticalness of the club's patrons. Lambdaistanbul volunteers were frustrated with the fact that the crowds who filled the club did not show any interest in their work as political organizers and marked this refusal to participate as being apolitical. While they articulated no clear connection between the fights that took place in the club and the apoliticalness of the club goers, the fact that they often critiqued the violence because it reproduced "cultural practices of manhood" and not because people actually got hurt spoke to the political nature of their critique. In other words, the women activists of Lambdaistanbul in particular perceived the bar's violence as politically problematic and attributed it to the patrons' lack of a critique of "cultural practices of manhood." As I will discuss later, the fact that many of these fights were rather performative and did not cause any serious harm to anyone resulted in the club's workers and clients perceiving politics as an abstraction, merely theoretical and disconnected from life.

Patrons of Kadınca were mostly *baç/buç* or *feminen*, as they referred to themselves and each other.[12] No one seemed to remember where they had heard the terms first, but by 2008 they seemed to have been in circulation for a few years. They were used by almost everyone at the club, if not always as an identification, at least as a reference, yet none of the Lambdaistanbul activists I knew used these categories. *Baç* women of Kadınca indeed performed highly masculine genders, sporting short haircuts, baggy pants, and T-shirts, no makeup, no manicures, and flat, masculine shoes. The *feminen* clients, on the other hand, mostly had long hair, makeup, and manicured nails; they wore tight jeans or short skirts with feminine tops and heels. The *baç/feminen* dynamic of the club stood in contrast to the lesbian and bisexual women of Lambdaistanbul, most of whom were neither as feminine as feminens nor as masculine as baçs. Over time, complaints I heard about the rather abstracted gender performances of the baçs of Kadınca took on qualities other than being simply about masculinity and violent tendencies. These included critiques of masculine Kadınca clients carrying *tesbih* (worry beads), which are seen as markers of unsophisticated, rural, and sometimes religious masculinity, carrying cigarette packs in their socks, or acting like *kamyoncu* (truckers). All these "inappropriate" behaviors, including frequent fighting, were markers of particularly working-class masculinities, indicating Kadınca clientele's lack of cultural capital that would follow from an educated, civilized background.

It is important to note here that not all Lambdaistanbul activists came from middle- and upper-middle-class backgrounds. And while some even worked in order to financially support their families, almost all were then attending university or had a college degree.[13] Kadınca clients, on the other hand, were mostly from the lower middle and working classes, working at retail and other service sector jobs, such as hairdressers or as staff at restaurants and hotels. Few attended college.[14] If class forms a set of dispositions that structure practices and perceptions, as Pierre Bourdieu suggests, then narrowing respectability to what hetero- and homonormativity dictates can result in missing out on other moral dimensions of respectability and of class.[15] In this case, it was possible for Lambda activists to be critical of neoliberal capitalism and simultaneously to be invested in markers of civility and bourgeois respectability (not always the same as neoliberal respectability) vis-à-vis queers whose gender performance they disapproved of and understood as political failures. The fact that I never personally observed any of the club's patrons fiddling with worry beads or carrying cigarette packs in their socks speaks to the power of such classed behaviors becoming markers of the space, even if they have been observed only once, continuously reproducing Kadınca as a space of unacceptable, uncivilized masculinities.

Yet it was not simply the masculinities performed by Kadınca's baç women that were (politically) problematic; it was also the fact that they did not have the *proper language* to express and defend their gender performances. For instance, Eren, the Lambdaistanbul volunteer cited earlier, told me during our interview that initially he, too, was called out as a trans man for "reproducing cultural practices of manhood" by Nevin, a lesbian Lambdaistanbul activist. In return he had responded that Nevin was equally reproducing the cultural practices of womanhood with her long hair and feminine and often heavily accessorized outfits. This retort of course required that Eren be able to grasp the nature of Nevin's critique and also have an equally apt understanding of the social reproduction of binary gender as a framework through which to think about gender performance critically. As a result, Eren was able to turn Nevin's argument on its head to show that the reproduction of normative gender was not simply the territory of trans men and therefore did not constitute a proper critique. Over time, his masculinity became very much accepted by Lambdaistanbul members, along with other members of the newly emerging trans men category.[16] As a new category of queer, they knew how to *make sense* of themselves to other Lambdaistanbul activists in a way the baç clients of Kadınca did not know how, or did not care, to do.[17]

Thus the inappropriate masculinities of baç clients of Kadınca merged with their inability to politically defend their gender performance, doubly marking their class. Their particular performance of masculinity, as well as their lack of cultural capital regarding current theories of gender and sexuality, positioned them as apolitical in a framework where politics was already predicated on the command of certain knowledges and on particular forms of embodied as well as verbal self-expression. I myself experienced both being challenged for the Kadınca club's women-only door policy when I worked at the club and being corrected about my narrative of my own sexuality.[18] As I was talking to three activists at another Istanbul-based LGBT organization about growing up and living in Istanbul until moving to the United States to continue my education, I casually said that I "had been heterosexual [*heteroseksüel*] back then." I was immediately corrected by one of the activists who said I had always been a lesbian, but I had just not known it at the time. I insisted that I really had been straight as a younger woman—I had dated boys and found them attractive, and I had experienced no sexual attraction or romantic interest in women or queer and nonbinary people until my early twenties. After some back and forth, another activist encouraged everyone to accept me as I was—I was different, yes, but it was possible to be like me, too. To be included on the list of legitimate kinds of queers, it was not enough, for instance, to challenge the prevalent frame of *cinsel yönelim* (sexual orientation) by suggesting one could inhabit different sexualities at different stages of life. That, too, was necessary of course, but having confidence in my knowledge, and being persistent in my narrative, were, in the end, what resulted in the activists ultimately acceding to my account of my sexuality. The issue was not that the activists would not listen or change their minds; it was that their default position was to assume that narratives that did not reflect their existing frameworks were wrong and in need of correction—this was part of their political and activist work.

I will speak a little more about what it meant to the Kadınca bar crowd and management to be blamed for being apolitical (see the next section) and about how they experienced politics in return. But before I do that, I want to pause and ask: What does it mean for an LGBT association to have such a sophisticated criticism of global neoliberal capitalism and to feature intersectional principles in their political organizing but nevertheless enact classist distinctions and exclusions? The shift of discussions from capitalism to neoliberalism at large has meant that certain important features of class, such as habitus and cultural capital, are rarely found in analyses regarding political organizing. Yet an acknowledgment of the role of cultural capital in accessing and evoking what counts as political language needs to accompany our analyses of social justice movements if our analyses are to be informed by social justice concerns.[19] The case of Lambdaistanbul and the Kadınca club shows that class can and does inform normativities beyond neoliberal ideas of what is profitable, fundable, and respectable. Paying attention to the classed dimensions of how politics are defined is especially expedient in times when right-wing populism positions the Left as elitist know-it-alls who see themselves above the people. This is precisely how Kadınca management and clients experienced queer activists of Lambdaistanbul. Since they often did not have the tools or the interest in making themselves legible to activists, and since they understood the terms through which they were being dismissed as a matter of politics, they, perhaps inevitably, turned to critiquing and rejecting politics itself.

Politics as Critique, Critique as Politics

The management and workers, as well as some of the clients of Kadınca, were aware of activists' critical stance toward the club and its clientele, and they had their own criticisms of the LGBT organization.[20] For instance, Lambdaistanbul's hosting of parties at straight venues came up as a major complaint in interviews, yet such complaints were not voiced as critiques of Lambdaistanbul's politics, but rather as (affective) resentments. I discuss the management and workers' understanding of Lambdaistanbul's preference for *heteroseksüel* venues as a failed solidarity, which itself can be understood as a political critique, elsewhere.[21] For my purposes here, I will turn to how Lambdaistanbul activists shaped Kadınca management's understanding of politics as critical and interventionist and as rigid and disrespectful of other ways of being in the world.

When members of the bar management complained about Lambdaistanbul activists' preference for straight venues as party locations, what they found disappointing was that the activists preferred these clubs to Kadınca *despite* the higher prices and poor—and, at times, openly *homofobik*—treatment they received at those venues. In the face of such treatment, the fact that Lambda activists made such a big deal out of the fights at Kadınca was puzzling to them. During our interview, Heval made a point of dispelling one particular story of a pride week fight that took place at Kadınca. Not only was the level of violence as narrated inaccurate, Heval said, but they personally had checked on the two people involved in the fight to find that they had resolved the issue between themselves without involving the police or going to a hospital.[22] I witnessed a similar case where, after rolling on the club floor fighting and being practically impossible to separate, not an hour later I saw the two baç women hanging out, one's arm around the other's shoulder. This mostly performative aspect of the fights made Lambda's reaction seem out of touch with reality and further removed what they perceived as life versus politics as expressed by Doğa: "They [Kadınca clients] are not interested in politics. People are living. The place fills up only on Saturdays if you noticed. People have fun and then leave. They have no relationship to politics or anything like that." Referring to Lambdaistanbul's critique of the bar fights, Bahar, the club's DJ, said: "You do not have to make such a big deal out of it [*büyütmek*]. If you want homosexuals to be accepted somehow, or somehow for them to have fun, to prove themselves, to live the way they want to live, you should not stone a tree that gives fruit." Here Bahar's statement echoed Doğa's point that (LGBT) politics was out of touch with life. Being out of touch with life inevitably indicated a kind of uselessness, an impracticality to politics. What was presented as politics to apolitical queers was also experienced as a rigid rejection of forms of existence that did not fit into particular ideologies. In this case, such a refusal worked to not accept LGBT people themselves and to not appreciate the club as a "tree that gives fruit." Not only did the activists *not* understand the nature of fights, they were also out of touch and, in fact, in denial of LGBT people's ways of living. Rigidly applying rules and principles with no attention to context under the rubric of being political presented activists as both uninterested in *and* incapable of grasping what was considered life: the everyday, as embodied by queers who worked all week in mostly lower-middle-class jobs and once a week needed to relax and have a good time. Politics, on the other hand, was serious, boring, and finger-wagging. No wonder the queers at Kadınca preferred life over politics.

I found that this association of politics with constraint produced a couple of important effects. First, it had implications for whether women who did not identify with Lambda activists' *attitude* or *political style* found themselves able to support Lambdaistanbul's larger goals regarding LGBT rights at all: Once their stance was perceived as pushy, know-it-all (*ukala*), and corrective, their larger political project looked like a bundle of impositions on others who did not believe in their ideals or were simply not interested them. Bahar told me, for instance: "Our people, including me, we leave things to life's flow. After all what I am living is right according to me, but it might not be right according to other people, and I would not try to get them to accept it. . . . I have my own truth [*doğru*], and they have their own after all." Bahar did not necessarily word her request for openness and allowing others to have their own truth as a political position—to her, this was the opposite of a political (read: critical) stance. Becoming political would mean becoming critical, which she understood as a lack of openness to difference, something queer women of Kadınca did not find inviting.

The second outcome of equating Lambdaistanbul with politics-as-intervention was the experience of any form of interventionist (*müdahaleci*) behavior as political. For instance, among several stories of Lambda's "political" reactions, Heval recounted Lambdaistanbul volunteer Elif's critique of a lesbian couple's desire to get a combination of their names tattooed on their ring fingers as a sign of commitment to each other. I assumed that this must have been a reaction stemming from Elif's politics around the institution of marriage, but Heval corrected me: "No, because the tattoo was going to be a combination of their names. She said that they might break up some day, and they will regret it; they should not do it." The reason this reaction became conflated with other moments of Lambda being too political was its *style*—Elif had been corrective and had taken the liberty to impose her own "truth," to use Bahar's term. Hence, the lines between reactions of a political and nonpolitical nature became blurry, and all responses of a corrective, interventionist style came to stand in for the political.

The features of this political *style*, as well as its reception by the apolitical queers bear similarities to the ways in which scholars have suggested critique operates within the humanities and social sciences.[23] Departing from Eve Sedgwick's response to the hegemony of paranoid reading practices in queer theory (and in other "critical" humanities), Rita Felski has invited us to think about critique as "a style of interpretation" where the content often takes the backseat. Critique, she proclaims, is a particular reading style that is charismatic and authoritative to the extent that it has become "synonymous with intellectual rigor, theoretical sophistication, and intransigent opposition to the status quo."[24] It authorizes the assumption that "whatever is not critical is therefore *un*critical"[25] and, therefore, unqualified to challenge the status quo. Humanities and social sciences continue to train students and scholars in critical reading and critical thinking practices, Bruno Latour notes, even at a time when skepticism of science and facticity and what we might call "deconstruction" have become common practice among the right wing (think: climate change deniers).[26]

While Sedgwick, Latour, and Felski are primarily concerned with the hegemony of critique among all interpretive hermeneutics in higher education and the increasingly thin line between critique, on one hand, and paranoia and conspiracy, on the other, I suggest that similar tendencies are surfacing in grassroots activism, especially in such areas as feminist and queer politics, where knowledge and activism are often deeply intertwined. And while I share Latour's worry that the weapons of social critique take shape as right-wing conspiracy theories that are predicated on denying scientific facts, my central concern is informed by my conviction that the currently prevalent form of critique does not have the same effect on the left and the right.[27] This is because, I suggest, in a post-ideological, neoliberal world where politics is supposed to be a technocratic endeavor, the Right has other forms of meaning and belonging to offer that can be packaged as unpolitical/nonideological. When employed by the Left, critique sounds jaded and disenchanted, demanding that people give up on things they might hold dear without offering anything in its stead. On the right, critique takes the form of conspiracies that sound magical and mystical and is supplemented by things to believe in, such as racial nationalisms, religious orders, and charismatic leaders. In a deeply disenchanted social and political world, it should not come as a surprise that many subjects find these more appealing than critique. This differential effect becomes especially important when we move from critique as a mode of interpretation and inquiry in the humanities and social sciences to critique as a form of political engagement with the social world among activists. As we are instructed by the example of Kadınca management and clients, most subjects are uninterested in being admonished or corrected for their "wrongs."[28] This political style signals to them a significant gap in their own dispositions and those of activists and results in them experiencing politics as disconnected from their lives.

Of course, this mode of activism is not unique to Turkish LGBT grassroots organizers and volunteers. In my years of teaching in the United States I have observed similar tendencies among my students, many of whom were involved in on- and off-campus feminist and queer organizing. Discussions of calling out versus calling in and opening up meetings with ground rules of what is OK and not OK to utter in various feminist and queer groups and organizations seem fairly common practice. An enthusiastic welcome of the position of the feminist killjoy among students and activists also contributes to such dynamics: theorized by Sara Ahmed, the feminist killjoy is an affect alien—a subject that refuses to be properly oriented toward happy objects, such as the family, and cannot help but disrupt the happy feelings in spaces that are made possible only by continuously ignoring the ongoing racisms, sexisms, or homophobias.[29] The feminist killjoy indicates the political potential of simply killing joy, which is understood to be the extension of not participating in the happy orientation toward objects a feminist or queer activists should be critical of. Since, as Felski reminds us, critique as a style commands that if you are not being critical, you are being *un*critical, a joyful orientation toward the world can only be naïve at best, failing the affective requirements of critique.

How can we strive for social change without assuming we are the only ones with "an unmystified view of systemic oppression"—an assumption that leads social justice activists to act as if their mission is to enlighten everyone else, which they often do by disenchanting their worlds?[30] If the critic is "not the one who lifts the rugs from under the feet of the naïve believers, but the one who offers the participants arenas in which to gather," how can we (re)imagine the role and affect not only of the academic critic but also of the activist who fights for social justice?[31] Being open to surprise, a quality of reparative reading, would correspond in activism to openness and indeed the expectation of leaving political conversations as transformed as we expect others to be.[32] Can we imagine a way of engaging politically with the world that features such openness? And, equally important, can we imagine a politics that centers feminist and queer *joy*? Below I turn to the Gezi Park protests of 2013 in order to discuss commons as a political project with radical potential that provides an alternative to critique. As we will see, Gezi commons provided a vision of queer worldmaking that managed to fold many previously apolitical subjects into its utopian fold. It re-enchanted politics by giving participants a taste of what it feels like to work in solidarity with complete strangers for a better world and to do so in a political climate of increasingly divided and polarized people. Queer slogans became popular during the uprisings, centering *aşk* (love) in the political project at hand. They also produced a vernacular that was not predicated on cultural capital, but inspired by a joyful humor used as a weapon against a neoliberal Islamist government whose task, it seemed, was, among other things, to kill joy.

The Promise of the Commons

Neoliberal Islam's Morality Politics and the Deployment of Marginality

Under what conditions did the critical attitude toward improperly political subjects discussed above shift to an approach that emphasized differential yet interconnected injustice and suffering? What were the circumstances under which activists and others stopped imagining particular groups to be the rightful leaders of political movements and enlighteners of the people? Below I detail the ways in which the Turkish government's moralization of citizens' economic behavior with an emphasis on Islamic virtue led to an increasing number of citizens feeling marginalized by the regime. Despite Erdoğan's deeply polarizing discourse that distinguished between morally upright responsible believers and disreputable irresponsible nonbelievers (often also marked as terrorists), this deployment of marginality in the nation led many citizens to reject such distinctions. Recognizing that the regime could render anyone marginal and precarious, the protesters refused a politics of respectability along with the government's neoliberal transformation projects, instead of demanding to be folded back into their rightful respectable place.

As recounted in the introduction, starting around 2010 and accelerating with their reelection for a third term in 2011, the AKP and its leader Erdoğan's tone shifted significantly, accompanied by changes in their undertakings. The government and the nation had more enemies it needed protection from and more players on the world stage envious of Turkey's robust economy and, therefore, more responsibility that fell on the shoulders of citizens to do their part. There were frequent references to various lobbies—the interest lobby, the capital lobby, the alcohol lobby, the porn lobby, the war lobby, the terror lobby—that were presented as both mystical entities and real threats to the republic under AKP rule. Whenever the government was the target of criticisms, for hiccups in the economy, leaked tapes revealing high-level government corruption, or contested moves in international relations, these lobbies were blamed. National politics was animated and enchanted: Talk of national politics was full of stories of dark and evil forces continuously conspiring against then prime minister (and, later, president) Erdoğan, the AKP government, and the Turkish nation, inviting those who were viewed as responsible citizens to national duty.

References to the glorious days of the Ottoman Empire proliferated in governmental discourses as guarantees for contemporary Turkey's abilities to stand against such threats. Ottoman ancestry, which had always been incorporated into the national imaginary through mandatory Ottoman history courses from elementary school throughout secondary education, was no longer simply the country's past but had temporary relevance: Ottoman revivalism made its way to such public rituals as celebrating Istanbul's conquest by the Ottoman emperor Fatih Sultan Mehmet in 1453.[33] The AKP's neoimperial ambitions became clear during the country's invasion of Syria. The AKP government positioned itself not only as the savior of the Sunni rebels against President Bashar al-Assad's regime but also of masses of Syrian refugees created as a result of the civilian conflict (partially enabled by Turkey's interventions and supply of arms). Mimicking discourses of colonial humanitarianism, President Erdoğan frequently framed Turkish superiority to European nations in terms of its humanitarian rescue—a rhetorical move often attributed to old and new imperial centers in the West. "Today many countries can build virtual walls on their borders while they live according to advanced human rights, high levels of democracy and welfare (within those borders)," Erdoğan proclaimed. "Those countries who see their own people as entitled to universal human values, democracy, and welfare are capable of watching tragedies next door . . . as if they are watching a thriller" on-screen.[34] While Erdoğan's humanitarian claims are clearly contradicted by the wretched living conditions of the now more than 3.5 million Syrian refugees in Turkey as well as by his continued use of them to extort the European Union for financial aid in return for keeping the Turkey-EU borders closed,[35] his rhetoric of exposing the hypocrisies of the so-called democratic Western civilizations has found increasing resonance both within and beyond national borders.[36] President Erdoğan's alleged true humanitarianism and critique of Western powers continues to ring true *and* genuine to many in a world where Orientalism's critical opponent easily becomes an equally reductionist Occidentalism, continually reproducing anthropological difference.[37]

Erdoğan continually narrated Turkey as both perpetually under threat and as thankfully supplied with the glorious past and the benevolent present it needs to overcome such challenges. Yet it is important to note that he is not the inventor of international conspiracies against Turkey, and neither is his government the origin of the complex relationship with the West marked by simultaneous fear, desire, and frustration.[38] Erdoğan's contribution to this old narrative is a new object of international envy: the robust Turkish economy. In this framing, the Turkish economy does not feature as a sheer technicality, but as a magical, enchanted entity that attained its strength under various liberal and neoliberal governments throughout Turkish history, all of which as a result had been targets of attacks. For instance, in an address at a TÜSİAD (Turkish Industry and Business Association) gathering, President Erdoğan simultaneously crafted a genealogy of economically successful Turkish governments as historically politically persecuted (including his own) *and* positioned the AKP as exceptional, as the only economically successful party that has persevered in the face of powers trying to bring down the nation: "There is a particular cycle constructed in Turkey so that whenever things are going well, there is a coup," he stated.[39] Erdoğan mentioned that the late prime minister Adnan Menderes had grown the economy and spread the (national) wealth to the people yet was brought down by a coup. Similarly, in the 1970s, when Turkey's growth was accelerating, anarchy had taken over the streets of the country followed by another coup. The reform process that had been initiated by the late prime minister Turgut Özal had stalled as a result of the February 27, 1997, postmodern coup, during which then prime minister Necmettin Erbakan had been asked to step down by the military.[40] Explicitly positioning himself in political kinship with the 1950s right-wing populist Menderes and the 1980s right-wing liberal Özal,

Erdoğan simultaneously accomplished several goals. For one, he placed his party in a (neo)liberal economic and political genealogy instead of a pro-Islamist political one. Second, he crafted the national history as one full of mysterious conspiracies, including a chain of military coups targeting not the radical Left but the center Right. This particular move, which positions liberal economic growth in opposition to military intervention, also enabled him to align the AKP with liberalism and its archenemy, the Kemalist regime, with raison d'état. The Kemalist combination of military government, single-party rule, and a closed-market, state-led economy, now all merged in an image of authoritarianism and lack of freedom, positioning AKP rule as liberal, democratic, and populist, thus disappearing the history of socialist, communist, and other Left alternatives to *both* orders. He also situated himself as not only the final but also the invincible member of this lineage. Erdoğan continued his speech alleging that the ambiguous powers he spoke of desired excessive gain for only a handful of people, but he reassured the audience that his government had created an economy where the working classes, the peasants, and everyone else had prospered thanks to both the low interest rates the AKP government made available as well as its investments in extensive development projects. He then proceeded to explicitly cite the Gezi protests as one such threat that his government had successfully upended and complained about credit-score companies that had recently issued a low score for Turkey: "This is the logic of 'we could not topple them politically, so we will topple them economically.'"[41]

Carefully suturing the international credit-rating systems to protests organized against the Turkish government's neoliberal privatization projects, calling them participants of an international ploy to "topple [Turkey] economically," Erdoğan preempted demonstration as a meaningful civilian action. There were those who were Turkey's friends and responsible loyal citizens, and there were those who were its enemies. National loyalty and financial loyalty were one and the same, since national security was continually under attack financially. The astronomical foreign debt Turkey has accrued under various AKP governments was bracketed, and so was the shrinking of industry and national production on many fronts, including agriculture, and the increasing reliance on trade and import as well as foreign investment. Thus, surrounded by various internal and external enemies, which President Erdoğan has come to term *faiz lobisi* (the interest lobby), the Turkish economy required all the safety it could muster and deserved all the securitization its safety required. As a result, Turkey experienced securitization not instead of, but as an extension of, neoliberalism: The weaving together of economy and security in Erdoğan's rhetoric is evident in the narrative where the Turkish economy is presented as strong yet under continuous international threat. The critique and resistance that result from actual precarities produced by neoliberalism are then delegitimized as the doing of ambiguous foreign powers conspiring against the Turkish economy (and thus its politics) and performed by, as we will see below, alcohol-drinking, religion-disrespecting, disloyal subjects.

But what did this prosperity under AKP rule, this object of global envy, look like? The discourse of Turkey's increasing glory and the resulting heightened risk the nation was facing unfolded in the context of various neoliberal austerity measures as well as nationwide privatization projects. The first AKP government was elected in 2002 following a major economic crisis (see the introduction). As a result, the AKP government raised taxes, capped government salaries and social spending,[42] and also encouraged consumer spending and real estate development.[43] These moves initially resulted in significant economic growth.[44] This early economic expansion was accompanied by the emergence of finance and credit markets that put homeownership as well as consumption of luxury items within the reach of many citizens, which led the working classes to be able to live middle-class lives and *feel* national prosperity, all at the cost of steadily increasing household indebtedness.[45] As recounted in chapter 3, the construction business experienced a significant boom under AKP governments as part of AKP's large-scale urban redevelopment projects—many of which led to the gentrification of low-income neighborhoods as well as the replacement of squatter homes by new housing units built by the housing development administration (TOKİ; Toplu Konut İdaresi Başkanlığı). These projects often involved the evacuation and dispossession of ethnic minorities and the urban poor as well as their initiation into a vicious debt cycle.[46] In addition, many of the government's development projects capitalized on natural resources and presented significant environmental hazards, causing protests by environmentalist groups as well as such professional organizations as the Union of Chambers of Turkish Architects and Engineers.[47]

Finally, the rise of finance and credit markets, urban renewal projects, and the commodification of public lands and forests for neoliberal restructuring have been accompanied by increasing labor repression. For instance, the privatization of TEKEL (Tobacco and Tobacco Products, Salt, and Alcohol Administration) led to plant closings, changing labor conditions, and mass layoffs, leading to an almost three-month strike in 2010.[48] The secretary general of the union's statement was poignant in its comparison of the state of labor domestically and the AKP government's humanitarian aid internationally: "While we endure a tragedy here in front of the world's eyes, our Prime Minister is working for other people's rights in Syria (and Palestine). Of course . . . [w]e will stand by anyone enduring pain anywhere in the world. Our call is to those who lamented cruelty yesterday but do not see the victims of today."[49] While these forms of labor repression are familiar everywhere under neoliberalism, what was particular to Turkey was the narrative with which Erdoğan countered grievances. In a speech he gave following the 2010 explosion in Zonguldak in which thirty miners died, Erdoğan expressed his own, and the government's, sadness about the trapped miners. Yet, he added, the people of the region were used to these kinds of events. Looking back twenty years he could see all kinds of mining accidents in the Zonguldak region. He told the audience he knew the working conditions in the mines well. He had been "down in the mines" and had broken fast with the miners. Yet "this" sadly was in the fate (*kader*) of this profession: those who entered this line of work did so with the knowledge that "these kinds of things" were possible.[50] When he was criticized for reducing work-related accidents to fate, he countered: "If you don't believe [*imanın yoksa*] in accidents, in fate, that is a different matter. I will not discuss that with you. Speak about that with the president of religious affairs, not with me. I am talking about something else. It is in the *fıtrat* [God-given nature] of this [business], in its fate."[51]

Religion figured here in a number of ways. First and foremost, it naturalized work-related death *and* changed the conversation from labor conditions to matters of faith. Religion was also evoked by Erdoğan talking about breaking fast with citizens as an apparent fellow believer in an imagined religious brotherhood yet also declaring that religion was not his expertise. That, he suggested, was a position occupied by the president of religious affairs, thereby also ensuring the distinction between religion and politics. In other words, Erdoğan was not a man of religion, but a politician-believer. Explaining conditions of labor under neoliberalism away with an alleged Islamic social order, he replaced "the worker" with "the believer" as the relevant category in question. Following this incident, fıtrat became a staple in Erdoğan's narratives regarding labor—four years later, he used it again in relation to work-related deaths of hundreds of miners in Soma after a firedamp explosion. This expression would extend to other spheres as well, as marginality was pressed on larger populations within the country.

Thus, unlike in the early to mid-2000s, the focus of the government's rhetoric was no longer on civil liberties, ethnic rights, and democratization, but on a strong country with a strong economy, which the citizens were asked to actively support. In other words, if the state followed the logic of market veridiction, part of citizens' economic responsibilities resided in ensuring this mechanism by which a strong economy signaled a strong government. Married couples were encouraged to have three children in order to contribute to Turkey's young population, which was presented as the backbone of its robust economy. President Erdoğan uttered this wish in various forums, ranging from opening ceremonies to lectures he gave at KADEM (Kadın ve Demokrasi Derneği [Association for Women and Democracy]), where his daughter Sümeyye Erdoğan serves as deputy chairwoman. As early as 2009 he was reported as asserting that families needed to start having three children before it was too late. Citing various World Health Organization as well as United Nations data on aging populations and longevity, he was convinced that for Turkey to protect its powerful position in the world it had to maintain a young generation. The burden of that, as with anywhere in the world, fell on families. Yet Erdoğan found the idea of financial worries absurd. "Look, what are the current populations of China, or India?" he asked. They were among the wealthiest nations in the world.[52] In other instances he dismissed financial concerns by stating that Allah will provide for each child (*Allah rızkını verir*). His pro-natalist and pro-family vision has led to the state providing financial incentives for married couples to have children and a reduction in the amount of childcare subsidies for working mothers.[53] Citizens' economic duties would later also take the form of exchanging their foreign currencies, especially US dollars and euros, or refusing to invest in them during periods of devaluation of Turkish lira. Such behavior that goes against all tenets of neoliberal or, for that matter, any kind of liberal rational action might seem to contradict neoliberalism itself, but let us not forget a couple of things: Firstly, this demand follows directly from the logic of market veridiction: the AKP cannot fail thus the economy cannot fail and vice versa. Therefore, the robust economy needs to be put back on track at whatever cost—a mechanism we might call a *neoliberal state of exception*.[54] As states of exception are constitutive of sovereignty under liberal governance, so are neoliberal states of exception necessary and foundational to the state-market relationship under neoliberalism. Secondly, invitations to invest in the national currency were always accompanied by rampant privatization of any and all public resources. In other words, citizens were responsibilized to save the national economy in a nation where everything was continually de-nationalized.

Erdoğan's growing authoritarianism became glaringly evident whenever his administration was criticized. When feminists protested his declarations that women were entrusted to men (by Allah), he admonished them for not understanding this important Islamic value.[55] His statements on women's reproductive roles as mothers and wives also rested on men's and women's difference in fitrat: Pronouncing gender equality as a breach of the God-given nature of men and women, he added that women's fragile bodies should not be expected to do the same kinds of labor as men, as they had been forced to do under old communist regimes.[56] When citizens critiqued Erdoğan's lack of concern for the civilians killed in an airstrike against Roboski (in Kurdish)/ Uludere (in Turkish) in December 2011, he lashed out, stating that abortion was actual murder, thus continuing his pro-natalist discourse.[57] Such unhealthy behaviors as alcohol consumption and smoking were personally scorned by Erdoğan. His earlier remarks that focused on the health hazards of alcohol, and that invited citizens to eat fruits instead of drinking,[58] were later replaced by his statement that our bodies have been lent to us by Allah, and therefore no one has the right to betray them.[59] Ultimately, alcohol sales would be prohibited between 10 P.M. and 6 A.M. in the country, which led to more protests by TEKEL workers. In other words, citizens both experienced Erdoğan's increasingly authoritarian style and watched his personal approvals and disapprovals turn into legislation. As I will discuss below, alcohol consumption as a marker of not being a true believer would, by extension, eventually signal marginal subjectivity in the president's narratives as he distinguished proper and improper citizen subjects.

Inderpal Grewal has argued that responsibilized American citizens under late neoliberalism are invited to participate in (Christian) humanitarian rescue projects as well as in "national security."[60] While Grewal carefully points out that her discussion of "exceptional citizens" is specific to the US context, neoliberalism is indeed breeding security regimes all over the world since states are facing the challenge of containing increasing desperation, demands and revolts. Turkish citizens, too, find themselves as responsibilized national subjects to economically save the nation, both through their reproductive labor and through such economic behaviors as investing in Turkish currency. For instance, a 2014 announcement tweeted by the Ministry of Family and Social Policy targeted those who lived alone as wasteful consumers, with graphics showing figures carrying their cut-off heads in plastic shopping bags.[61] Citing statistics showing increased consumption levels of food, packaging, electricity, and gas superimposed on this visual representation of alleged selfish wastefulness, the campaign invited citizens to a life that married the conventional family form with economic responsibility.

Further, Turkish citizens were invited to uncritically support the AKP government's humanitarian politics and participate in national pride via Turkey's humanitarian superiority to Western nations—a contradiction, as the TEKEL union leader for miners noted, in the face of continued miseries and tragedies at home.[62] Finally, during the evening of July 15, 2016, in the midst of the unfolding coup attempt, citizens found themselves invited into the streets and the squares in order to stop the military tanks. Nonstop announcements were heard throughout the night from the sound systems of tens of thousands of mosques, calling all the people to the squares in order to protect "our democracy."[63] Many civilians followed this call to confront soldiers and tanks, and a number of them lost their lives. Declaring a state of emergency that lasted for three years, the government continually capitalized on having been under attack and positioned itself as the representative of democracy despite growing authoritarian repression, including sweeping arrests of journalists, intellectuals, judges and attorneys, politicians, and military personnel, with claims of terrorism or coup attempts. Thus on July 15, 2016, a large group joined an already existing population of purported terrorists throughout the nation (recounted in chapter 3).[64]

I return to how the state of emergency and heightened security measures after the coup attempt influenced LGBT organizing in the next section. For now, let us remember that back in 2010 little international coverage focused on the Turkish government's targeting of politicians, academics, and intellectuals who were speaking up against the oppression and persecution of Kurdish citizens in the country, and Turkey was being heralded as a role model for the Arab world.[65] When Kurdish political prisoners went on a hunger strike in 2010, the minister of justice dismissed pleas for a government response, stating that there were absolutely no problems in Turkish prisons and no reason to be worried about anyone's well-being. By 2011, Turkey had the largest number of jailed journalists in the world.[66] As the government grew and the police were fortified, the occasional protests, such as demonstrations against the demolishing of the historic Emek theater in Beyoğlu to be replaced by a shopping mall, were increasingly met with tear gas and water cannons. It was in this context of authoritarian morality politics of neoliberal Islam that the Gezi protests of 2013 took place, when so many average citizens felt marginalized in ways they had not experienced before. As this growing authoritarianism and deployment of marginality was felt by many in the nation, yet was not organized under any recognizable political entity, the Gezi Park protests were a surprise not just to international observers but also to many citizens of Turkey.

Resistance Everywhere: Queer Commons
and the Re-enchantment of Politics

On May 28, 2013, a handful of protesters gathered in a small park in the Taksim district of Istanbul to stop municipality bulldozers from removing the trees in order to make space for a shopping mall to be placed in a restored Ottoman military barracks. At the time, this particular incident did not stand alone in the neoliberal restructuring policies of the AKP government. Only very recently had the historic Emek theater building been sold to be converted into a(nother) shopping structure and the Beşiktaş ferry station—a public waterfront property on the Bosporus Strait—had been purchased by the Shangri-La hotel chain. Talks about construction of the widely protested third Bosporus bridge that was expected to cause significant environmental damage also were on the table. When the initial protesters camping on the park grounds were countered by water cannons and tear gas and their tents were burned by security forces, more citizens rushed to the park to join them. As the demonstrations spread throughout the country, clashes with the police took an increasingly violent turn. In the two weeks that followed May 28, 8 protesters were killed, some 4,000 were injured, 104 of them suffering serious head injuries, and 11 people lost an eye due to plastic bullets and tear gas canisters.

Most of the coverage of the Gezi Park protests has inevitably focused on the scale of the neoliberal state violence unleashed onto civilian bodies— photos have depicted highly pressurized water being sprayed at unarmed civilians, bodies flying in the air from the force of it, and bodies disappearing into clouds of tear gas. The importance of these details notwithstanding, we would not be doing justice to these demonstrations if we limited the story to unabashed authoritarian state violence. The ways in which bodies under attack interacted with each other and the worlds that were formed as a result speak to the possibilities of resistance under neoliberal authoritarianism that can and do go beyond critique and actively imagine a different form of coexistence. Below I will discuss the spirit of the protests—often referred to by the protesters as the Gezi spirit—which led to the production of a Gezi commons that in many ways was a queer commons.[67] The links protesters made between various forms of state and market violence, between social and economic dispossession, between recognition and redistribution tell us of both the need for and potentialities of collective organizing against increasingly unbearable conditions of life. The protests also tell us about political potential of subjects who often remain illegible to the conventional critical Left.

These dynamics were evident in the fact that the demonstrations quickly multiplied both spatially and ideologically despite the starting point of the park and its demolition. Recognizing the regime's deployment of marginality onto an increasingly larger and more heterogeneous body, protesters quickly drew connections between the government's physical reengineering of the country and its social and moral reengineering of its public. Responding to Erdoğan's unabashed call for three children per family, banners and signs read, "Would you like three more children like us?" Underlining the shortsightedness of sheer pro-natalist politics that cannot conceive of the revolutionary possibility of a new generation, these slogans not only rejected the government's reproductive futurity and its contours of respectability, they also undermined the very plan-ability of such a future. Similarly subverting the government's morality politics and attempts to responsibilize its citizenry, when government officials called mothers to come collect their children from the park, infantilizing the protesters and delegitimizing their political demands, many women rushed to the park as mothers, forming a human chain around their so-called delinquent children to protect them from police violence.[68] The more the government hailed citizens into neoliberal and national responsibility, the more irresponsible and irreverent they seemed to become.

As the protests spread out from Gezi Park to various public venues across the country, the emphasis of the slogans oscillated between various positions: standing up against the demolishment of Gezi Park, recognizing other important neoliberal redevelopment or extraction projects across the country, and protesting the authoritarian and autocratic AKP government that had marginalized many and now referred to all those involved in the protests as morally suspect. This also required an oscillation between unity and difference: Protesters were at once both one and many. At people's forums organized in the park in order to share experiences—a format that would be replicated in many parks across the city once the Gezi commons was finally dispersed by the police—queer subjects told stories of the park as a central cruising ground for gay men and a place for trans sex workers to pick up clients.[69] Gezi Park itself, Armenian groups reminded everyone, was an edifice of erasure, since the historic Ottoman barracks the government wanted to restore were partially built on an Armenian cemetery that also was demolished in the process.[70] As crowds that gathered and lived in the park composed a document with their Gezi demands, the Muslim minority Alevis and other people of Dersim came forth with their Dersim demands, thereby decentering Gezi Park as *the* political environmental disaster resulting from neoliberal politics.[71] They demanded cancellation of "licenses which effectively allow the parcel and sale of our mountains in Dersim for mining purposes and result in severe distortions of the landscape." In other words, Gezi became a forum through which various groups made gendered, sexual, racial, and classed claims to public spaces that nevertheless featured uneven histories of dispossession. The protesters were one and not the same.

Others who joined the protests humorously challenged AKP's moralization of alcohol consumption and Erdoğan's push toward limiting alcohol sales: Proclaiming "Ayık kafayla çekilmiyorsun AKP" (AKP, you are unbearable when we are sober) turned the recently introduced limitation on alcohol sales on its head, positioning their very governance as the reason citizens are drinking.[72] Another chant, "Huzur İsyanda" (Inner peace is in revolt), a play on the words "Huzur İslam'da" (Inner peace is in Islam), both challenged the government's use of religion to tame the public and proposed rebellion against repressive regimes as the very thing subjects would not live without. Chants often ended in "faşizme karşı omuz omuza" (shoulder to shoulder against fascism), positioning the revolt not only against the neoliberal, but also the authoritarian, autocratic, pro-natalist biopolitics of the AKP regime. Yet fascism was not treated in a presentist way, as if it were a matter of AKP exceptionalism. This was perhaps best exemplified in a banner that gained significant social media circulation, which stated: "You hung us when we were the sea, so we are returning as an ocean" (Deniz olduk astınız, okyanus olduk geliyoruz). Referring by name to Deniz Gezmiş, one of the radical Left student leaders in the 1960s who was executed along with three others following the 1971 military coup, this slogan reminded the government that radical histories of the country were not forgotten despite its attempts to re-narrate the history of coups as targeting liberal economies. Revolutionary generations recognized both the genealogies of authoritarianism in the country as well as the histories of revolt against them.

Demonstrators tied these critical sites together through *direniş* (resistance), which itself was a common keyword in banners, stencils, and hashtags both in Turkish and English. Direnistanbul/Resistanbul and Direngezi/Resistgezi became widely used slogans; yet they were quickly decentered by messages that recognized the nationwide occurrence of revolts, such as the slogan "Taksim everywhere; resistance everywhere." This was indeed the power of the protests—the recognition that centering the privileged metropolitan area of Istanbul would have repeated the very injuries the protesters aimed to address. The resistance could not mimic the existing hierarchies. It had to provide instead a space where all those who had felt displaced, dispossessed, and cast out of the structures of national belonging and respectability could continuously decenter any center that emerged. This rhetorical and political decentering of Istanbul and eventually of Gezi Park and the proliferation of protests against *faşist devlet* (the fascist state) quickly resulted in a governmental dismissal: The protesters did not know what they wanted, Erdoğan claimed. The whole thing had started as an innocent environmentalist movement but had been taken over by anti-government political factions, fooling naive environmentalists into participating in chants asking the government to resign. The dismissal of the very nature of the critique by dividing it into "initial apolitical (and legitimate) environmentalist innocence" and "anti-governmental (and illegitimate) political violence" was accompanied by Erdoğan's claims that aimed at politically discrediting demonstrators by questioning their moral behavior. He infamously called the protesters a handful of plunderers/looters and drunkards.[73] He claimed they had entered a mosque with their shoes on and had drunk beer inside and that they had assaulted his "sisters with headscarves."[74] He shuttled back and forth between stating that the protesters were a handful of marginals *and* that they were organized antigovernmental groups taking over an innocent environmentalist movement. *Marjinal* is a term derived from the French *marginal*, and its everyday use in Turkish evokes not so much a sense of triviality but a sense of abnormality, a deviation from mainstream norms and values. Whether the demonstrators were a handful of looters or a significant anti-governmental organization, their location on the morality spectrum remained the same.

Finding themselves doubly marginalized in the government's narratives, prior to Gezi as unmarried women, as nonmothers, as bachelors, as university students in coed housing, as drinkers and smokers, as Kurds, as critics of the government, and during Gezi as "anti-government insurgents," the demonstrators emphasized their collective spirit and their commitment to engaging in the "impossible politics of difference."[75] First, instead of erasing the differences evoked by Erdoğan to divide the public into respectable and disreputable, they recognized and transformed those very differences. Since Erdoğan often superimposed the division between morally sound/morally loose onto the binary of pious Muslim citizens versus immoral drunkards whom he claimed especially disrespected Muslim women with headscarves,[76] the protesters both stated their respect for pious citizens and refused to be folded into the government's respectability politics. The former was evident in Gezi protesters' collective decision not to consume alcohol at the park during the two nights of Isra and Mi'raj, in their keeping watch over the group Revolutionary Muslims as they prayed at the Gezi Park five times a day, and in their participation in collective fast-breaking whether they were fasting or not. Yet they still inhabited the space of the marginal, the immoral, the plunderer, and the drunkard. In other words, they rejected the government's respectability politics *and* performed acts that interrupted the religious/moral versus secular/immoral binary perpetuated by governmental discourses.

This was perhaps most evident in the protesters' embrace of the term *çapulcu* (plunderer/looter) employed by Erdoğan when referring to the protesters in order to politically and morally discredit the demonstrations. The term was everywhere in the city and around the country: on banners, on T-shirts, graffitied and stenciled on walls and the pavement. The slogan "Ne sağcıyım ne solcu, çapulcuyum, çapulcu" (I am not right-wing or left-wing; I am *çapulcu*, I am *çapulcu*) suggested it as a political position that challenged old divisions and rose above them—a means for protesters to distance themselves from politics as usual and embrace the political potential of the disreputable. This move was especially significant in the context of Gezi, where most participants had previously thought of themselves as apolitical subjects and admitted that they had never been to a protest before. In a country where there had been numerous protests to join, both historically and during the AKP reign, this is particularly striking. The politicization of these participants had happened not through subscribing to some previously established right-wing or leftist political ideology, but through embracing a marginal subject position that was imposed on them. Some of the youth explicitly noted that previously they had viewed politics as the domain of professionals to which they had believed they would have nothing to contribute. Participating in street politics had made them realize that that was not the case—because politics was about core values and principles, and no one needed be a professional to have them.[77] *Çapulcu* became the marker of the dare to stand up against an authoritarian and oppressive government's othering rhetoric in mass and the refusal to be intimidated by police violence.[78]

However, as I discussed above, the çapulcu formation did not work to homogenize the protesting publics and erase historical and current realities. The distinctions among various histories and current forms of marginalization did not seem to divide, but to strengthen the alliances that were emerging from this social movement. Thoughtful reconsiderations of the Turkish state's historical regimes of truth proliferated on social media, which had become the only site for reliable news due to the government's tight control of most mainstream channels. Both the utter lack of proper coverage of protests, and the amount of misrepresentation on mainstream television caused citizens to question the truth of the representation of Kurdish citizens as terrorist bodies from the 1990s onward on those very same channels. Further, the recognition of these varied relationships to marginalization were central to critiques of neoliberal policies becoming multivocal and complex: Secular critiques of neoliberal privatization of public goods married with in-faith critiques by the Revolutionary Muslims, who objected to the booming mosque construction business during the AKP regime. Emphasizing that Islam provides everyone with the *kıble* (the direction of Mecca) for prayer and thus turns entire skies into a dome (under which one can pray facing the kıble), they exposed the rapidly proliferating mosques all over the country as resulting from business interests and not piety. Revolutionary Muslims had their own mosque-tent setup in the park marked as Gezi Mescidi, where they prayed every day outdoors, next to a banner that read, "Property belongs to Allah." In July of that year, a month and a half after the end of the protests, thousands would gather on İstiklal Street following the call of the Revolutionary Muslims and the Anticapitalist Muslim Youth group to form *yeryüzü sofraları* (tables of the earth). An alternative to the AKP's exclusive *iftar* tents, where their guests broke fast during Ramadan, the yeryüzü sofraları were for the people. Tablecloths lay on the ground all along İstiklal Street, with thousands sitting on the pedestrian road, extending for hundreds of meters, sharing food and beverages they had brought along. Everyone who wanted to join, whether fasting or not, whether contributing food or not, was invited to these tables that were proposed as an alternative to "the capital's luxury tables and the sovereign's exploitation tables."[79] Tables of the earth have remained a Ramadan tradition, repeated every year since the first gathering following Gezi in 2013 until May 2019, when the tables and members of the Revolutionary Muslims were finally attacked by police.

It is important to note that Gezi was not simply an ideological commons but also a material one in ways that rendered the ideological/material binary obsolete. Its ideology of resisting erasure of publics arose from the living circumstances created at the park, within which protesters theorized together—as they spent time and resisted side by side with others they might have never met under other conditions, received help from complete strangers under tear gas or pressurized water or when facing risk of detention, attended impromptu concerts or dance performances (some of which were politicized ethnic minority dance forms), read books at the Gezi library, were fed, and received medical assistance, all for free. No monetary exchanges were allowed in the park, and participants remembered this as a time when they "did not touch money."[80] For many participants, including many of my friends, what made Gezi like a dream was the commons it created along with the spirit of mutual caring. Numerous accounts mention moments of receiving help from complete strangers as transformative experiences, as the magic of Gezi. This physical coexistence in marginalization resulted in many participants questioning their own previous practices of othering Kurds, Alevis, or queers.[81] When the stenciled slogans and graffiti took sexist and homophobic tones, feminists and queers organized workshops to collectively imagine ways to curse without reproducing existing forms of marginalization of women, queers, or sex workers.[82] It was due to physical coexistence that when soccer fans, who surprised the public with their active participation in the resistance, used their regular swearwords "sons of whores" for the police, actual sex workers who were among the protesters let them know that they were resisting side by side with whores and that it was time they changed their language.[83] There were openly queer activists who, organized as LGBT Blok with the characteristic rainbow flag, distributed food, water, and medical supplies to thousands. Other queers did not join the blok but did participate in the resistance individually or with friends, joining whoever was around them. Trans women sex workers living in the area opened their homes to demonstrators escaping police violence.[84] In return, the Istanbul-based soccer team Beşiktaş's fan group Çarşı attended the trans pride march at the end of June.[85] The LGBT pride march of 2013 reached a historical high in attendance, with some accounts reporting around fifty thousand present.

As Gezi commons created its own dreamworld in which previous strangers became comrades and friends, where everyone took care of everyone else, where money was of no use and protesters experienced the arbitrariness of state violence and abjection, they continued to blur common distinctions between straight and queer. Queer vernacular became common vernacular during and after Gezi. For instance, *ayol*, one of the untranslatable idioms in Turkish language and widely employed in the queer subculture, became integrated into the language of the uprisings. Ayol is untranslatable partially because it does not mean anything literally but, rather, constitutes a gesture and an effect of effeminacy and limp-wristedness. *Diren ayol* (resist ayol) emerged both as a slogan and a key hashtag during the protests as protesters had to rely heavily on social media for news and communication.[86] Through their banners asking, "What is prohibition ayol?" protesters mocked various government prohibitions, reversing the unintelligibility often placed on their lives and bodies back onto the authoritarian rule. The chant *"Ay, this is literally a revolution ayol!"* queered the protest style and attitude of hypermasculinized, teargas-mask wearing, barricade-building bodies, redefining the subject of revolution. *Aşkım* (my love), another queer colloquialism, spread through the crowds, with tens of thousands chanting in a call-and-response manner throughout the day, "Neredesin, aşkım? Buradayım, aşkım!" (Where are you, my love? I am here, my love!). Among the two words that would both translate as love into English, *sevgi* and *aşk*, the latter connotes a romantic love that is blinding, marked by burning desire and irrationality. Voicing the irrational, unexplainable love and affirming the presence of thousands of others *in love*, protesters, just like the trans sex worker activists in chapter 3, recognized the regime as structured around hate, which required a structure of love to resist. Aşk named both the relationships formed among strangers in Gezi commons as well as the enchantment they felt when they realized that they had been strangers only prior to being transformed by love.

The relationships of the Gezi commons created by love also reimagined the connections between the living and the dead. When I suggested it would be unfair to capture Gezi solely with the numbers of dead and injured, it was both because this would do no justice to the commons created during Gezi and also because the lives lost to police violence during the demonstrations were rendered as part of the commons. If "Where are you, *aşkım*? I am here, *aşkım*!" was one common call-and-response, another consisted of calling out the names of those who had died during the protests and declaring their presence still with them. "Ethem Sarısülük!" chants a woman's voice in the documentary #*direnayol* and crowds respond, "Present!" "Medeni Yıldırım!," she continues. "Present!" "Abdullah Cömert!" "Present!" Conjuring the dead, our dead, protesters refused to accept that these young lives were lost. There is an eerie quality to this chant; it fails to replicate the excitement of "Where are you, my love?" The presence of the living and the dead does not form an equivalence but does constitute a necessary corollary reminding us that social solidarities require both the living and the dead as well as the refusal of erasures that neoliberalism performs on collective memories of public space.[87] The protesters refused to leave their dead behind: the resistance would continue with them.

Gezi, therefore, is not simply a tale of queer activism coming into contact with a larger and fairly heterogeneous resistance movement and generating moments of mutual care that transformed the approach of heterosexual cis citizens to queer and trans people. Such transformations certainly took place, yet what was critical to Gezi commons was the conjuring of a dreamlike space and forming social solidarities that overcame social distinctions historically introduced and fostered by nationalism, neoliberal capitalism, and, most recently, by neoliberal Islam, thus redefining what was *possible*. It was possible for a nationalist to chant with Kurds against militarism, for soccer fans to resist alongside trans sex workers, for upper-class queers to come into contact with working-class queers and stand up against a system that marginalized anyone in its way. It was possible for people to share all their resources without reservations and to live in common with those they had never thought they would come in contact with in a city of more than seventeen million. It was possible for the living and the dead to form social solidarities and to reject neoliberal Islam's definitions of morality, respectability, and life.

The Subject of Politics

In this chapter, I began with a story of how LGBT activists' sophisticated understanding of global neoliberalism and neoimperialism, as well as their intersectional politics, did not suffice to prevent them from perpetuating class distinctions vis-à-vis the baç clients of Kadınca club, who presented working-class and unsophisticated masculinities and did not have the language to make sense of their gender performances. The travel and translation of now mainstay gender and queer studies theories, such as the social construction and performance of binary gender, seeped into the language of LGBT activists and other college-educated queers and transformed into cultural capital, excluding those who did not have access to this purportedly legitimate language of queer politics. As a result, these apolitical queers were pushed out of the limits of legible political subjectivity. In return, Kadınca clients and management experienced politics as an elitist interventionism and as something that directly opposed both freedom and life.

The Gezi Park demonstrations, on the other hand, constituted a moment in which the subjects of politics were abundant, heterogeneous, and often previously apolitical. Anyone concerned about the park, the intensifying privatization of public goods, and the rising authoritarianism in the country was welcomed. There were certainly people who were surprised to see queers or pious Muslims or soccer fans at the park, but these constituted moments of transformation of citizens' own preconceived notions of who made a proper subject of politics. No one was expected to speak a legitimate political language—in fact, Gezi created its own vernacular that relied on humor and politicization of unconventional subjectivities and performances, such as çapulcu.[88] It was due to this heterogeneous mass coming together in person that feminist, queer, and sex work activists were able to speak to those who used sexist and queer-/trans-/sex-worker–phobic language. They did so not in ways that questioned their political subjectivity, but through workshops where people collectively imagined a new language of anger and revolt that did not need to demean the already marginalized subjects of the system. One of the most significant outcomes of the uprisings was the fact that it redefined political capital and, therefore, who had access to political subjectivity. When demonstrators defined Gezi as a dream, they did not oppose it to life. What they meant was rather that they knew they could wake up from this dream someday and find that life carried on as before but that "there were things those bodies that shared the dream would remember when they woke up."[89] As a political utopia, Gezi redefined political life in ways that made politics and life no longer oppose each other.

Nonetheless, it would be misleading to present the Gezi demonstrations as a utopian dream completely devoid of exclusions and distinctions. As critics note, what brought the protesters together was a critique of the commodification of natural resources and public spaces, not a critique of the commodification of labor or of class. As Cihan Tuğal notes, this resulted in nonsocialist participants at Gezi voicing their disdain for what they saw as an ignorant public continuing to vote for the governing party, which echoes my earlier point that a critique of neoliberalism without a critique of class resulted in queer activists' performance of distinction vis-à-vis other queers.[90] For Tuğal, such elitist statements as well as a critique of neoliberalism-induced marginality that did not marry criticism of capitalism and class led to the movement not extending to greater masses. Öykü Potuoğlu-Cook, on the other hand, along with Ayşe Parla, asks what bodies were not able to participate in the human chain formed by mothers at the park and draws our attention to the ideologies of selfless sacrifice and maternal instinct that were reproduced by the participants even as they mobilized them to stand up against state violence.[91]

Yet, as an imperfect dream, Gezi nevertheless points to possibilities for solidarities that can open doors for understanding past marginalization and for standing up against current forms of state and neoliberal violence. Gezi also constitutes a nightmare for the AKP government, with Erdoğan comparing Gezi to other alleged coup attempts in his talks and AKP deputies objecting to the June–July 2017 march for justice (Adalet Yürüyüşü) claiming that it was an attempt to "resurrect the Gezi events" and stating that they "will not allow a second Gezi" in response to protests of deforestation of the Middle East Technical University campus.[92] The threat posed to the authoritarian and autocratic Turkish government by collectivities that resist without fear of police violence is real. Equally real is the menace posed by a people who do not fear the difficult task of facing their own privileges and the ways in which they have contributed to the marginalization of others. Gezi, as an imperfect dream, nevertheless speaks to the power of bodies that do not fear marginalization and who in fact can proudly embrace it—knowing that being the marginal subjects of the neoliberal Islamic regime that thrives by dispossessing peoples of commons and of dignified lives is perhaps the only way one can be sure one is in a quest for a life worth living.

Conclusion

Queer Studies
and the Question
of Cultural Difference

If one of the main goals of this book has been to show the importance of studying sexual liberation politics to understanding neoliberal Islam, the other one has been to open up room for queer studies to discuss Islam as something other than a homogenous and victimized other of Western modernity. This necessitates a historical, contextualized approach that understands all religions, including Islam, as multiple lived realities and does not focus only on their representation and symbolic significance.[1] It also requires that we forgo totalizing notions of the West and understand it as "a play of projections, doublings, idealizations, and rejections of a complex, shifting otherness."[2] In other words, it necessitates an approach that is as committed to avoiding Occidentalisms as it is to debunking Orientalisms. Throughout the book I have tried to show what is to be gained from thinking about *neoliberalism* and *Islam* together, the two terms that make up the object of this study, despite their mutually exclusive treatment in queer studies. The question I have bracketed thus far—*why* it is that these terms have been kept separate—is what I try to answer in this conclusion.

In order to look for answers, I suggest we turn to queer studies' foundations. Foucault's analysis of modernity, which centers on the medical and psychiatric establishments and, in particular, on sexual subjects, has been key to most scholarship that falls within the parameters of queer theory/studies. The field's special attention to the production of normalcy/abnormality in the context of biopolitical regimes, as well as these systems' power to name their subjects, quickly distinguished queer studies from LGBT studies. Refusing to locate "proper objects" of analysis, queer studies claimed all areas in and through which normativity is produced to fall within its purview.[3] This ultimately opened up the field to pay attention to the carceral state, immigration, and diaspora as well as the global war on terror, discussing how sexuality and the liberal logic of sexual minority can be deployed to further congeal normalizing regimes.[4] As LGBT was mainstreamed over time, it no longer constituted queer existence—other sites of abjection, such as criminalization, poverty, and citizenship, came to mark the others of Western modernity. This move eventually worked toward decentering not only minoritized sexual subjectivities and identities but partially sexuality itself from the program of queer studies.[5]

Foucault's centrality to the field has not meant, of course, that he has been immune to criticism. Some queer studies scholars have (re)claimed psychoanalytic theory despite Foucault's strong rejection of it as a proper approach to analyzing sexuality and modern power,[6] while others have questioned his clear-cut division between *scientia sexualis* and *ars erotica* and the neat mapping of these formations onto modern/premodern and West/East.[7] This binary was made possible partially by Foucault's general lack of attention to the colonial context of the metropolitan, modern Europe he theorized.[8] Finally, queer studies scholars have sought ways to reconcile Foucauldian biopolitics and governmentality with questions of capitalism and the categories of labor, value, and interest that are also central to theorizing modernity.[9] It is these last two Foucauldian omissions—colonialism and capitalism—and how queer studies as a field has dealt with them that are important to understanding the separation of neoliberalism from Islam. Despite previously drawn connections between capitalist modernity and colonialism, and between (unruly) desire and (calculated) interest,[10] queer studies' attention to capitalism and colonialism developed through two different and separate venues: Whereas the former focused on neoliberal cooptation of progressive social movements in the West and sex-cultural homogenization in the rest of the world, the latter has been primarily concerned with questions of representation and their neoliberal outcomes, such as the contemporary global war on terror. Despite these interventions, however, Foucault's larger proposal of the rise of modern/sexual subjectivity as *the* signifier of modernity continues to be central in the field. I argue that it is this bifurcation between tending to omissions of capitalism and colonialism in Foucault that led to the field's separation of neoliberalism and Islam. Once this separation is accomplished, and Islam is properly relegated to the realm of the cultural (versus the economic, itself a faulty separation), the emphasis on sexual subjectivity as *the* marker of modernity enters analyses in order to evaluate contemporary sexual cultures in the non-West as modernity's neocolonial effects. Let me elaborate on each of these points in turn.

Since John D'Emilio's critical argument linking capitalism and gay identity, queer studies has featured a set of scholarship that has paid attention to capitalism's and, later on, neoliberalism's effects on sexual identities and subcultures.[11] Yet it is important to note that while (neoliberal) capitalism seems to be always imagined as transnational, its effects in the West have been mostly discussed domestically. These analyses have focused on the effect of neoliberal values on queer movements, positioning queers as respectable, productive members of society with purchasing power, formulating such agendas as gay marriage, gays serving in the military, and hate crime laws. Gays and lesbians, as a result, scholars have argued, moved from being undesirable inhabitants to gentrifiers of neighborhoods, from targets of police violence to subjects of protection by law enforcement, and from abnormals to married couples and responsible parents—briefly, from queers to normative gays and lesbians. Of course, only *some* queers have been welcomed into such national belonging, critics have emphasized: Increasing economic precarity and criminalization continue to target queer and trans people of color, especially those who are from lower-class and poor backgrounds, contributing to a system where some queers seek protection by a state that continually oppresses other queers.

Even though D'Emilio's observations were limited to Western urban spaces, Dennis Altman's reading of global capitalism as a homogenizing force resulted in debates in the social sciences in particular regarding whether global capitalism had indeed flattened out heterogeneous forms of gender and sexual nonnormativities "elsewhere."[12] In "Capitalism and Global Queering," Peter Jackson suggests: "The political economy of global queering needs to relate the market to *both* the localizing and the transnational dimensions of cultural globalization, and explain how capitalism produces both modern forms of sex-cultural differentiation in some domains alongside convergence in others. . . . [T]he analytic task is to explain how the market produces both new local forms of sexual difference and indigenous commonalities."[13]

In other words, since capitalism seems to be indigenous to the West, its effects there are discussed within the rubric of increasing normalization of previously othered publics, whereas in locations outside the so-called West, capitalism's effects are understood as a form of cultural imperialism. This parallels the issue of the purported indigeneity of modernity and, therefore, of modern sexual categories to the West: While gays, lesbians, bisexuals, and trans people in the West are understood to have been oppressed in the past by the heteropatriarchal state and its juridical and medical structures, modern sexual others in the non-West are at best products of capitalism = cultural imperialism and, at worst, its perpetrators. This reductive understanding of capitalism as cultural imperialism in the non-West begs some questions.

For one, what does it mean to discuss capitalism and its effects only in terms of the production of sexual identities and cultures in the non-West, which are then measured against their Western counterparts in terms of their likeness and unlikeness? What effects does this move produce? Is sex-cultural differentiation the only thing that capitalism produces that is to be of concern to scholars of sexualities in the non-West? And if among what capitalism produces are responses to it that are not only identities but also ideologies, such as communism, socialism, or other critiques of capitalism, are those equally signs of Western imperialism? Are there any political positions that are not produced by capitalist modernity and therefore authentic to the non-West? Is the non-West only to be relegated to the realm of precapitalist sexual indigenous identities and practices when assessed for its levels of subjection to cultural imperialism? If so, what does this tell us about the location of cultural difference in the epistemic unconscious of queer studies?

In *Queer Marxism and Two Chinas*, Petrus Liu has postulated that arguments over the coloniality of applying (North American) queer theories to elsewhere conceal that cultural difference undergirds the epistemic unconscious of queer theory.[14] Departing from Judith Butler's use of Claude Lévi-Strauss in *Gender Trouble*, Liu argues that cultural variation of gender and sexual norms has been central to much of queer theory's foundational arguments. If sexual difference has necessitated cultural comparability, then we must pause and ask: What work have "cultural Others" been asked to do to liberate the West from the "heterosexism of the Symbolic"?[15] While Liu limits his discussion to China, he recognizes that Foucault's geographies of *ars erotica* that constitute the cultural others of Western modernity included "China, Japan, India, Rome, the Arabo-Moslem societies."[16] Therefore, his argument that non-Western cultures have been made to serve as the West's conceptual limits in queer studies is equally relevant and useful for other others of Western modernity, including those in Muslim-majority countries.

Islam in fact today serves as a popular cultural alternative to Western modernity, whether it is denounced or embraced as difference. Arif Dirlik suggests in his critique of "alternative modernities" that the search for alternatives to capitalism is nothing new but that since the 1980s, cultural difference has become the most important marker of these alternatives.[17] As alternatives are increasingly sought among other cultures, Islam's emergence as an alternative has further culturalized Islam. Under neoliberal incorporation, this has meant, among other things, that Islamic civilization could be packaged and marketed by the Turkish AKP government in such branding projects as its Alliance of Civilizations (recounted in the introduction).[18] I do not make these points in order to deny the existence of difference but to ask: When and to what end is difference deconstructed in our analyses and its neoliberal incorporation critiqued, and when is it embraced as an alternative or resistant reality to Western modernity?

In fact, so strong is the alternative culture status of Islam in queer studies that when the field analyzes the Islamic non-West, capitalism is often completely absent from discussions. Vis-à-vis Islam, modernity's central defining feature shifts from capitalism to secularity. In other words, there is yet another split when studying queer sexualities and cultures in the non-West: Scholarship on capitalism's effects in terms of global queering focuses on East and Southeast Asia (and less so Africa) and rarely discusses religion, whereas analyses of queer cultures in Muslim-majority regions are rarely discussed in terms of the effects of neoliberal capitalism.[19] Instead, the focus has been on the Orientalist representations of an allegedly patriarchal and homophobic Middle East and the ways in which these representations have been evoked in the context of the war on terror by queer and non-queer actors and organizations alike. As an effect of these analyses, in queer studies Islam is doubly removed from the political economy and rendered as cultural twice over (as compared to the cultures of other non-Western elsewheres). This means, among other things, that Islam and in conjunction with it the Middle East bear an additional burden in queer studies' relationship to cultural difference. To be clear, I am not arguing that queer studies scholars are unaware of the operations of neoliberal capitalism in Muslim-majority regions. I am, rather, speaking of a field formation that has prioritized and, at times, rendered paradigmatic particular approaches that have the effect of separating Islam and the political economy and rendering Muslim-majority zones, especially the Middle East, as doubly cultural.

Of course this rendering of the cultural of the Middle East and the treatment of Islam as cultural difference is not unique to queer studies.[20] What I find significant in the context of queer studies is the role language has played in the field vis-à-vis both sexuality and culture. Let me return here to my proposal that despite various engagements with Foucault's omissions in the field, queer studies has not radically questioned the proposal that sexual subjectivity is *the* marker of modernity. What signifies sexual subjectivity in return are linguistic markers of (sexual) kinds of people. In fact, so powerful has been the proposal that linguistic sexual categories index modernity that the emergence of the very categories of gay or lesbian have been treated as potential signs of cultural imperialism, and the persistence of local (presumed to be indigenous) gendered and sexual formations, such as *waria*, *kathoey*, *bakla*, *hijra*, and others, have been understood as signs that Western modernity and globalization are not totalizing forms.[21] While scholars who have contributed to this body of work vary in their positions regarding what the travel of modern sexual identity categories indicate vis-à-vis colonial modernity and globalization, and while a number of them have worked to complicate the binaries of global/local and modern/traditional, no other formations of modernity seem to be questioned regarding their indigeneity when they are located in the non-West.[22] This includes, but is not limited to, the existence of the nation-state form, stock exchanges, modern public transportation systems, police force, prisons, welfare systems, modern legal systems, or a modern army.[23] This view/understanding is made possible by a reading of modernity as a colonizing, imperial force with sexual subjectivity as its defining center.

What seems to be common to these debates is an ahistorical and usually rigidly discursive treatment of language itself. The only linguistic change is imagined to be mobilized by global modernity, where the English language and Western categories travel to the rest of the world: This is true whether they are imagined to produce epistemic violence or more complex, localized forms of meaning. Even though, I, too, have traced terms that have traveled from US/Euro contexts to Turkey, my treatment of linguistic travel has not taken either one of these positions. By turning to translation theories, I have argued that meaning is always fractured and that language is more than discourse. This is not to undermine the discursive power of language, and throughout the book I have traced such discursive effects, but it is to recognize that the semantic dimension of language requires that we acknowledge that oftentimes what is produced is a complex, disjunctive, and heterogeneous field of meaning. Chapter 1, for instance, traced not only the multiple responses produced when LGBT rights were weaponized against headscarf rights in Turkey (mainly by non-queer secularists) but also the multiplicity of Muslim positions vis-à-vis the question of LGBT rights. This story revealed both the complexity and multiplicity of what easily gets reduced to the local and, in this case, the Islamic position, rendering the secular/religious binary untenable, but it also showed the various ways in which Islamic positions are transnationalized today, whether they embrace discourses of human rights or its poststructuralist critiques.

Translation studies scholars who have focused on the question of homolingualism have deeply historicized language to show that what we understand to be language as a unit today contains a long history of violent erasures of indigenous languages and of oral traditions, of reducing many languages to dialect, and of standardizing what would count as language.[24] This stands in stark contrast to, for instance, Talal Asad's evoking of language in his chapter "The Concept of Cultural Translation in British Social Anthropology" in *Genealogies of Religion*.[25] Asad takes issue with Ernest Gellner's objection to anthropological accounts he finds to be "too charitable" to the "primitive" by attributing too much reason to particular non-Western cultural forms. In his critique, Asad rightfully points out that cultural translation in anthropology is not devoid of power—it affects who gets to be the observer/translator of which society, for whom traditions or rituals of "others" need to be rendered intelligible, and the ways in which such production of knowledge might affect how said societies understand themselves. So far, it is impossible to disagree with Asad. However, when his desire to bring concerns about power into this discussion are formulated in terms of the "inequality of languages," which then map onto "unequal societies," and "languages of dominated and dominant societies" that a problem arises:[26] If Arabic, for instance, which stands in an asymmetrical position vis-à-vis English, unproblematically becomes the powerless language, do we not overlook the histories that produced Arabic as a national language in various nations and at what cost such standardization took place? The homolingual understanding of languages as separate and commensurable entities that Asad operates with overlooks the fact that native speakers of all national languages are made, not born. Forgetting this historicity of language and assuming power to solely operate along a first/third world axis performs other erasures even in otherwise commanding accounts of power/knowledge.

I suggest that a similar homolingual treatment of language and a similar understanding of power existing only along the first/third world axis inform Joseph Massad's *Desiring Arabs*, which has perhaps single-handedly framed the question of epistemic violence via Western categories of thought as dispersed by LGBT activism in the context of the Middle East.[27] In fact, when I started my fieldwork, so significant was Massad's scholarship to analyzing queer activism that activism itself was understood as a normalizing mechanism (and thus the least queer subject of them all, unless the goal was to produce similar critiques of activists). Massad's book is predominantly a study of "the influence and impact that Orientalism has had in shaping the Arabs' own perceptions of themselves and each other since the Arab renaissance to the present."[28] Yet Massad is not only interested in the construction of a particular Arab history but also of "the modern projects that this effort serves."[29] The modern projects he refers to here are international human rights groups and, in particular, LGBT activism. In chapters 1 and 3 I have shown the complex nature and effects of travel of human rights and LGBT rights frameworks to Turkey. Here I simply want to emphasize that Massad's critique rests on an unacknowledged relationship between modernity, language, discourse, power, and sexual subjectivity when he posits that an internationalization of "gay rights" as such erases "cultural formations whose ontological structure is not based on the homo/hetero binary" and as a result engages in epistemic violence.[30]

How can a critique of US imperialism or Western hegemony repeat the very binaries of tradition/modernity, East/West, and universal/particular that it presumably sets out to disrupt? Deploying such concepts as the Arab world, the third world, or the Muslim world continue to reproduce the logic of culture = religion and language = difference, erasing the violent histories through which these entities have come to be understood as bounded and homogeneous. Some of the violence has been colonial and imperial and continues to be so, but not all of the violence can be so designated. I suggest that instead of projecting a kind of purity onto the precolonial past and continuing to search for it in non-Western, non-Christian elsewheres, we recognize complex historical, transnational intersections as well as complicities.

Therefore, instead of looking for cultural alternatives, or for places untainted by colonial modernity, I suggest we remember that while linguistic change is neither natural nor devoid of power, no cultures, geographies, or communities remain unaffected by historical erasures and epistemic violence, and not all of that has been the work of colonial modernity. Epistemic and other forms of violence are not exclusive domains of the historical fantasy called the West. In *Queer in Translation*, I have sought to document this by showing the ways in which Islam today does not occupy a pure place of indigeneity or local culture that is simply outside of the political economy. The Turkish-Islamic synthesis and the introduction in Turkey in the 1980s of a so-called moderate Islam in conjunction with neoliberalism (recounted in the introduction) requires that we pay attention to the various political histories of Islam. The AKP regime has a citational relationship to this history and has engaged in a particular moral marriage between neoliberalism and Islam.[31] I have also shown that Islamic positions on the issue of LGBT rights are varied and at times contradict each other. Further, they are all in conversation with various transnational forms of knowledge, such as human rights discourses or post-structural criticism, which inevitably disrupt both the religious/secular binary and the local as a reified, homogeneous form.

Finally, using translation as a queer methodology, I have sought to interrupt a simplistically hegemonic understanding of linguistic travel. Instead of assuming that the travel of vocabulary, such as LGBT rights, outness, hate crimes, or sexual orientation, perfectly translates to either colonizing the spaces where they arrive, wreaking epistemic havoc, or liberating them, I have shown that all translation involves social disjunctures. Understanding translation as a disjunctive social relation enables us to illustrate "the unstable, transformative, and political nature of . . . the differentiation of the inside from the outside, and of the multiplicity of belonging and nonbelonging."[32] Instead of a wholesale assumption that LGBT activism and queer politics has normalizing effects everywhere around the world, I have sought to lay out the various normalizing and moralizing regimes perpetrated by the economic, religious, and military structures of Turkey, which also include the current government's deployment of Islamic morality. Queer activism registers the challenges of neoliberal capital, US imperialism, secular militarism, *and* conservative Islamic morality without seeing these as being in ontological contradiction. The queer politics that result trace the wide deployment of marginality in the nation, the increasing debt and precarity, the widening securitization, the rising deep citizen violence, the sexist pro-natalism, and other forms of moralist regulation and violence done under the name of Islam as interconnected without citing proper subjects of state and neoliberal violence. These of course are legible only when we think beyond the logic of homolingualism, which reproduces crude understandings of cultural difference. Far from forming normalizing mechanisms, or demanding to be included in the respectable few, queer activism in Turkey exceeds politics for and about LGBT subjects and seeks social change that will make life livable for all. This, at times, may be activism without hope, but it nonetheless refuses to give up on joy or on imagining and working toward a queer commons for all.

Appendix

On Method and Methodology

As might have been clear to readers in the social sciences, design-ing the research for this book was not a simple and straightfor-ward process. And in many ways I do not think I could have de-signed the final version it ended up taking—that this project is even designable. This was partially because I was researching a dynamic and shifting social ground: How can any proposal predict what is to come in the following years? (This turned out to be exceptionally true in my case.) I had only a loose sense of what to expect. The inability to properly and tightly de-sign this research was also partially due to the fact that there was barely any literature on queer politics in Turkey at the time. I imagined my curiosities to be shaped by a state structure and a history marked by Westernization, so I tried to prepare for the field by reading feminist literature on Turkey and pe-rusing the online publications and videos of queer activist groups. The queer studies literature I had access to was mostly US-based and therefore almost inevitably US-centric. Even as it greatly informed my thinking, I could not locate my research very easily in queer studies literature or think of a gap to fill as we are told to do in classic research design classes. Looking back, I understand the un-designability of this project to be a blessing and one that is rarely mentioned in design courses. Formulating why I had a difficult time fitting this project in the literature ended up becoming the very framework of this book.

When I arrived in Istanbul in June 2008 for fieldwork, I initially selected Lambdaistanbul as an obvious location to observe queer politics. At the time studying activism or resistance was not very popular in queer studies. In 2007, the year before I started my research, both Joseph Massad's *Desiring Arabs* and Jasbir Puar's *Terrorist Assemblages* were published, and they included provoking and important critiques of queer activism. While it certainly is not these two authors' doing that their work became so paradigmatic and shaped years of queer approaches to activism and social change, this scholarship heavily informed how to understand LGBT activism, especially in the Middle East. I found Lambdaistanbul's political positions to be fairly different from the suggestions of the literature on homonormative or homonationalist queer organizing. The organization could have provided a conventional site from which to respond to the existing, if slim, literature on queer activism. It was physically, if not temporally, bounded with a clear sense of what events to observe and which subjects to interview and would have yielded a more conventional ethnography of how politics was experienced at and conducted by one queer activist organization. But that is not how political discourse or affect works. As I encountered political overflows from Lambdaistanbul, I decided to trace them. I traveled the political discourse of sexual politics wherever it led, which took me to various sites, some physical, some discursive, some both.

Approximately a month after I arrived in Istanbul, Ahmet Yıldız was murdered. This incident brought subjects to the premises of Lambdaistanbul who otherwise did not attend its meetings, protests, or events. This was the first time I encountered members of the bear subculture in Istanbul, and I was interested in the ways in which this story was unfolding, exposing, among other things, some disjunctures between Lambda activists and the bears (though these groups did sometimes overlap socially). In addition to attending Lambdaistanbul's biweekly coordination meetings and protests, parties, and special meetings organized by the group, I was introduced to some of the members of the bear community by friends at Lambdaistanbul. I interviewed several bears and went several times to a pub owned and managed by one of the founding members of Anadolu Ayıları (Anatolian Bears). As the Ahmet Yıldız story unfolded in the news and then disappeared from the daily mainstream agenda, the actions taken for him transnationally and the continuing lawsuit made it clear that this was an excellent example of how complex the travel of outness and honor killings was and how the state, family, religion, and law intersected under neoliberal Islam. The movie *Zenne*, inspired by Ahmet's story, was released in 2011. I interviewed a group of bears one evening about their thoughts about the movie as well as four people who had worked on or consulted for the movie in some capacity. While I initially thought about writing more extensively about the film, it ultimately made it only briefly to the conclusion.

Also fairly early on in my research, I frequently heard about the women-only Kadınca club, especially from the lesbian and bisexual activists of Lambda. Because I was interested in queer politics, I was especially intrigued by the activists' complaints that the queer women who frequented the club were apolitical. When I saw a listing online that the club was looking for waitstaff, I wrote to the owner of the club, explaining my research and the reason for my interest in potentially writing about it. They were sympathetic to my interest, and I worked at the club on Friday and Saturday nights, usually from 10 P.M. until 5 A.M., for five weeks, as those were the only nights the club was open and I was in my last weeks of field research. (In my follow-up trips, I attended the club as a client numerous times.) As the club had a connected coed café downstairs, I made a habit of arriving a couple of hours earlier than opening time and hanging out downstairs with the owner, workers, their friends, and some of the clients who frequented the club every weekend. I also interviewed the owner, the workers at the time, and a number of clients. It is an ethnographer's methodological habit to ask, "What is this a case of?" when we encounter a social phenomenon. Over the years I gave many answers to this question about the Kadınca club, some of which have since been published: The club is a space that complicates the notion of commercial space, as it is a site where affective economies work differently from what the literature imagines and where subjects understand themselves to be the others of politics. I kept coming back to questioning who is the subject of politics and ended up telling this last version of the Kadınca story in conjunction with the Gezi protests to show how two different political imaginaries exclude, or hail, apolitical subjects.

In the first couple months after entering the field, I found out from a very close friend who had been a Lambdaistanbul volunteer for two years that a large group of trans women who had been organizing within the association had recently left the group to start their own group. At the time they were organized under Istanbul LGBTT (currently, Istanbul LGBTİ+). I had also known of Pembe Hayat (Pink Life), which was organizing trans women in Ankara, and that, too, consisted of transfeminine subjects who had found it difficult operating within larger LGBT organizations. Ultimately I decided to spend time with and interview Pembe Hayat activists. I made this choice mostly because at the time they were more established and active than Istanbul LGBTT, and perhaps due to the smaller size of Ankara, they seemed more able to reach a larger group of trans women and organize them. Not limiting my research to Istanbul has also meant that the claims I make about urban redevelopment, sexuality, and the transformation of public space are not limited to one metropolitan site but point to important shifts in urban spaces in neoliberal Turkey. One of the activists of Lambdaistanbul at the beginning of my fieldwork, who became a good friend and who knew the Pembe Hayat activists well, accompanied me on several trips to Ankara. Each time I stayed at the home of Esra, one of the Pembe Hayat activists, which gave me a chance to experience their daily life in addition to interviews.

Finally, "Subjects of Rights and Subjects of Cruelty" is the only chapter that features almost no ethnographic detail. It traces the unfolding of headscarf rights versus LGBT rights debates in Turkey that were particularly intense with the declaration of Selma Aliye Kavaf (then head of the Ministry of Women and Family Affairs) that homosexuality is an illness that should be cured. This rich and complex discursive site of public debates ensued mostly in newspaper columns, news pieces, and on TV shows. LGBT activists themselves were not invited to actively participate in these debates. Nevertheless, my knowledge of some of the queer activists' political positions regarding the AKP and the headscarf issue in 2008 informs my readings of these debates and the ensuing loss of potential solidarities. When I found out that there had been an in-person meeting between some Lambda activists and headscarf activists (the only one I am aware of) a few months *prior* to my fieldwork, I was nonetheless able to interview one activist about the meeting and obtain the meeting notes.

I spent an initial nine months in the field during 2008 and 2009 and then returned to the field for two months each in 2010, 2012, and 2014. I ended up interviewing a total of sixty-five people: this number includes Lambdaistanbul activists, Pembe Hayat activists, and a few trans women activists in Istanbul; managers and clients of the Kadınca club; and members of the bear community and a few others who were involved in Ahmet's case, such as his boyfriend at the time of his murder and Ümmühan Darama, the primary witness in the case. My interviewees also included one member of LISTAG, the Lambdaistanbul family group. For a while I thought I would write a chapter about this organization but ultimately did not include it in the research. No interview lasted less than an hour and a half, and a number of interviews were spread out over two sessions, lasting well over five hours. All of the interviews were conducted in Turkish, and all of the translations in the book are mine. All of the subjects' names have been changed, save for

Ümmühan Darama, since she was a public figure in the news, and Ahmet Yıldız, since he was deceased.

All in all, the archive of *Queer in Translation* features ethnography, interviews, and content analyses of news and social media. This form of mixed methods was the only way I was able to trace discourses as keenly as possible without stopping at the door of some physical field and to tell the stories in the book in ways that I can only hope do justice to their complexity.

Notes

Introduction

Portions of this chapter previously appeared in "Ethnography and Queer Translation," in *Queering Translation/Translating the Queer: Theory, Practice, Activism*, ed. Brian James Baer and Klaus Kindle (New York: Routledge, 2017), 72–83; and "Translation as Queer Methodology," in *Other, Please Specify:_____: Queer Methods in Sociology*, ed. Kristen Schilt, Tey Meadow, and D'Lane Compton (Berkeley: University of California Press, 2018), 249–61.

    1. I have chosen to use LGBT in referencing various queer organizations in Turkey despite the fact that the abbreviations of the names of most of the organizations I have either worked with, or known of, have changed several times over the past decade. During the summer of 2008, when I first started this fieldwork, most organizations used LGBTT, which stood for Lezbiyen, Gey, Biseksüel, Transseksüel, Travesti. Over the next couple of years, one of the *T*s was dropped from the abbreviation, with the remaining *T* now standing for *trans*, in order to avoid hierarchies that might be suggested by differentiating between *transseksüel* (transsexual) and *travesti* (transvestite) based on different trans subjects' status vis-à-vis hormone use, surgery, or both. There was yet another change in 2015, when *İ* was added for *interseks* (intersex), making the abbreviation LGBTİ. Currently most organizations prefer LGBTİ+ in order to signal inclusivity of various gendered and sexual others. (I thank Beren Azizi for verifying this information.) I settled on LGBT for this project after much thinking for three reasons: First, during the bulk of my research, intersex activism was not on the agendas of activists groups; therefore, LGBTİ/LGBTİ+ would wrongly suggest that the book covers intersex politics when it does not. Second, inasmuch as the acronym has changed several times over the course of this project, there is reason to think that

further changes might occur before publication of this book, rendering futile any attempt to ensure currency. Third, and connected to the second point, while I fully respect queer organizations' name changes, which often are guided by concerns about inclusivity, I also harbor an uneasiness regarding some of the politics that accompany these changes. In addition to questions scholars have raised already about the politics of inclusion (see Butler, *Gender Trouble*), I am also wary that the corrective nature of the name changes—after all, the change is made to ensure a more "correct" abbreviation—suggests that we are always improving the practices of naming. This position plays into a particular modern narrative of progress, suggesting that we are always moving toward better futures. This position is also used at times to correct and discipline those subjects who do not employ what is viewed as the accurate terminology. For the violence enacted by such erasures, see Valentine, *Imagining Transgender*. While I refer to LGBT politics, activism, and organizing throughout the book, when I refer to particular activist groups, I use their own current abbreviation.

2. The term "moderate Islam" (*ılımlı İslam*) has been used in conjunction with President George W. Bush's Greater Middle East Project to refer to US think tanks' and the US government's interest in encouraging nonradical, US-friendly Islamic governments, especially after the September 11 attacks, even though US interest in a nonradical Islam dates back at least to the 1979 Iranian Revolution. Several thinkers have voiced criticism of the AKP government's affiliations with moderate Islam as a US project (Macit, *Küresel Güç Politikaları: Türkiye ve İslam* [Global politics of power: Turkey and Islam]; Emre Kongar, "Ilımlı İslam, demokrasi ve antiemperyalizm" [Moderate Islam, democracy and anti-imperialism], *Cumhuriyet*, September 14, 2018, http://www.cumhuriyet.com.tr/yazarlar/emre-kongar/ilimli-islam-demokrasi-ve-antiemperyalizm-1082298). In 2008, Attorney General Abdurrahman Yalçınkaya opened a case requesting the closure of AKP and the ban of a number of its key politicians from politics for five years, citing the party's and its leaders' relations to moderate Islam as well as their connections to Muslim cleric Fethullah Gülen who resided (and continues to do so) in the United States ("İşte AKP iddianamesi tam metin" [Here is the AKP indictment full text], *Hürriyet*, March 19, 2008, https://www.hurriyet.com.tr/gundem/iste-akp-iddianamesi-tam-metin-8467042). The term has been criticized by both Islamists and secularists. I, too, find the radical-versus-moderate binary problematic and in this book use *Islamists* to refer to AKP politics. See note 8 for an explanation of my use of *Islam* in the book. For more on moderate Islam and Turkey see Büyükkara, "Ilımlı İslam Tartışmaları Zemininde Günümüz Türkiyesi'nde Laikliğin Anlam ve Sınırları" [The meanings and limits of secularism in the context of moderate Islam debates in contemporary Turkey].

3. This defense of Turkish democracy had historically manifested itself not only in quite undemocratic and violent ways—military coups, shutting down Islamist parties, barring Islamist politicians from engaging in official politics, crackdowns on intellectuals and journalists, and the headscarf ban for public employees and students at public schools, including universities—but also in an elitist positioning of the pious subjects of the country as backward, ignorant, and undeserving of the democratic rights, freedoms, and privileges bestowed on them by Kemal Atatürk, founder of the

republic. Turam, *Between Islam and the State*; Atasoy, *Islam's Marriage with Neoliberalism*. For more on Atatürk as a military leader and founder of the secular republic, and for an overall introduction of militarism as a defining feature of Turkish national culture, see Altınay, *The Myth of the Military Nation*.

4. Turam, *Between Islam and the State*; Cizre, *Secular and Islamic Politics in Turkey*.

5. Özbay, *Queering Sexualities in Turkey*.

6. Trans activists started organizing a separate trans pride march in 2010 as they felt that the larger LGBTİ+ pride march did not provide the space or the level of visibility they desired. The Trans Pride March (Trans Onur Yürüyüşü) regularly takes place the Sunday before the LGBTİ+ pride march in June, and many trans activists also still participate in the larger LGBTİ+ march.

7. Özkırımlı, *The Making of a Protest Movement in Turkey*. The fact that the pride march was the first and for a time the only sizable gathering permitted at Taksim Square following the resistance rendered this delayed reaction rather surprising. In fact, even as successive AKP governments started showing signs of authoritarianism and corruption, the pro-AKP LGBT group AK LGBTİ emphasized the AKP's (alleged) liberal position on gay and other civil rights issues by noting that their administration was the only one under which a stand-alone annual pride march had been allowed to take place.

8. While there is no such thing as a single logic of Islamic morality, I use *Islam* critically throughout the book in order to both outline and challenge Turkish government claims to it. The AKP's neoliberal Islam project has been a strictly Sunni one, but calling it neoliberal Sunnism would not be accurate, since the AKP often claims to speak on behalf of Islam in general and not Sunnism in particular.

9. Atasoy, *Islam's Marriage with Neoliberalism*; Yücesan-Özdemir, "The Social Policy Regime in the AKP Years"; Balkan, Balkan, and Öncü, eds., *The Neoliberal Landscape and the Rise of Islamist Capital in Turkey*; Yeşilyurt-Gündüz, "The EU and the AKP."

10. I do not mean to suggest that when not conjoined with Islam neoliberalism is otherwise without contradiction. This would equate to imagining that there is a pure form of neoliberalism, which, following Stuart Hall, I refute. According to Hall, "Neo-liberalism is . . . not one thing. It combines with other models, modifying them. It borrows, evolves and diversifies. It is constantly 'in process.' We are talking here, then, about a long-term tendency and not about a teleological destination." Hall, "The Neo-liberal Revolution," 708. Also see Ferguson and Hong, "Sexual and Racial Contradictions of Neoliberalism."

11. There are certainly scholars who study gender and sexuality in Muslim-majority contexts who are not blind to the nation-state context or the political economy and whose work can easily be folded into "queer studies"; these include Afsaneh Najmabadi (*Women with Mustaches and Men without Beards*) and Minoo Moallem (*Between Warrior Brother and Veiled Sister*). Yet this scholarship is often historical in nature, leaving contemporary queer formations and sexual politics to be represented as signs under the framework of homonationalism. For an exception to this, see Najmabadi, *Professing Selves*.

12. There are notable exceptions to this, such as Rofel, *Desiring China*; and Amar, *The Security Archipelago*.

13. Petrus Liu makes a similar point in his *Queer Marxism in Two Chinas*. I engage his work in more detail in the conclusion of the book, where I discuss the question of cultural difference in queer studies.

14. Long, "Unbearable Witness."

15. Moallem, *Between Warrior Brother and Veiled Sister*.

16. See Firat Bozcali, "Turkey's Three-Front War?," *Jadaliyya*, August 31, 2015, https://www.jadaliyya.com/Details/32412/Turkey's-Three-Front-War; Patrick Kingsley, "Who Are the Kurds, and Why Is Turkey Attacking Them in Syria?," *New York Times*, October 14, 2019, https://www.nytimes.com/2019/10/14/world/middleeast/the-kurds-facts-history.html.

17. Iran also features a similar noncolonized past, yet the Islamic Republic of Iran's current relationship with the United States positions it neatly within the "victim of US imperialism" category—a different political situation from that enjoyed by Turkey until recently, that is, as the second most important ally of the United States in the Middle East following Israel.

18. There have been a number of critics of such tendencies, but let me refer to two of them in order to raise two particular issues. In her critique of understanding Turkish history as "Westernization," Yael Navaro-Yashin states, "It is interesting that there should be such an implicit overlap between [the] modernization/Orientalist construct of 'Westernization' and postmodernist/post-Orientalist references to 'modernity.' The concept of Westernization . . . is based on the assumption, by default, that an essentially separate 'culture' existed prior to the development or the shift." Navaro-Yashin, *Faces of the State*, 10. Such studies, as a result, "have risked reproducing essentialism in leaving a precipitation of cultural authenticity or tradition underneath the layers of European costume, thereby overlapping, by default, with cultural revivalisms or nationalisms in the contexts studied" (8). In his critique of the "alternative modernities" paradigm as a crude "culturalist" approach, Arif Dirlik notes that people have always conceived alternatives to capitalist modernity, but only starting in the 1980s did those "alternatives" come to be conceived in cultural, rather than systemic, terms. Dirlik, "Thinking Modernity Historically," 17. Dirlik continues, "In fact, 'cultural difference' in conversations about modernity has relied on a systemic overlooking of worldwide capitalism" (19). In the conclusion of this book, I return to the question of cultural difference in scholarly searches for alternatives to (colonial) modernity in order to unpack the implications they have had for queer studies in particular.

19. The methodology I used in choosing the particular debates to focus on is presented in the appendix.

20. I am aware of the significant differences between postcolonial and decolonial critique, as well as the different histories each draws from. I am using postcolonial and decolonial in the same context here to refer to the folding of the various geographies they cover into the Global South, which is then overburdened with revolutionary expectations. While I am lured by feminist and queer imaginaries for less destructive and more just futures, I am weary of the romanticization of the past in much of deco-

lonial and indigenous studies. Kēhaulani Kauanui voices a similar concern regarding indigenous studies' conceptualization of a pre-settler colonial time as devoid of patriarchy. Kauanui, "Native Hawaiian Decolonization and the Politics of Gender."

21. Scholars have noted that these arguments have often been used by conservative governments located outside of "the West." To use perhaps the most relevant example here, former AKP prime minister Ahmet Davutoğlu, who was trained as a political scientist, notes in his 1993 book *Alternative Paradigms* that "the Islamic paradigm" is "absolutely alternative to the Western" (cited in Dirlik, "Thinking Modernity Historically," 14n11).

22. Sakai, *Translation and Subjectivity*.

23. Joseph, *Against the Romance of Community*; Blackwood, "Transnational Sexualities in One Place"; Boellstorff, *A Coincidence of Desires*; Carrillo, *The Night Is Young*; Cruz and Manalansan, *Queer Globalizations*; Jackson, "Capitalism and Global Queering"; Jackson, *Queer Bangkok*; Blackwood, "Transnational Discourses and Circuits of Queer Knowledge in Indonesia"; Gopinath, *Impossible Desires*; Manalansan, *Global Divas*; Moallem, *Between Warrior Brother and Veiled Sister*; Puar, *Terrorist Assemblages*; Reddy, *With Respect to Sex*; Rofel, *Desiring China*; Wilson, *The Intimate Economies of Bangkok*.

24. Edelman, *No Future*; Halberstam, "The Anti-Social Turn in Queer Studies."

25. For a discussion of the radical political potential of misinterpellation, see Martel, *The Misinterpellated Subject*.

26. Gordon, *Ghostly Matters*, 4.

27. As the editors of the 2005 special issue of *Social Text* titled "What's Queer about Queer Studies Now?" put it: "A renewed queer studies . . . insists on a broadened consideration of the late-twentieth-century global crises that have configured historical relations among political economies, the geopolitics of war and terror, and national manifestations of sexual, racial, and gendered hierarchies." Eng, Halberstam, and Muñoz, "Introduction," 1.

28. Scholars of neoliberalism have, and continue to point out the various and at times contradictory uses of the term "neoliberalism" to mark economic, political, social and cultural changes during late capitalism. While there is no consensus about what is exactly meant when the term is evoked, the common denominator of the existing literature points to at least three key "schools" of neoliberalism: one that understands neoliberalism as mainly an economic shift resulting in massive upward redistribution (Harvey, *A Brief History of Neoliberalism*); a second one that sees neoliberalism most significantly as a transformation of statecraft and the shift from a welfare state to a carceral state (Wacquant, *Punishing the Poor*); and finally the school that sees neoliberalism as a normative reason and a governing rationality that extends itself into all dimensions of everyday life, including realms that have no relationship to the economy (Brown, *Undoing the Demos*). This is of course not to say that scholars in one camp refute the changes pointed out in the others. What is at stake here is rather an emphasis on which transformation exactly (economy, state, culture) lies at the heart of neoliberalism, what makes neoliberalism *neo*. Bernstein and Jakobsen, "Introduction"; Brown, "American Nightmare: Neoliberalism, Neoconservatism, and

De-Democratization"; Springer, "Neoliberalism as Discourse: Between Foucauldian Political Economy and Marxian Poststructuralism"; Wacquant, "Three Steps to a Historical Anthropology of Actually Existing Neoliberalism."

29. Duggan, *Twilight of Equality?*

30. Duggan, *Twilight of Equality?*, 16–17.

31. Duggan, *Twilight of Equality?*

32. Duggan, *Twilight of Equality?*; Eng, Halberstam, and Muñoz, "What's Queer about Queer Studies Now?"; Eng, *Feeling of Kinship*; Ferguson and Hong, "Sexual and Racial Contradictions of Neoliberalism"; Puar, *Terrorist Assemblages*; Reddy, *Freedom with Violence*; Spade, *Normal Life*; Ward, *Respectably Queer*.

33. Ward, *Respectably Queer*.

34. Foucault, *"Society Must Be Defended."*

35. Boyd, "San Francisco's Castro District"; Hanhardt, *Safe Space*; Haritaworn, *Queer Lovers and Hateful Others*; Manalansan, "Race, Violence, and Neoliberal Spatial Politics in the Global City"; Schulman, *Gentrification of the Mind*.

36. Spade, *Normal Life*. Spade argues that the very demand for state and police protection places middle- and upper-middle-class respectable queers at the heart of LGBT politics, as they would be the only ones who can imagine being protected by these structures. I take issue with this proposition in chapter 4, where I discuss the campaign demanding a hate crime law initiated by trans sex workers in Turkey.

37. Puar, *Terrorist Assemblages*.

38. Hochberg, "Introduction"; Puar, *Terrorist Assemblages*.

39. This is certainly not exclusive to Muslims. Other communities of color or immigrant groups have been designated as locations of homophobia as well. Puar, *Terrorist Assemblages*.

40. Puar, *Terrorist Assemblages*.

41. Puar, *Terrorist Assemblages*, 36.

42. Bracke, "From 'Saving Women' to 'Saving Gays'"; El-Tayeb, *European Others*; Haritaworn and Petzen, "Invented Traditions and New Intimate Publics"; Puar, *Terrorist Assemblages*; Ritchie, "How Do You Say 'Come Out of the Closet' in Arabic?"

43. Examples abound, but to just name a couple, in the summer of 2016, Turkey's pending membership in the EU was used as a key reason for the Brexit vote; also, one of the early actions taken by the US Trump administration was an executive order preventing the citizens of seven Muslim countries from traveling to the United States, even if they held documents authorizing their entry.

44. See Ritchie, "Pinkwashing, Homonationalism, and Israel-Palestine," for a critique of the conceptual limits of homonationalism.

45. There are other critiques of this focus as well, including the erasure of anti-Black racism in France due to the emphasis of Islamophobic racism.

46. Bereket and Adam, "The Emergence of Gay Identities in Turkey"; İflazoğlu and Demir, eds., *Öteki Olarak Ölmek* [Dying as the other]; Bereket and Adam, "Navigating Islam and Same-Sex Liaisons among Men in Turkey"; Berghan, "Patronsuz ve Pezevenksiz Bir Dünya!" [Boss- and pimp-free world!]; Çakırlar and Delice, eds., *Cinsellik Muamması* [Sexual enigma]; Erdem and Ergül, eds., *Fetiş İkâme*

[Fetish substitute]; Gorkemli, "'Coming Out of the Internet'"; Gorkemli, *Grassroots Literacies*; Güneş, *Göğe Kuşak Lazım* [The sky needs a rainbow belt]; Güngör, *Öteki Erkekler* [Other men]; Hocaoğlu, *Eşcinsel Erkekler* [Homosexual men]; Alkan, *Cins Cins Mekan* [Queer space/place]; Mutluer, ed., *Cinsiyet Halleri* [States of gender]; Özbay, "Nocturnal Queers"; Özbay, *Queering Sexualities in Turkey*; Özbay and Soydan, *Eşcinsel Kadınlar* [Homosexual women]; Ozyegin, "Reading the Closet through Connectivity"; Ozyegin, *New Desires, New Selves*; Şeker, ed., *Başkaldıran Bedenler* [Revolting bodies]; Yardımcı and Güçlü, eds., *Queer Tahayyül* [Queer imaginary]; Zengin, "Sex for Law, Sex for Psychiatry"; Zengin, "Violent Intimacies." It is worth noting that a number of presses in Turkey are committed to publishing feminist and queer work. While a number of the books noted here have come out of Metis Publishing House's general research series Siyah-Beyaz (Black and white), Sel Publications has two series committed to sexuality and queer studies: Queer Düş'ün (Queer dream/thought) and LGBT Kitaplığı (LGBT library). These series include both original publications by scholars from Turkey as well as fully translated works, such as Sara Ahmed's *The Cultural Politics of Emotion* and *The Promise of Happiness*, Jack Halberstam's *The Queer Art of Failure*, Monique Wittig's *The Straight Mind*, Virginie Despentes's *King Kong Theory*, and Sherry Wolf's *Sexuality and Socialism*. While not translated as entire books, the work of other queer studies scholars have appeared in the various edited collections published in Queer Düş'ün that mix original work and translations, such as Lauren Berlant, Michael Warner, Guy Hocquenghem, David H. Halperin, Robert McRuer, Mario Miele, Paul B. Preciado, Lisa Duggan and Kathleen McHugh, Del LaGrace Volcano and Ulrika Dahl, and Leo Bersani, among others. Metis Publishing House does not have a particular queer series but does put out translations of queer studies' texts, such as Judith Butler's *Gender Trouble*, *Precarious Life*, and, with Athena Athanasiou, *Dispossession*. Butler's *Bodies That Matter* and *Psychic Life of Power* also have been translated by other presses. Much of Foucault's work appears in Turkish, including *The History of Sexuality*, *The Birth of the Clinic*, *Discipline and Punish*, and *The Archaeology of Knowledge*. Bilgi University Press is publishing his Lectures at Collège de France, with six volumes having been published at the time of this writing (April 2020). Finally, since November 2014, Ankara-based KaosGL has been putting out the biannual peer-reviewed magazine *KaosQ+*, which features translated works as well as original publications. This volume of translated works will come as no surprise to anyone born and raised in countries with a non-English primary language, but I found it useful to include this incomplete list to give all readers a sense of what forms of queer thought are translated into Turkish, what kinds of works audiences come into contact with, and with what works Turkish scholars imagine themselves in conversation. This might be particularly useful since *Queer in Translation* might inadvertently promise the study of translations of queer studies work itself, which is not the goal of this book. That being said, the sexuality and queer studies research being translated into Turkish is an important backdrop to this study, the aim of which is to trace how contemporary categories of thought regarding nonnormative genders and sexualities are publicly debated in Turkish. Most of those who translate these works are themselves queer academics, artists, or activists.

47. It is also worth noting that this amount of scholarship has been produced despite the challenges of doing academic work in the area of sexualities in Turkey. Özbay, *Queering Sexualities in Turkey*.

48. This is with the exception of Gul Ozyegin and Cenk Özbay's work: Ozyegin, *New Desires, New Selves*; and Özbay, *Queering Sexualities in Turkey*.

49. The work of both Tarik Bereket and Barry Adam and Şebnem Keniş constitutes exceptions. See Bereket and Adam, "Navigating Islam and Same-Sex Liaisons among Men in Turkey"; and Keniş, "Islam and Homosexuality Debates in Turkey."

50. These works also focus mostly on the effects of neoliberalism on sexual subjectivities. In the conclusion, I discuss in detail queer studies' focus on sexual subjectivity as the key marker of modernity and what the implications of this focus have been for queer analyses that lie outside of the so-called West.

51. I am not suggesting that neoliberal subjectivity and homonormativity are nonexistent among Turkey's gays and lesbians. As Özbay's careful study demonstrates, Istanbulite middle-class gay male clients of reportedly heterosexual rent boys distinguish between good and bad rent boys. See Özbay, *Queering Sexualities in Turkey*. So-called good rent boys are marked by a desire for upward mobility, a tendency to treat clients as potential contacts for networking and future jobs, and an expressed desire for a more respectable life than sex work. Bad rent boys, on the other hand, are understood as more criminal, less trustworthy, and in many ways less legible to middle-class gay men because they do not act as proper entrepreneurial subjects and refuse to see sex work as an investment in a future defined by neoliberal parameters. In other words, homonormative gay subjects (very much in the sense that Duggan means it) exist in Turkey. However, those values have not yet infiltrated queer activism, which remains fairly grassroots and critical of neoliberal capitalism and respectability politics. Further, the strong presence of sex workers in the queer movements in Turkey shapes all activists' orientation toward sex work as a matter of labor and not as a matter of respectability. See chapter 3 for more details about the politics of trans sex work.

52. I want to acknowledge that some of these scholars, including myself, currently live and work in the diaspora. Yet, to my knowledge, we all have been born and raised in Turkey, and our commitment to writing about home is testimony to attachments that go far beyond intellectual interest.

53. For more on the limits of homonationalism as a framework see Ritchie, "Pinkwashing, Homonationalism, and Israel-Palestine"; Haike Schotten and Haneen Maikey, "Queers Resisting Zionism: On Authority and Accountability Beyond Homonationalism," *Jadaliyya*, October 10, 2012, https://www.jadaliyya.com/Details /27175/Queers-Resisting-Zionism-On-Authority-and-Accountability-Beyond -Homonationalism.

54. Mikdashi and Puar, "Queer Theory and Permanent War." Mikdashi and Puar's question of whether "queer theory (still) require[s] a sexual or gendered body or a sexual or gendered injury—particularly if part of the project of homonationalism is to produce and stabilize transnational, imperial, and settler colonial forms of sexual and gendered injury?" is an apt one. However, I do see the strength of queer inquiry

asking questions about the production of an asymmetrical value of human life and the historical centrality of sexuality in racializing mechanisms, which have been key to colonialism, dispossession, extraction, and other forms of exploitation.

55. Amar, *Security Archipelago*; Arondekar and Patel, "Area Impossible"; Mikdashi and Puar, "Queer Theory and Permanent War"; Shakhsari, "Weblogistan Goes to War." While I otherwise agree with Mikdashi and Puar's analysis about this emerging field, I diverge from their assessment that this work ultimately "provincializes" the United States. I maintain that it is crucial to entertain multiple sovereign centers simultaneously, which constitutes part of the strength of this work. US imperialism does not, and need not, disappear from analyses that discuss the history and contemporary world of the Middle East. I hold this position very much in alliance with Grewal and Kaplan's suggestion that we think of hegemonies as scattered. Grewal and Kaplan, eds., *Scattered Hegemonies*.

56. Amar, *Security Archipelago*.

57. Amar, *Security Archipelago*, 6–7. While Amar declares that human security states, with discourses that veer away from markets and the rational-liberal consumer, signal the end of neoliberalism, I understand securitization as an extension of neoliberal regimes that produce different discourses of rescue based on the political economic context. For instance, unlike in Egypt, current Turkish government's humanitarian discourses target not a particular segment of its own citizens, but Syrians who had to take refuge in Turkey as a result of the civil war fueled by the Turkish government itself alongside the United States and Russia. Turkey's admission of millions of refugees is often evoked in President Erdoğan's rhetorical addresses to "the West," where Europe in particular and the West in general are called out for their failed humanitarianism. See chapter 4 for more on Erdoğan's rhetorical uses of the Syrian refugee crisis.

58. Shakhsari, "Weblogistan Goes to War."

59. Ferguson and Hong, "Sexual and Racial Contradictions of Neoliberalism," 1063.

60. Arondekar and Patel, "Area Impossible." Important exceptions to this are of course translation studies scholars who have analyzed sexualities. See, for instance, Baer, "Russian Gays/Western Gaze"; Baer and Kaindl, *Queering Translation/Translating the Queer*; Bassi, "Displacing LGBT"; and Gramling and Dutta, "Translating Transgender."

61. A big thank you to my colleague Julie Hua for pointing out affect as a universal proposition. Elsewhere, I have discussed the specific problems with the universalism of Sara Ahmed's "happy objects." See Savcı, "On Putting Down and Destroying."

62. Just to share a small example, Kathryn Bond Stockton's wonderful work that theorized a queer child's growth as "growing sideways" (versus the normative "growing up") is utterly untranslatable to Turkish, as the only term applicable to it is "to grow"—neither up, nor in any other particular direction. This is one of many examples one could give, of course, but it is useful because it exposes queer (and all other) theory's dependence on vocabulary both to critique and to imagine otherwise. Stockton, *The Queer Child*.

63. Butler, *Gender Trouble*; Butler, *Excitable Speech*.

64. See Sakai, *Translation and Subjectivity*. Puar and Mikdashi refer to the United States– and Western Europe–centeredness of queer theory as queer theory's own homonationalism. This is certainly a suggestion worthy of consideration, but a queer theory that shifts geographic focus while remaining English centered might get us out of homonationalism without getting us out of queer theory's homolingual address. Neither does it interrupt the naturalization of the nation form through the homolingual regime of languages. Mikdashi and Puar, "Queer Theory and Permanent War."

65. Mezzadra and Sakai, introduction, 10. Also see Gal, "Migration, Minorities, and Multilingualism"; Gramling, *Invention of Monolingualism*; Makoni and Pennycook, *Disinventing and Reconstituting Languages*.

66. Gal, "Migration, Minorities, and Multilingualism."

67. Rafael, *Motherless Tongues*; Yildiz, *Beyond the Mother Tongue*.

68. Mezzadra and Sakai, introduction; Yildiz, *Beyond the Mother Tongue*.

69. Rafael, *Motherless Tongues*.

70. Navaro-Yashin, *Faces of the State*.

71. Sakai, *Translation and Subjectivity*.

72. Sakai, *Translation and Subjectivity*, 3; Mezzadra and Sakai, introduction; Solomon, "Postimperial Etiquette," 185.

73. Sakai, *Translation and Subjectivity*, 6.

74. Solomon, "Postimperial Etiquette," 185.

75. This of course conveniently overlooks the fact that when other languages are translated into American English, translation is often employed as a mechanism of domesticating and incorporating what is alien and unfamiliar. Rafael, *Motherless Tongues*.

76. Some of these points will be familiar to those who work with transnational feminist scholarship. Transnational feminists have long critiqued such tendencies that produce third world difference (Mohanty, "Under Western Eyes"), that assume and reproduce clear distinctions between the global and the local (Nagar and Swarr, *Critical Transnational Feminist Praxis*), that locate hegemony squarely in the West (Grewal and Kaplan, *Scattered Hegemonies*; Hoang, *Dealing in Desire*), as well as the nostalgic yearning for a precolonial, authentic past of the Global South (Abu-Lughod, "Do Muslim Women Really Need Saving?"). What translation studies contributes to these debates is the complication of *the linguistic*, which seems to remain the marker of culture par excellence.

77. Mezzadra and Sakai, introduction.

78. Mezzadra and Sakai, introduction, 11.

79. Afsaneh Najmabadi notes, "Perhaps one of the problems with the current heated debates between proponents of 'global gay' or 'gay international' resides in the presumption, common to both groups, that 'I am gay,' or 'I am transsexual' means the same thing anywhere it is pronounced." Najmabadi, "Transing and Transpassing," 37.

80. Dirlik, "Thinking Modernity Historically."

81. Sakai, *Translation and Subjectivity*.

82. See Joan W. Scott's seminal essay "The Evidence of Experience" for a very useful discussion on how experience is linguistically bound.

83. Abu-Lughod, ed., *Remaking Women*; Alexander and Mohanty, eds., *Feminist Genealogies, Colonial Legacies, Democratic Futures*; Grewal and Kaplan, eds., *Scattered Hegemonies*; Nagar and Swarr, *Critical Transnational Feminist Praxis*.

84. Also see Mourad for a critique of equating translated sexual terminology with cultural inauthenticity in the context of Lebanon. Mourad, "Queering the Mother Tongue."

85. Williams, *Marxism and Literature*.

86. Sakai, *Translation and Subjectivity*.

87. Sakai, *Translation and Subjectivity*.

88. Williams, *Marxism and Literature*.

89. Eng, Halberstam, and Muñoz, "Introduction," 15.

90. In this sense Turkish economic neoliberalization bears eerie similarities to that in Chile, often noted as the first neoliberal experiment. Harvey, "Neoliberalism as Creative Destruction."

91. Yirmibeşoğlu, "Women and Trade Unionism in Turkey."

92. Senses, "Turkey's Experience with Neoliberal Policies."

93. Altınordu, "The Politicization of Religion"; Akın and Karasapan, "The 'Turkish-Islamic Synthesis'"; Atasoy, *Islam's Marriage with Neoliberalism*; Coşar and Yeğenoğlu, "New Grounds for Patriarchy in Turkey?"; Özbay et al., *The Making of Neoliberal Turkey*; Tuğal, *Fall of the Turkish Model*; Turam, *Between Islam and the State*; White, *Islamist Mobilization in Turkey*.

94. Ahmad, *The Making of Modern Turkey*, 221.

95. *Laiklik*, the Turkish-style secularism, which many scholars compare to the French *laïcité*, has always required full regulation of religion by the state, including, for instance, the regulation of religious education and textbooks and the training and appointment of imams. It was established as one of the six Kemalist principles during the early years of the republic and became constitutionally protected in 1937. Atasoy, *Islam's Marriage with Neoliberalism*. As discussed in chapter 2, undermining the *laik* principles of the republic have historically been grounds for criminal investigation and charges for individuals as well as political parties and associations.

96. Altınordu, "Politicization of Religion." Cihan Tuğal refers to Turkey in this context as the "global system's best bet for rendering Islam governable." Tuğal, *Fall of the Turkish Model*, 8.

97. Turam, *Between Islam and the State*, 49.

98. Ahmad, *The Making of Modern Turkey*; Altınordu, "Politicization of Religion"; White, *Islamist Mobilization in Turkey*. According to the Presidency of Religious Affairs website, around 8,600 more mosques were added between 2008 and 2018, putting the number of mosques in the country at 88,681 (https://stratejigeli stirme.diyanet.gov.tr/sayfa/57/istatistikler [accessed April 17, 2020]). The reported population of Turkey in December 2018 was 82,003,882 ("Son Dakika: Türkiye'nin Nüfusu Açıklandı [2018 TÜİK verileri]" [Last minute: Turkey's population an-

nounced (2018 TÜİK data)], *NTV.com.tr*, February 1, 2019, https://www.ntv.com.tr
/turkiye/son-dakikaturkiyenin-nufusu-82-milyonu-asti,QzFOktjusUex4xpyjjDRaw).
This corresponds to one mosque for every 924 people.

99. Altınordu, "Politicization of Religion."

100. This constitutional and military *regulation* of Islam is nevertheless accompanied by the popular impression of its *repression*. This is due to Atatürk's legacy
as a military hero and the founder and leader of the secular republic, symbolically
positioning the armed forces as the protector of secularism. It is also due to various
military-staged formal and semiformal interventions in what was perceived as Islamic
insurgency in the 1990s. Two things are worth noting here regarding this forgetting
of the earlier marriage of the military, religion, and neoliberalism in Turkey. First,
as Berna Turam notes, "Atatürk believed that 'the modern state would be shored
up by *civic religion*' and used it as another force to glue the nation together. In sharp
contrast to the Shah's estrangement of the clergy by his anti-religious arbitrary rule,
Atatürk often used religious idioms in his discourse and refrained from anti-religious
attitudes and discourses. . . . Hence, any argument that pits the Republic against the
Muslim faith misses the contingent relationship between them." Turam, *Between
Islam and the State*, 41. Second, the current shape of the political collective memory is
also perhaps partially due to the fact that Turgut Özal, who is known as *the* historical
figure responsible for the liberalization of the economy and starting down the path of
Turkish neoliberalism, had run and won the 1983 general election—the first one after
the coup—against the opposing junta party. This opposition is misleading, however,
given that Özal had been appointed as deputy prime minister during the postcoup
military regime and had resigned from the post in 1982 due to disagreements over
economic policy. Later, this early delinking of the military's ties to neoliberalism and
the liberalization of Islam would aid the successive AKP governments in aligning the
military with authoritarianism, the old Kemalist regime with a state-led economy,
and their own rule with anti-militarism and democratic (neo)liberalism.

101. Tuğal, *Fall of the Turkish Model*, 4. These two issues are connected, as some
of the poverty in urban areas resulted from the forced migration of citizens inhabiting
the predominantly Kurdish regions in southeast Turkey that have become targets of
the Turkish state's counterterrorism measures, including burning down entire villages
suspected of providing aid and accommodations (*yataklık yapmak*) to terrorists.

102. Altınordu, "Politicization of Religion"; Arat, *Rethinking Islam and Liberal
Democracy*; White, *Islamist Mobilization in Turkey*. White and Altınordu are in dis-
agreement here. Jenny White argues that the Islamist rhetoric played no role in the
Welfare Party's success at the ballot box, emphasizing instead their focus on the urban
poor and especially the growing immigrant populations residing in squatter settlements. Ateş Altınordu, on the other hand, critiques the arguments that attribute the
Welfare Party's success solely to the failure of the center-Right parties, the party's
successful grassroots organizing, or their appeal to the urban poor, arguing that the
successful politicization of Islam in the 1990s was due to the reactionary measures
taken by secularist governments against the Islamic revival of the 1970s and especially
1980s.

103. White notes that voters in squatter neighborhoods were very informed about different party platforms but mostly saw "voting and petitioning local officials . . . as the primary means to bargain for community needs with political parties and with city and national authorities." White, *Islamist Mobilization in Turkey*, 106.

104. Özbay et al., *The Making of Neoliberal Turkey*, 4.

105. Altınordu, "Politicization of Religion"; Arat, *Rethinking Islam and Liberal Democracy*; Tuğal, *Passive Revolution*; Turam, *Between Islam and the State*; White, *Islamist Mobilization in Turkey*.

106. Erdoğan came to power as the leader of the AKP following a six-month prison sentence in 1998 for "inciting religious hatred"—an instance many see as part of a series of early signs of his long game (along with public statements that he did not think of democracy as an end, but as a means). Erdoğan was charged for reading passages from a poem and was also banned from politics after finishing his prison sentence. He later claimed that he believed the passage belonged to a poem by Mehmet Akif Ersoy, who also wrote the lyrics to the Turkish national anthem. The particular lines that resulted in the charges against him read: "minarets [as our] bayonets, domes [as our] helmets."

107. Coşar, "AKP's Hold on Power"; Duran, "Justice and Development Party's 'New Politics'?"; Tuğal, *Passive Revolution*; White, *Islamist Mobilization in Turkey*.

108. Zabcı, "Internalisation of Dependency." Turkey's economic growth was measured at around 8.8 percent in 2010 and 2011, but it dropped to (nevertheless high levels of) 2.2 percent in 2012 and 3.8 percent in 2013. See "Turkey Economy Profile 2019," Index Mundi, http://www.indexmundi.com/turkey/economy_profile.html.

109. Cindoglu and Unal, "Gender and Sexuality in the Authoritarian Discursive Strategies of 'New Turkey.'" Zuhal Yeşilyurt-Gündüz notes that while AKP efforts to meet the criteria for admittance to the EU are often analyzed in terms of civil rights–related policy changes, a number of neoliberal measures also were taken to encourage the accession process, especially an emphasis on privatization in order to enhance the candidate's "capacity to cope with competitive pressure and market forces within the Union." Yeşilyurt-Gündüz, "The EU and the AKP," 277. Cihan Tuğal argues that the key distinction of AKP from previous Islamist regimes was its successful incorporation/absorption of radical Islamists into their neoliberal politics. Tuğal, *Passive Revolution*.

110. Acar and Altunok, "The 'Politics of Intimate'"; Dedeoğlu and Elveren, eds., *Gender and Society in Turkey*.

111. Atasoy, *Islam's Marriage with Neoliberalism*; Turam, *Between Islam and the State*.

112. These included talks about education in the mother tongue for all, including Kurdish, as well as the launching of the first Kurdish-language public TV station and talks about the mutual opening borders and reviving of diplomatic relationships. There also were talks about relaxing the ban on wearing the headscarf by students at public universities and employees at public offices. As the Turkish state had been the largest employer until the liberalization of the economy in the 1980s, most women who wore headscarves could not find employment or simply had to not wear them at

work. This ban was not equally enforced on each campus, yet it became more regularly and strictly imposed after 1997. I tell the story of this ban and its repercussions in more detail in chapter 1.

113. Dirlik, "Thinking Modernity Historically." Davutoğlu left the AKP to form a new political party in the summer of 2019.

114. Iğsız, "Brand Turkey and the Gezi Protests." Such a reification of difference makes it easy to package and sell nations worldwide via neoliberal branding projects. For a similar neoliberal branding project in India, see Puri, "Sculpting the Saffron Body."

115. Atasoy, *Islam's Marriage with Neoliberalism*; Dedeoğlu and Elveren, eds., *Gender and Society in Turkey*; Özbay et al., *The Making of Neoliberal Turkey*; Tuğal, *Passive Revolution*; Yücesan-Özdemir, "Social Policy Regime in the AKP Years."

116. The imam of the mosque immediately renounced Erdoğan's claim, stating that the protesters had escaped from police violence and had turned the mosque into an infirmary for those wounded by tear gas canisters and plastic bullets. The imam was reassigned a few months after refusing to testify that the protesters had consumed alcohol in Dolmabahçe Mosque. See "Dolmabahçe Camisi'nin imam ve müezzini gitti" [Dolmabahçe Mosque's imam and muezzin reassigned], *Hürriyet*, September 21, 2013, http://www.hurriyet.com.tr/dolmabahce-camisinin-imam-ve-muezzini-gitti -24756039.

117. Another instance where economic obligations and betrayals were presented as moral ones was at the end of 2016, when the value of the US dollar was rising steadily vis-à-vis the Turkish lira, indicating a pending economic crisis. Erdoğan openly asked citizens to exchange their US dollars for Turkish lira in order to help the government fight what he called the "interest lobby" and foreign powers conspiring against Turkey. See "Erdoğan'dan 'Dolarınızı bozdurun' çağrısı" [Erdoğan's call to "exchange your dollar"], *Hürriyet*, December 2, 2016, http://www.bbc.com/turkce /haberler-turkiye-38179921.

118. Grewal, *Saving the Security State*, 4. David Harvey also briefly notes, in his infamous essay "Neoliberalism as Creative Destruction," that "the neoliberal emphasis on individual rights and the increasingly authoritarian use of state power to sustain the system become a flashpoint of contentiousness. The more neoliberalism is recognized as a failed if not disingenuous utopian project masking a successful attempt at the restoration of class power, the more it lays the basis for a resurgence of mass movements voicing egalitarian political demands, seeking economic justice, fair trade and greater economic security and democratization." Harvey, "Neoliberalism as Creative Destruction," 157.

119. Yüccsan-Özdemir and Coşar, eds., *Silent Violence*.

120. Berna Yazıcı notes another particularity of the Turkish case, which is the government's insistence on the significance of an extended, three-generational family structure in AKP's Return to the Family project. Yazıcı, "Return to the Family."

121. Dedeoğlu and Elveren, eds., *Gender and Society in Turkey*; Korkman, "Blessing Neoliberalism;" "Erdoğan, 'kadınlığın tanımı'nı da yaptı: Anneliği reddeden kadın eksiktir, yarımdır" [Erdoğan also defined "womanhood": A woman who refuses motherhood is incomplete; she is half a woman], *Diken*, May 6, 2016, http://www

.diken.com.tr/erdogan-kadinligin-tanimini-da-yapti-anneligi-reddeden-kadin
-eksiktir-yarimdir.

122. "Cumhurbaşkanı Erdoğan: Çocuk yapmanın parayla pulla alakası yok, rızık Allah'tan" [President Erdoğan: Having children has nothing to do with financial means; Allah provides for them], *T24*, March 4, 2015, http://t24.com.tr/haber /cumhurbaskani-erdogan-sigarayla-mucadelede-mahalle-baskisi-yapmak-lazim ,289349.

123. Iğsız, "Brand Turkey and the Gezi Protests."

124. Sinem Adar, "Paradoxes of 'New Turkey,'" *Jadaliyya*, May 26, 2017, http:// jadaliyya.com/Details/34310. Updated data are available at the website www.turkey purge.com.

125. Foucault, *"Society Must Be Defended"*; Grewal, *Saving the Security State.*

126. Details on the methodology used are presented in the appendix.

Chapter One. Subjects of Rights

Portions of this chapter previously appeared in "Subjects of Rights, and Subjects of Cruelty: The Production of an Islamic Backlash against Homosexuality in Turkey," *Political Power and Social Theory*, no. 30 (2016): 159–86.

1. Faruk Bildirici, "Eşcinsellik Hastalık, Tedavi Edilmeli" [Homosexuality is an illness; it should be cured], *Hürriyet*, March 7, 2010, http://www.hurriyet.com.tr /kelebek/escinsellik-hastalik-tedavi-edilmeli-14031207.

2. Bildirici, "Eşcinsellik Hastalık, Tedavi Edilmeli." It is unclear from the short excerpt whether the minister felt the need to acknowledge the existence of homosexuals to distinguish herself and the government she was a part of from Iran's previous president, Mahmoud Ahmedinejad, who infamously had claimed that there are no homosexuals in Iran. This lack of clarity is partly due to the fact that the questions posed by the journalist were not published in the profile piece.

3. "Homosexuality Is a Disease" (translated from Turkish), letter to Selma Aliye Kavaf, head of the Ministry of Women and Family Affairs, Escinsellikhastaliktir. blogspot.com, March 21, 2010, http://escinsellikhastaliktir.blogspot.com. The letter, posted in its entirety (the URL itself translates as homosexualityisanillness.blogspot .com), is dated March 20, but the public reading of the letter took place on March 21, and most news outlets reported on it on March 22. See, for instance, "STK'lardan Bakan Kavaf'a destek mektubu!" [Letter of support from NGOs to minister Kavaf], *CNNTurk*, March 22, 2010, https://www.cnnturk.com/2010/turkiye/03/22/stklardan .bakan.kavafa.destek.mektubu/568892.0/index.html.

4. Asad, *Formations of the Secular.*

5. Atatürk's address to the nation at the republic's tenth anniversary, October 29, 1933. "10. Yıl Nutku" [(Atatürk's) 10th Year Address], *T.C. Kültür ve Turizm Bakanlığı*, https://www.ktb.gov.tr/TR-96294/10-yil-nutku.html.

6. I acknowledge the initial employment of Islam in Atatürk's (national) narratives as well as the continuity of these reforms with those of the mid-nineteenth-century Tanzimat era. However, ultimately the republican reforms worked toward an almost

total submission of religion to the state. They also constituted significantly more abrupt interventions in everyday social life as compared to the Ottoman Tanzimat reforms.

7. It is important to note that while the Islamic *fez* (hat) was replaced by the European *şapka* (hat) in the 1925 Şapka Devrimi (Hat Revolution), no other forms of Islamic dressing and head covering were outlawed by the republic. While many republican historians have suggested that the chador, which was the common form of hijab, especially in urban Turkey, was gently advised against, accounts by feminist scholars counter that those who did not comply, or spread "counterpropaganda," were dealt with severely. Kandiyoti, "End of Empire." A Westernized look became the way in which citizen-subjects displayed loyalty to the new regime.

8. Şeyhülislam is a position in the Ottoman cabinet ranked just below the grand vizier and is in charge of religious affairs.

9. Ahmad, *Making of Modern Turkey*; Finkel and Sirman, introduction; Kandiyoti, "End of Empire"; Margulies and Yildizoglu, "Political Uses of Islam in Turkey."

10. Acar and Altunok, "Understanding Gender Equality Demands"; Arat, "Project of Modernity and Women in Turkey"; Arat, *Rethinking Islam and Liberal Democracy*; Göle, "Quest for the Islamic Self"; Sirman, "Feminism in Turkey"; Tekeli, "Emergence of the New Feminist Movement in Turkey." Turkish feminists have voiced skepticism about this state-led emancipation of women by pointing to the pragmatic nature and, at times, pragmatic timing of the reforms and the inclusion of women in political and public spheres. Tekeli, "Emergence of the New Feminist Movement in Turkey."

11. Tekeli, "Emergence of the New Feminist Movement in Turkey."

12. Mutluer, "Kemalist Feminists in the Era of the AK Party."

13. Shively, "Religious Bodies and the Secular State."

14. The headscarf is inevitably a gender issue, as it is a head covering worn only by women. There is no equivalent piece of clothing that is believed to be a religious requirement of men, and hence no men have been similarly banished from public education due to their beliefs.

15. Amar, "Turning the Gendered Politics of the Security State Inside Out?"

16. It is important to also note the subject-forming effect of the ban. As recounted by one of the interviewees in the documentary *Böyle Giremezsiniz* (You cannot enter like this) that covers the enforcement of the ban at Boğaziçi University, many female students with headscarves did not know each other at college until they were all stopped at the main gate. The ban therefore literally made the veil a significant common denominator among female students who previously might have selected friends based on their major or participation in social clubs and might have thought of themselves simply as Boğaziçi students and not Boğaziçi students with headscarves.

17. For instance, the civil constitution would decrease the power of the military to stage interventions.

18. I was present when the collected signatures were handed over to then BPD deputy Sebahat Tuncel in front of Parliament. Barış ve Demokrasi Partisi (BPD; Peace and Democracy Party), established in 2008, was dissolved in 2014.

19. Not limited to headscarf wearing, the idea of neighborhood pressure was initially conceptualized by sociologist Şerif Mardin, who pointed out the small-scale pressures of conforming to social norms in the neighborhood, a significant social unit in contemporary Turkey. Çakır, *Mahalle Baskısı*.

20. Çolak and Karakuş, "Eşcinseller de Eşitlik Istiyor, Verecek Miyiz?"

21. Ruşen Çakır, "Başörtülülerden 'Herkese Özgürlük' Bildirisi" ["Freedom to everyone" declaration from women with headscarves], *Gazete Vatan*, February 14, 2008, http://www.gazetevatan.com/rusen-cakir-162117-yazar-yazisi-basortululerden —herkese-ozgurluk—bildirisi. Also cited in "Söz Konusu Özgürlükse Hiçbir Şey Teferruat Değildir" [If freedom is the issue, nothing is detail], *Birikim*, February 24, 2008, https://www.birikimdergisi.com/guncel/214/soz-konusu-ozgurlukse-hicbir -sey-teferruat-degildir. Title 301 of the Turkish penal code criminalizes anyone who threatens the unity of the nation, secularism, and the republic and historically has been used to put on trial intellectuals who have critiqued the political order in general or the government of their time. YÖK (Yüksek Öğrenim Kurulu) is the Turkish council for higher education, established after the 1980 military coup that had followed years of political unrest and bloodshed mostly due to conflict between fascist and communist contingents within the nation. These groups had organized most notably within universities, thus turning the university into a politically risqué venue in need of close state supervision. YÖK was created precisely with the goal of preventing any "politicizing" within spaces of higher education.

22. Çakır, "Başörtülülerden 'Herkese Özgürlük' Bildirisi."

23. Hilâl Kaplan would in fact title her very first column published the following year by the daily *Taraf Gazetesi* "Herkese Müslüman" (Muslim to everyone). Hilâl Kaplan, "Herkese Müslüman," *Taraf Gazetesi*, September 23, 2009, http://www .taraf.com.tr/hilal-kaplan/makale-herkese-musluman.htm (accessed July 31, 2011; site discontinued).

24. Hrant Dink was an Armenian Turkish journalist who was assassinated on February 19, 2007, after receiving death threats for three years while being tried under title 301. This case resulted from the claim that a piece published in the Armenian paper *Agos*, which Dink was editor of at the time, "insulted Turkishness" by suggesting that one of Atatürk's adopted daughters could be one of the numerous orphans of the Armenian massacre.

25. Here the Turkish word used is *zulüm*, which translates as cruelty, but within Islam it can also refer to committing injustice, to oppression and torture, and to overstepping boundaries in word and deed. See Ekin Kadir Selçuk, "Kısır Tartışmaya Dişi Darbe" [Female intervention to a barren debate], *Radikal*, February 23, 2008, http:// www.radikal.com.tr/hayat/kisir-tartismaya-disi-darbe-867824.

26. Kaplan, "Herkese Müslüman."

27. Nur Çintay, "Başörtüsü Çeşitlemeleri" [Headscarf medley], *Radikal*, February 25, 2008, http://www.radikal.com.tr/yazarlar/nur-cintay-a/basortusu-cesitlemeleri -841217.

28. Selçuk, "Kısır Tartışmaya Dişi Darbe." *Nefs* refers to a subject's will, which is to be controlled through meticulous training of the body and of the soul. It is also

important to note that what is being discussed here under the issue of cruelty against homosexuals seems to be referencing mainly the violence faced by trans women sex workers—this is true in particular for references discussants made to being forced into prostitution and police oppression. The word used in almost all of these public discussions in media was *eşcinsel*, which literally translates into English as homosexual. None of the discussions seemed to distinguish the various and differential difficulties that differently othered sexual and gendered subject experience. LGBT activists themselves at the time used LGBTT (*lezbiyen, gey, biseksüel, transseksüel, travesti*) and currently use LGBTİ+ (*lezbiyen, gey, biseksüel, trans, interseks*) to mark the sexual and gendered subjectivities their politics address. Therefore, I use *homosexual* when referring to the public debates by non-LGBT activists and LGBT in my own analyses. This is not to erase the complexities of LGBT under the term *homosexual*, but to represent the ways in which it worked as a singular signifier in these debates.

29. Here I am using "Muslim/Islamist" as a formulation, fully aware that *Muslim* and *Islamist* are distinct subject positions. I do so, however, to capture the secular framework in Turkey that has reduced the two to each other, where any woman wearing a headscarf, for instance, is presumed to have an Islamist outlook and not want to live in a secular democracy.

30. Interestingly, this image of the veiled woman as an unfair judge was also brought up by interviewees in Nil Mutluer's 2016 study of Kemalist feminists, thus speaking to its potency and appeal as a case against allowing state officials to wear headscarves. Mutluer found that even Kemalist feminists, who were open to lifting the ban for students and other women seeking state services, were not amenable to allowing headscarf wearing by providers (teachers, nurses, judges, and other state employees) because they represented the state. Mutluer, "Kemalist Feminists in the Era of the AK Party."

31. Fatih Altaylı, "Türban Tartışması" [Headscarf debate], *Teke Tek,* June 9, 2008, https://www.youtube.com/watch?v=SCe-Rspv-_E (link discontinued).

32. On Erdoğan's reference to democracy as a train you get off of at the stop you need see Ruşen Çakir, "Erdoğan: Demokrasi tramvayında ihtiraslı bir yolcu" [Erdoğan: A passionate traveler on the democracy train], *Vatan,* November 6, 2012 http://www.gazetevatan.com/rusen-cakir-491426-yazar-yazisi-erdogan— demokrasi-tramvayinda-ihtirasli-bir-yolcu.

33. Özkan, who made stereotypical Kemalist arguments for why she was against headscarf wearing at universities, was never asked whether she supported gay rights and liberties. Neither did Altaylı openly state his own stance on LGBT rights.

34. Acar and Altunok, "Understanding Gender Equality Demands in Turkey."

35. Fatih Altaylı, "Türban Tartışması."

36. See *Kaos GL,* "Kavaf: 'Eşcinseller Evlenemiyor, Evlat da Edinemezler'" [Kavaf: Homosexuals cannot get married; they cannot adopt either], *Kaos GL,* February 23, 2010, https://www.kaosgl.org/haber/kavaf-escinseller-evlenemiyor-evlat-da -edinemezler; Yasemin Öz, "Türkiye Eşcinsellerin Evliliğine de Ebeveynliğine de Karşı" [Turkey is against homosexual marriage and parenting], *Bia Haber Merkezi,* February 24, 2010, http://m.bianet.org/bianet/toplumsal-cinsiyet/120251-turkiye

-escinsellerin-evliligine-de-ebeveynligine-de-karsi. While Turkey is not a full member of the EU, it is a full member of the European Council and hence is endowed with the right to request changes to resolutions/statements published by the Council. The requests Kavaf made on behalf of Turkey were incorporated into the final declaration.

37. Mahmood, *Religious Difference in a Secular Age.*

38. See "Kavaf: Dizilerdeki Erotizmden Irite Oluyorum" [Kavaf: I am irritated by the eroticism on TV shows], *Radikal*, February 19, 2010, http://www.radikal.com.tr/politika/kavaf-dizilerdeki-erotizmden-irite-oluyorum-981259.

39. Bildirici, "Eşcinsellik Hastalık, Tedavi Edilmeli."

40. See "STK'lardan Bakan Kavaf'a destek mektubu!" [Letter of support from NGOs to minister Kavaf], *CNNTurk*, March 22, 2010, https://www.cnnturk.com/2010/turkiye/03/22/stklardan.bakan.kavafa.destek.mektubu/568892.0/index.html.

41. Bawer Çakır, "MAZLUMDER'DE İnsan Hakları Eşcinsel Deyince Bitiyor" [Human rights end at Mazlum-Der when it comes to homosexuality], *Bia Haber Merkezi*, March 25, 2010, https://bianet.org/bianet/toplumsal-cinsiyet/120894 -mazlumder-de-insan-haklari-escinsel-deyince-bitiyor; Yıldırım Türker, "Müslüman'a En Büyük Imtihan" [Muslims' biggest exam], *Radikal*, April 12, 2010, http://www.radikal.com.tr/yazarlar/yildirim-turker/muslumana-en-buyuk-imtihan-991007; Ozanser Uğurlu, "Hani Mazlumun Yanındaydınız?" [So you were supporters of subjects of cruelty?], *Radikal*, March 28, 2010, http://www.radikal.com.tr/radika12 /hani-mazlumun-yanindaydiniz-988209; D. Yaras, "Mazlum-Der'in Turnusol Kağıdı: Eşcinsellik" [Mazlum-Der's litmus test: Homosexuality], *Internethaber*, March 30, 2010, http://www.internethaber.com/mazlum-derin-turnusol-kagidi -escinsellik-9536y.htm?interstitial=true (accessed July 31, 2011; link discontinued).

42. Hilâl Kaplan, "İslâm ve Eşcinsellik Meselesi" [Islam and the issue of homosexuality], *Taraf*, April 3, 2010. *Taraf* newspaper has been closed down and its website discontinued, but Kaplan's piece can be found in its entirety in the following site: *T24*, April 3, 2010, https://t24.com.tr/haber/islam-ve-escinsellik-meselesi,74117.

43. Kaplan, "İslâm ve Eşcinsellik Meselesi"; Fadime Özkan, "Eşcinsellik Hastalık Değil Günah Ama Zulüm Yasak: Süyebh Öğüt'le Söyleşi" [Homosexuality is not an illness but a sin, but cruelty is forbidden: An interview with Süyebh Öğüt], *Star Gazetesi* 2010, http://www.stargazete.com/%0Aroportaj/yazar/fadime-ozkan/escinsellik -hastalik-degil-gunah-ama-zulum-yasak-haber-251180.htm (accessed July 31, 2011; link discontinued).

44. Özkan, "Eşcinsellik Hastalık Değil Günah Ama Zulüm Yasak."

45. Boellstorff, "Between Religion and Desire."

46. Boltanski, *Distant Suffering.*

47. Because the meeting took place a couple of months before I started my fieldwork, my retelling relies on Lambdaistanbul volunteer Eren's account of it as well as meeting notes taken by another LGBT activist who was present.

48. At this point in the meeting notes, the recorder states that the Muslim activists must not be aware of some more reformist Muslim clerics' approaches to homosexuality.

49. In 2008 pride week did indeed feature a panel with LGBT activists from Lebanon and Palestine alongside Hendricks. However, as I recounted, and as the events of the following couple of years demonstrate, these initial signs of good will and a desire to support each other did not result in more concrete political solidarities.

50. Mahmood, *Religious Difference in a Secular Age*, 114.

51. Mahmood, *Religious Difference in a Secular Age*, 9.

52. The original piece by Süheyb Öğüt was published on August 15, 2015, under the link www.aktuel.com.tr/yazar/suheb-ogut/2015/08/17/butch-lezbiyenler-ve -hdpkk (accessed July 1, 2017; link discontinued), which also appears in Slavoj Žižek's book *The Courage of Hopelessness*. While the original link has been discontinued, a Turkish-language reprint of the piece titled "HDP ve PKK'ya çakacağım diye lezbiyenliği anlattı" [He recounted lesbianism in an attempt to bash HDP and PKK] is available at https://odatv.com/hdp-ve-pkkya-cakacagim-diyelezbiyenligi-anlatti -2108151200.html. A response to Öğüt by Žižek, which features an English translation of Öğüt's piece, is available at https://yersizseyler.wordpress.com/2016/02/14/butch -lesbians-in-turkey-slavoj-zizek. Unpacking Öğüt's "psychoanalytic" approach and his collapsing of secularism, Kemalism, and Israel deserve their own paper, which unfortunately falls outside of the confines of this chapter.

Chapter Two. Who Killed Ahmet Yıldız?

1. Bülent Aydoğdu, "Üniversiteli Genç Eşcinsel Diye Mi Öldürüldü?" [Was the college youth murdered because he was a homosexual?]," *Gazete Vatan*, July 17, 2008, http://haber.gazetevatan.com/Haber/189445/1/Gundem (accessed July 31, 2011; link discontinued); "Ailesinden de Tehdit Alan Gencin Korunma Talebi de Bir İşe Yaramadı" [The request for protection of the youth threatened by his family did not help]," *Bugün*, July 17, 2008, http://www.bugun.com.tr/haber_detay.asp?haberID =32526 (accessed July 15, 2011; site discontinued); Bawer Çakır, "lgbtt Dernekleri: Öğrenci Yıldız Eşcinsel Olduğu İçin Öldürüldü [LGBTT associations: Student Yıldız was murdered because he was a homosexual]," *Bia Haber Merkezi*, July 18, 2008. https://bianet.org/bianet/bianet/108414-lgbtt-dernekleri-ogrenci-yildiz-escinsel -oldugu-icin-olduruldu; Mustafa Maydan, "İstanbul'un Göbeğinde Silahlı İnfaz" [Weaponized execution in the middle of Istanbul], *Star Gazete*, July 17, 2008, http:// www.stargazete.com/guncel/istanbul-un-gobeginde-silahli-infaz-114062.htm (accessed July 15, 2011; link discontinued); Selamet Öz, "Kurşunlardan 3'ü Göğsüne Saplandı" [3 of the bullets hit his chest], *Hürriyet*, July 17, 2008, http://www .hurriyet.com.tr/gundem/kursunlardan-3-u-gogsune-saplandi-9454604; "Üniversite Öğrencisi Genç Otomobilinin İçinde Tek Kurşunla Vuruldu [University youth shot in his car with a single bullet]," *Takvim*, July 17, 2008, http://arsiv.takvim.com.tr// 2008/07/17/gnc121.html; İstihbarat Servisi, "Üniversiteli Gence Cafe Önünde Kanlı Pusu" [Bloody trap for the university youth in front of a cafe], *Yeni Şafak*, July 17, 2008, https://www.yenisafak.com/gundem/universiteli-gence-cafe-onunde-kanli-pusu-129236.

2. The ANAP came to power under the leadership of Turgut Özal soon after the military coup, and it has been *the* instrumental party in Turkey's neoliberalization

starting in the early 1980s, as I recounted in the introduction. ANAP remained one of the strongest right-wing parties of the country until the mid-1990s. While little detail was reported on the cause of Akarçeşme's murder, the papers mentioned that he was known to have mafia connections.

3. Islamic marriages are referred to as *imam nikahı* (imam's marriage/Islamic matrimony) and are extremely common in Turkey. Studies show that 91 percent of married couples in contemporary Turkey are both officially and religiously married. See Civelek and Koç, "Türkiye'de İmam Nikahı." The majority of couples get married religiously in addition to officially, and in fact, getting married religiously before getting married officially is illegal.

4. Nicholas Birch, "Was Ahmet Yildiz the Victim of Turkey's First Gay Honour Killing?," *Independent*, July 19, 2008, https://www.independent.co.uk/news/world /europe/was-ahmet-yildiz-the-victim-of-turkeys-first-gay-honour-killing-871822.html.

5. This is the customary burial for all Muslims, practicing or not.

6. Aydoğdu, "Üniversiteli Genç Eşcinsel Diye Mi Öldürüldü?"; "*Independent*: İlk Eşcinsel Namus Cinayeti Mi?'" [*Independent*: The first homosexual honor killing?], *cNNTurk*, July 19, 2008, https://www.cnnturk.com/2008/yasam/diger/07/19 /independent.ilk.escinsel.namus.cinayeti.mi/483020.0/index.html; " 'Türkiye'de İlk Gay Namus Cinayeti'" [The first gay honor killing in Turkey], *Radikal*, July 20, 2008, http://www.radikal.com.tr/turkiye/turkiyede-ilk-gay-namus-cinayeti-889390; "*Independent*: Ahmet Yıldız Ilk Eşcinsel Namus Cinayeti Kurbanı Mı?" [*Independent*: Is Ahmet Yıldız the first victim of a homosexual honour killing?], *Milliyet*, July 19, 2008, http://www.milliyet.com.tr/ilk-escinsel-namus-cinayeti/dunya/haberdetay/19.07 .2008/968886/default.htm; "'İlk Eşcinsel Namus Cinayeti Kurbanı Mı?'" [The first homosexual honor killing victim?], *Hürriyet*, July 20, 2008, http://www.hurriyet .com.tr/gundem/ilk-escinsel-namus-cinayeti-kurbani-mi-9473894; "İlk Eşcinsel Namus Cinayeti" [The first homosexual honor killing], *Sabah*, July 20, 2008, http:// arsiv.sabah.com.tr/2008/07/20/haber,83A76BFDFF0B497989FE7DFE1BD3B1FA .html.

7. Birch, "Was Ahmet Yildiz the Victim?"

8. Birch, "Was Ahmet Yildiz the Victim?"

9. Birch, "Was Ahmet Yildiz the Victim?"; emphasis added.

10. The 2001 economic crisis played a major role in the AKP's election to government in 2002.

11. Berlant, *Cruel Optimism*.

12. "'Türkiye'de İlk Gay Namus Cinayeti'" [The first gay honor killing in Turkey], *Radikal*, July 20, 2008, http://www.radikal.com.tr/turkiye/turkiyede-ilk-gay-namus -cinayeti-889390.

13. Ahmet had been a somewhat active member in the gay community and had worked for *Beargi*. Turkish bear subculture is similar to that of other international bear groups, and the middle- and upper-middle-class members of the subculture are in fact quite well connected to international bear circles.

14. See, for instance, "No Title," *Birgün*, July 26, 2008, http://www.birgun.net /actuel_index.php?news_code=1217060541&year=2008&month=07&day=26

(accessed July 31, 2011; link discontinued); Müjgan Halis, "Öldürüldü" [Murdered], *Sabah*, July 26, 2008, http://arsiv.sabah.com.tr/2008/07/26/ct/haber,EF7BA07EBA6 D4064B5BF45B989448A48.html.

15. Massad, "Re-orienting Desire"; Massad, *Desiring Arabs*.

16. Ahıska, "Occidentalism."

17. Ahıska, "Occidentalism," 353.

18. Here I follow Ahıska, "Occidentalism," and James Carrier in their contention that "Occidentalisms and orientalisms serve not just to draw a line between societies, but also to draw a line within them." Carrier, ed., *Occidentalism*, 22.

19. Quoted in Dirlik, "Thinking Modernity Historically," 14. See Davutoğlu, *Alternative Paradigms*.

20. Ahıska, "Occidentalism"; Dirlik, "Thinking Modernity Historically"; Iğsız, "From Alliance of Civilizations."

21. Dirlik, "Thinking Modernity Historically."

22. Cited in Iğsız, "From Alliance of Civilizations."

23. Koğacıoğlu, "Tradition Effect."

24. Kocamaner, "How New Is Erdoğan's 'New Turkey'?"

25. Massad, "Re-Orienting Desire," 362. Massad, *Desiring Arabs*.

26. Grewal and Kaplan, *Scattered Hegemonies*.

27. Foucault, *History of Sexuality*.

28. Ahmed, *Cultural Politics of Emotion*; Gopinath, *Impossible Desires*; Manalansan, "In the Shadows of Stonewall"; Puar, *Terrorist Assemblages*; Ritchie, "How Do You Say 'Come Out of the Closet' in Arabic?"

29. Manalansan, *Global Divas*, 27.

30. Massad, *Desiring Arabs*.

31. For critiques of Massad, see Amar, *Security Archipelago*; Amar and El Shakry, "Introduction"; Hochberg, "Introduction"; Mikdashi and Puar, "Queer Theory and Permanent War"; Mourad, "Queering the Mother Tongue"; Moussawi, "(Un)Critically Queer Organizing." See Moussawi, "(Un)Critically Queer Organizing," also for a discussion of *differing* strategies of Beirut-based LGBTQ organizations regarding coming out.

32. Grewal and Kaplan, "Global Identities," 667.

33. D'Emilio, "Capitalism and Gay Identity."

34. On kinship and alternative families and homes, see Reddy, "Homes, Houses, Non-Identity"; and Weston, *Families We Choose*. On the "rejecting the family" model, see Gopinath, *Impossible Desires*; and Manalansan, *Global Divas*. On women breaking free from the family, see Davis, *Racism, Birth Control and Reproductive Rights*; and Collins, "Black Women and Motherhood." On the legalization of gay marriage, see Duggan, *Twilight of Equality?*; Eng, *Feeling of Kinship*; and Spade, *Normal Life*. Interestingly, a brief repetition of the second argument took place via Lee Edelman's call for queers to refuse reproductive futurity and the critiques of this argument as a white and individualistic understanding of sociality. Halberstam, "The Anti-social Turn in Queer Studies"; Muñoz, *Cruising Utopia*; Smith, "Queer Theory and Native Studies."

35. Grewal and Kaplan, "Global Identities."

36. Sakai, *Translation and Subjectivity*.

37. Collins, "Black Women and Motherhood"; Davis, *Racism, Birth Control and Reproductive Rights*; Muñoz, *Cruising Utopia*.

38. Grewal and Kaplan, "Warrior Marks."

39. In fact, the Lambdaistanbul-organized protest I attended in front of the Üsküdar Courthouse attracted a number of journalists but, despite the press release, did not end up receiving any coverage.

40. "Onu Bu Kadar Çok Severken Nasıl Öldürürler?" [How can they kill him when they love him so much?], *Sabah*, July 26, 2008, http://arsiv.sabah.com.tr /2008/07/26/ct/haber,DE61D62EAE814EFE887D8339D33E45F6.html.

41. Ahmed, "Happy Objects."

42. Yazıcı, "Return to the Family," 112.

43. Yazıcı, "Return to the Family."

44. Manalansan, "In the Shadows of Stonewall."

45. Turkish heteromasculinity, as with all heteromasculinities, has various looks, of course. Here I am not referring to a particular ethnicized look, but rather to the tropes and performance of hegemonic masculinities. See Connell, *Masculinities*.

46. Yıldız, "Yalan Söyleme, Maskeni Çıkart ve Onur Duy" [Don't lie, take off your mask and feel proud]," *Beargi Dergi*, no. 31 (August 2008); this is the original source for the letter. Ahmet's letter in its entirety has been republished here: "Yalan söylememiş maske takmamıştı" [He did not lie or wear a mask], *Kaos GL*, July 21, 2008, https://www.kaosgl.org/haber/yalan-soylememis-maske-takmamisti.

47. Birch, "Was Ahmet Yildiz the Victim of Turkey's First Gay Honour Killing?" In fact, in the interviews with Ahmet's friends and others in the bear community who had known him, I encountered almost, without exception, the wish that Ahmet had not come out to his parents and had engaged in *idare etmek* (managing the situation) instead. Some of my interviewees mentioned, in a disapproving tone, that his decision was influenced by a couple of new *gey* friends he had made who, among other things, had the financial stability and independence to live *gey* lives. It is possible that what Ahmet had aspired to was this life in its entirety—a nice apartment, a life with your boyfriend, and a job that affords a middle- to upper-middle-class lifestyle which packages these possibilities into outness. While Ahmet himself was from an upper-middle-class family, as a university student he did not have financial independence from his parents.

48. Ahmet narrates his coming-out to his parents as not so much a story of wanting to come out but rather needing to: "They kept asking questions, cornering me, investigating. I lived through many incidents such as having my cell phone and computer gone through, being forced to live with my sister, having them listen to my door, none of which I want to think of. They were trying to take away my freedom in order to find out about my situation. We came to a point where I had to tell them." Yıldız, "Yalan Söyleme," 43.

49. See the memorial blog *Ahmet Is My Family* at http://ahmetyildizismyfamily .blogspot.com (last accessed March 8, 2020). See also Jonathan Robinson, "Ahmet Is My Family (Was Ahmet the Victim of a Gay Honour Killing?)," YouTube

video posted January 10, 2009, http://www.youtube.com/watch?v=TqqFwb HON3Y.

50. It is also worth noting that while there is a presumed equivalence among the languages uttered or on display in the video, the status of English as *the* universal language is discernable from the title of the clip, the captions toward the end, as well as the from fact that some of the participants chose to pronounce "Ahmet is my family" in English despite their country of origin not being English-speaking.

51. Foucault, *Discipline and Punish.*

52. On the so-called Oriental pathology of honor killings see Massad, *Desiring Arabs.* Regarding the role purportedly played by Islam in honor killings see Abu-Lughod, "Seductions of the 'Honor Crime.'"

53. Grewal, "Outsourcing Patriarchy."

54. Even scholars who argue that "honour crimes should not be treated in isolation from the phenomenon of violence against women in general" given such isolation might lead to "the stigmatization of migrant communities which might result in anti-immigrant sentiments," they nevertheless can claim that honor crimes are now a globalized phenomenon "occurring among immigrant communities in receiving countries." Ertürk, "State Responses to Honour Killing," 172. This keeps the category of honor killing and its attachment to particular geographies (that can travel via immigration) intact.

55. Berna Yazıcı analyzes the Return to the Family project of the SSCPA (Social Services and Children's Protection Agency) that for economic reasons aimed at sending children receiving institutional care in SSCPA residential homes back to their families. Yazıcı, "Return to the Family." While this project is partially a response to EU demands that Turkey better the conditions for children in institutional care, as Yazıcı notes, it was as much motivated by the AKP government's conservative family ideologies as well as their motivation to cut down on government spending.

56. Harkins, *Everybody's Family Romance.*

57. Puar, "Circuits of Queer Mobility" and *Terrorist Assemblages.*

58. Puar, *Terrorist Assemblages.*

59. Şermin Terzi, "Ahmet, töre cinayetine mi kurban gitti?" [Was Ahmet the victim of a custom/honor killing?], *Hürriyet*, February 1, 2009, https://www.hurriyet .com.tr/gundem/ahmet-tore-cinayetine-mi-kurban-gitti-10900920.

60. Darama clearly equated homosexuality with anal sex. Nonetheless, I did not ask her whether queer relationships in which the parties do not engage in anal sex are therefore exempt from haram status in order to not distract her from the topic at hand.

61. I make this suggestion for conceptualizing a right to sin tentatively and cautiously. As discussed in chapter 1, the word used for *right* in Turkish is *hak*, which is derived from Arabic and also has religious connotations, including, perhaps most importantly, one of Allah's ninety-nine names. Therefore, a subject having the (secular, liberal) right to commit a sinful act is a conceptual conundrum, even if a fruitful one.

62. As of this writing, homosexuality still qualifies as a reason for exemption from military conscription for male-assigned citizens of the Turkish Republic. As proof

of their homosexuality, subjects used to be asked to submit photographic or video evidence of their engagement in gay male sex acts during which they were anally penetrated. This practice seems to have been replaced by other markers, such as perceived presence of effeminate mannerisms, a soft voice, and questions about colorful, tight clothing and the use of accessories and makeup. Tarhan, "Zorunlu Askerlik ve Sivil Alternatif Hizmete Direniş Olarak Vicdani Red."

63. Amar, "Turning the Gendered Politics of the Security State Inside Out?"

64. Pervizat, "In the Name of Honour."

65. Koğacıoğlu, "Tradition Effect."

66. See, for instance: "The juridico-political structure of many Western democracies was reformed in the last quarter of the twentieth century in ways that it has constrained the violent exercise of male power." Mojab and Abdo-Zubi, *Violence in the Name of Honour*, 23.

67. The distinction needs to be made, however, between blaming Kurdish customs for violence against women and understanding structural constraints on one's ability to seek protection, such as not being a native speaker of Turkish (because one's first language is Kurdish) and therefore not being able to seek or feel comfortable seeking legal advice. See Tahaoğlu, "Kadına Şiddette Suçlu Kim?" This of course is very much a result of the standardization of Turkish as the mother tongue and official language of the republic.

68. All honor killing literature in Turkey, and to my knowledge also internationally, refers to honor killings as crimes against women perpetrated to control women's sexuality. In this sense, Ahmet's murder constitutes an exception. I will briefly discuss the significance of Ahmet's maleness in the context of this honor killing in the conclusion to this chapter.

69. Koğacıoğlu, "Tradition Effect."

70. Yalçın-Heckman, "Kurdish Tribal Organization and Local Political Processes," 291.

71. Yalçın-Heckman, "Kurdish Tribal Organization and Local Political Processes."

72. Bozçalı, "Türkiye'nin Kürt Sorunu."

73. Bargu, "Another Necropolitics"; Savcı, "Revolting Grief."

74. Bargu, "Another Necropolitics."

Chapter Three. Trans Terror, Deep Citizenship

1. I detail my decision to speak with trans sex workers in Ankara rather than Istanbul in the appendix. While my focus is on trans organizing and sex work in Ankara, I also met and spoke with several transfeminine sex workers and former sex workers in Istanbul.

2. This, needless to say, renders trans women vulnerable to a lot more violence, as they have to hitchhike on the freeway in order to make their way back into town.

3. Puar and Rai, "Monster, Terrorist, Fag."

4. Spade, *Normal Life*; Haritaworn, *Queer Lovers and Hateful Others*. These assumptions regarding the demand for hate crime laws necessitate a particular under-

standing of law and the function of the human in juridical liberalism. Feminist legal scholars have long regarded the law as the location of the production of modern subjectivity and the human and as a space for taming radical justice demands into liberal equality. See Esmeir, *Juridical Humanity*; Hua, *Trafficking Women's Human Rights*. One articulation of this critique maintains that the rise of the global human rights regime works as the juridical mechanism of economic and political neoliberal reforms with a neocolonial function. See, for instance, Atanasoski, *Humanitarian Violence*. While these critiques are invaluable and have shaped my own thinking and criticisms of liberalism and the subject of law, scholarship that looks at the *practices* of law demonstrates that subjects' engagement with the law is often complex and multifaceted. See, for instance, Koğacıoğlu, "Law in Context"; Kotiswaran, *Dangerous Sex, Invisible Labor*; Puri, *Sexual States*. Law, in other words, does not only discursively constitute subjects but is itself shaped by its social, economic, and political context as well as by subjects' engagement with it.

5. According to the website TurkeyPurge (https://turkeypurge.com/purge-in -numbers-2), the total number of judges and prosecutors was 4,424 as of March 10, 2020.

6. I thank İpek Bozkurt for alerting me to feminist legal activism. While I knew of this, of course, as someone who has followed feminist politics in Turkey for almost two decades, it was our conversation and her ideas for her master's project that made me, for the first time, put together this empirical reality with feminist theories of the law. Bozkurt, "Bir Feminist Aktivizm Yöntemi Olarak Dava Takibi."

7. I would like to note that there have been comparable moments in the United States, where the theoretical critique of law and the practice of it come into collision, such as when during the first days of the Muslim ban implemented by President Donald Trump, ACLU members as well as other volunteer lawyers flooded US airports, helping those detained at the border fill out habeas corpus petitions.

8. Ergut, "Policing the Poor in the Late Ottoman Empire," 149.

9. Shah, *Street Corner Secrets*; Wyers, *"Wicked" Istanbul*. Shah argues, citing David Arnold, that the Congress in India did not alter the composition of the police force after independence from the British, since congressional ministers viewed communism as a major threat at the time and the police had come to be understood as loyal not only to the British Raj but also to the propertied classes. Thus the police force was historically formed to reflect caste and religious difference as well as to curb urban crime and discourage working-class activity. Arnold, "The Police and Colonial Control in South India"; Shah, *Street Corner Secrets*, 131.

10. See Wyers, *"Wicked" Istanbul*. This class relationship is discernable from legislations regarding in what districts brothels were permitted (openly banning brothels from operating in close proximity to homes of distinguished families), as well as laws that distinguished between four tiers of brothels, ranging from lowest to highest class.

11. Wyers, *Wicked Istanbul*, 217.

12. Amar, *Security Archipelago*; Camp and Heatherton, eds., *Policing the Planet*.

13. In a private conversation, Ruşen Çakır, long-term researcher on Islam and the Left in Turkey, stated that while there had been a few people who wanted to craft

links between Islam and Left traditions, also inspired by the Iranian Revolution, there were no significant Left Islamist organizations whose activities were interrupted or banned in the post-coup period. Therefore, my claim remains a theoretical one about the inevitable *definition* of Islam itself as Right-leaning through its deployment against the Left.

14. Readers might be familiar with Gülen's name due to President Erdoğan's claims that Gülen and his organization were behind the July 2016 military coup attempt—since the coup attempt, the organization is referred to as FETÖ (Fethullah Gülen Terrorist Organization). Gülen currently resides in Pennsylvania, and since the summer of 2016 the Erdoğan regime has several times requested Gülen's surrender to the Turkish forces for a trial, to no avail.

15. Şık, *Dokunan Yanar (İmamın Ordusu)*.

16. This led to the police force organizing and structuring itself according its own internal logic, which was somewhat independent from the state despite an initial allowance from the military junta that made its staffing possible. In other words, the military junta produced the very Islamist threat that rapidly organized within the police force and that they continued to keep under control via (threats of) military interventions. For instance, the junta-appointed president Kenan Evren has been documented as speaking publicly about the centrality of religion for national unity and the need for the nation to hold on to its religion. In a speech delivered in Konya on January 15, 1981, Evren announced, "There is no way to tear apart a people who have one God, one Qur'an, one prophet, and who pray [*namaz kılmak*] in unison." Quoted in Şık, *Dokunan Yanar (İmamın Ordusu)*, 13. During the initial decade of AKP rule, and prior to the public animosity between the Gülen community and Erdoğan that was initiated by the July 2016 military coup attempt, those in the Gülen community were important supporters of consecutive AKP governments, and Erdoğan was a public ally of Gülen.

17. Alevis, a subdenomination of Shi'ites, constitute a Muslim minority in Turkey. While Turkey has constitutionally always been a secular republic, the unspoken Sunni Muslim norm in the country has historically meant that the *cemevleri*, which are the places of worship for Alevis, have not been recognized as religious spaces and instead have been categorized as cultural centers. This was also criticized by the freedom for everyone declaration of Muslim headscarf activists discussed in chapter 1. Alevis in various parts of the country have also been targets of physical violence. Perhaps the event that has been most strongly etched into Turkey's collective memory is that of Madımak, which I will return to at the end of the chapter.

18. Yonucu, "Devlet Şiddeti ve 'Mimli' Mahalleler."

19. Yonucu, "Devlet Şiddeti ve 'Mimli' Mahalleler."

20. Turkey's history of various Left organizing has also meant that the depoliticization tactics were only mildly successful—the large political-prisoner population in Turkey continuing from the 1990s to today and the organized resistance they have staged in terms of hunger strikes and fasts unto death are a testament to their failure. In fact, one of the highly organized moments of prisoner resistance was against the introduction of F-type, single-cell prisons in the 1990s. The prisoners understood this

proposed reform as simply an extension of what they called the neoliberal capitalist "cellularization" of life. These single-cell prisons were aimed at thwarting the political and social organizing and educational efforts then taking place in prison yards. Recognizing solitary confinement as an expression of a larger cellularization of life—a marriage between neoliberal capitalism and the authoritarian state that turned "citizens into consumers, solidarity into competition, and sociality into individualism"—political prisoners understood their resistance to F-type cell prisons as central to the fight against larger social transformations operative also outside of prison walls. The Turkish state argued in response that the new high-security prisons were modeled after the super-maximum security prisons in the United States and Europe and promoted them as civilized spaces that would contribute to the health and well-being of the prison population. See Bargu, *Starve and Immolate*, 164. In brief, the prison system, the judiciary, and law enforcement are understood as political entities in Turkey and not as neutral institutions that deliver justice or simply house criminals.

21. The Turkish case shows a significant difference from the literature on neoliberalism, policing, and the carceral state produced in the United States that has claimed that neoliberalism constitutes a statecraft that punishes the poor, especially evident in war-against-poverty policies and the growing prison-industrial complex. Camp and Heatherton, *Policing the Planet*; Wacquant, *Punishing the Poor*.

22. Habitat II was the second United Nations conference on human settlements, ironically themed "livable cities."

23. Kandiyoti, "Pink Card Blues"; Selek, *Maskeler, Süvariler, Gacılar*.

24. Selek, *Maskeler, Süvariler, Gacılar*.

25. Selek, *Maskeler, Süvariler, Gacılar*.

26. Savcı, "Queer in Translation."

27. Interview with Hülya Anne (Mother Hülya), July 1, 2010.

28. In her discussion of the closure of dance bars in Mumbai, Jyoti Puri notes that the extractability of dance bars via high taxes was no longer sufficient for Mumbai's neoliberal local government, which sought to position Mumbai as a world-class city and as a financial and consumerist hub. See Puri, *Sexual States*. This is also true for trans sex workers in both Istanbul and Ankara, yet because their existence is not fixed in space (such as a dance bar), they experienced systems that targeted them as both extractable labor and surplus existence.

29. Atasoy, *Islam's Marriage with Neoliberalism*.

30. Parla, "'Honor' of the State."

31. Especially following the 1985 Turkish Police Duty Law, which had endowed the police with extensive autonomy to detain people whose actions were considered to be violating "public morality and rules of modesty" or whose actions were "not approved by the social order," officers reportedly harassed and, at times, detained women who were walking or driving alone at night or spending the night at a hotel with a man they were not married to under the pretense of checking for unauthorized sex worker status. Parla, "'Honor' of the State."

32. Foucault, *Abnormal*.

33. Hong, *Death beyond Disavowal*.

34. Robin D. G. Kelley discusses a similar incident regarding arrest warrants in Ferguson, Missouri, in the United States and argues that they are used as a "racial tax, a direct extraction of surplus by the state that produces nothing but discipline and terror and the reproduction of the state—in other words, *revenue by primitive accumulation*." Kelley, "Thug Nation," 29–30.

35. To elaborate, the term *işgal* is most notably used in cases of one country occupying another.

36. Kotiswaran, *Dangerous Sex, Invisible Labor*; Puri, *Sexual States*; Shah, *Street Corner Secrets*.

37. I depart here from the suggestion of Lisa Sanchez, who uses the "prostitution-free zone ordinance" of Portland to suggest we look at which subjects stand on the right side versus the wrong side of the law in order to understand the contemporary dynamics of exclusion. See Sanchez, "Global E-rotic Subject, the Ban, and the Prostitute-Free Zone." While one surely can, and should, pay attention to the kinds of exclusions the law names, I maintain that we will only have a partial understanding of exclusion if we limit our analyses to reading exclusion directly off of laws.

38. This is perhaps most similar to stand-your-ground laws in the United States that do not specify who may stand their ground and who may be shot for transgressing yet categorically distribute protection to some and violence to others through the racist logics they rely on and perpetuate.

39. For a similar argument regarding the police treatment of hijra populations, see Puri, *Sexual States*.

40. "Eryaman'da Travesti ve Transeksüellere Sistemli Şiddet!" [Systematic violence to transvestites and transsexuals in Eryaman!], *Kaos GL*, May 3, 2006, https://www.kaosgl.org/haber/eryamanda-travesti-ve-transeksuellere-sistemli -siddet.

41. "To see someone" in Turkish slang means to give them their "share."

42. Melih Gökçek, a member of the AKP and the mayor of Ankara in the period 1994–2017, has become famous for his conservative stance on many issues, including the arts.

43. Merve Çağrışlı, "Eryaman'da Travesti Kırımı" [Slaughter of transvestites in Eryaman], *Toplumsal Özgürlük*, no. 14, July 2006, 25.

44. Hayat Çelik. "Avcılar'da ikiyüzlü bir deprem: Meis Sitesi olayı" [A two-faced earthquake in Avcılar: The Meis Community incident], *Sendika.org*, November 27, 2012, https://sendika63.org/2012/11/avcilarda-ikiyuzlu-bir-deprem-meis-sitesi-olayi -hayat-celik-75094/.

45. The only three trans women who remained in their buildings and refused to sell their homes and move away continued to be pressured by the other inhabitants as well as the owner of a new luxury restaurant in the complex.

46. See, for instance, Boyd, "San Francisco's Castro District"; Hanhardt, *Safe Space*; Puri, *Sexual States*.

47. Willse, *Value of Homelessness*; Hong, *Death beyond Disavowal*. For a discussion of sites of transnational investability, see Murphy, "The Girl."

48. Erman, *Mış Gibi Site*.

49. One precursor to the changes to come was the appointment of Korkut Özal, brother of Turgut Özal, as minister of interior and his appointment of Saadettin Tantan as Istanbul's police chief. A number of the trans women I spoke with who had lived through the 1977–1978 period recounted Tantan's arrival as the destruction of the infamous Abanoz Street that had housed many clubs and brothels where trans women worked. The accounts of older trans women I spoke with also echo the accounts featured in a collection of interviews documenting trans and queer lives in the 1980s. Gürsu and Elitemiz, eds., *80'lerde Lubunya Olmak*.

50. Gürsu and Elitemiz, eds., *80'lerde Lubunya Olmak*.

51. Öz, "Ahlaksızların Mekansal Dışlanması."

52. Altinay, "Reconstructing the Transgendered Self as a Muslim, Nationalist, Upper-Class Woman"; Ertür and Lebow, "Coup de Genre"; Stokes, *Republic of Love*; Öz, "Ahlaksızların Mekansal Dışlanması."

53. Martin Stokes argues that Ersoy's turn to elite classical Turkish music from the more popular genre of arabesk upon her return to Turkey might partially be due to her desire to prove her artistic merit and, hence, her deserving of an exceptional amnesty. Stokes, *Republic of Love*.

54. The first attempts to introduce a strict distinction between brothels, on one hand, and pavilions and night clubs, on the other, date back to a 1930 directive, which was legislated into the 1933 prostitution law in the republic, that outlawed brothels from providing music, entertainment, and alcohol. Wyers, *"Wicked" Istanbul*. By that point, the legal category of prostitute had been in effect since a 1915 Committee of Union and Progress legislation. Although this law had been passed during the final years of the Ottoman Empire, the Republican government continued regulation of sex work as a governance strategy, clearly defining the codes of when, where, and by whom sex work could be provided.

55. Wyers, *"Wicked" Istanbul*.

56. Government documents, including a state memorandum penned by the minister of interior in 1931, as well as citizen complaints at the time, voiced concerns about prostitution under the guise of entertainment—including references to "foreign prostitutes posing as entertainers coming to Turkey, particularly from Hungary, Bulgaria and Austria." Wyers, *"Wicked" Istanbul*, 188.

57. Scholars have also shown that sex work is a chosen and preferred line of work for many across the world since alternative forms of labor that are presented as honorable, such as factory or construction work, are often underpaid and involve endless hours of very difficult physical labor. Hoang, *Dealing in Desire*; Kotiswaran, *Dangerous Sex*; Shah, *Street Corner Secrets*.

58. See Wyers's account of the adoption of the Ottoman regulation model of sex work by the early Turkish Republic. Wyers, *"Wicked" Istanbul*.

59. Wyers, *"Wicked" Istanbul*; Zengin, *İktidarın Mahremiyeti*. This means that, for instance, the Turkish state approves the number of brothels and registered sex workers in each town; regulates the location of brothels, their operating hours, their exposure (e.g., the height and location of windows), their access (e.g., through a single door only), and the salaries of sex workers as well as the fees they need to pay.

Yıldırım, *Fahişeliğin Öbür Yüzü*; Zengin, "Devletin Cinsel Kıyıları." In addition to the regulation and evaluation of brothels, the ironically named commissions to battle prostitution are also in charge of the regular STD-testing and other health-related checkups of registered sex workers as well as the capturing and registering of unregistered sex workers. Zengin, *İktidarın Mahremiyeti*. Official acknowledgment of unregistered sex work is evident in the naming of two kinds of sex workers as *vesikalı* (licensed) and *vesikasız* (unlicensed).

60. Yıldırım, *Fahişeliğin Öbür Yüzü*.

61. Kandiyoti, "Pink Card Blues"; Kurtoğlu, "Cinsiyet ve Cinselliğin İnşası."

62. This is partially because many clients in the sex work market prefer transfeminine workers who have not undergone medical transition. For a similar finding, see Berg, *Porn Work*.

63. There are of course a large number of non-trans/cis women in the informal sex economy. While they are not within the scope of this book, I occasionally speak of one cis sex worker, Ayşin, who was a close friend of the trans women I spent time with. It is also important to note that while the number of cis women in the informal sex work economy is much larger than that of trans women, the latter are much more frequently affiliated with sex work in the media.

64. While today the use of *lubunca* is more widespread among queers, historically it was employed almost exclusively by trans women in order to communicate with each other without the police understanding them. See Kontavas, "Lubunca."

65. While unfortunately I do not have the space here to reflect on this in detail, I find this informally institutionalized training of gacıs to be an interesting complication of the duality of choice versus born-this-way arguments. Neither choice nor determination by birth, this understanding suggests that in some ways one is not born gacı but that one becomes one, without suggesting that this is a choice.

66. Gacıvari (gacı-like) is a derivative of gacı, which in Turkish queer slang refers to trans women. When I talked to trans women about older terms, before the entrance of *gey* (gay) and *lezbiyen* (lesbian) into Turkish in the early 1990s, they mentioned *lubunya* as an all-encompassing term for male-assigned queers, with distinctions made between *laçovari* (laço-like, with *laço* referring to masculine men) and gacıvari. Lubunya is still used in queer subculture, though I have heard gacıvari and laçovari mostly used by trans women. The addition of *-vari*/-like at the end of *gacı* and *laço* situates the terms as rather fluid instead of adhering to strict boundaries, referring to a state of being (gacı or laço) without fully arriving at it. Yet, as I was sitting in Esra's living room, interviewing Dilara, she referred to the young trans woman in formation as gacıvari, which shows that the term has multiple uses and can sometimes indicate a moment of possible future arrival at a more defined gacı state. One last thing that is important to note, however, is that there is significant variation among femininities of trans women—not all of them have had breast implants, for instance, and while some wear highly feminine clothing and attitude, others dress down, even tomboy-like, unless they were going out for work, all of which speak to the not too strictly defined territory of gacı.

67. *Koli* is a widely used term to refer to sex partners (in queer slang, *lubunca*). While in non-trans queer contexts one distinguishes between *koli* and *beldeli koli* (*beldeli koli* referring to a sex partner one would charge for sex), for trans women koli always refers to customers—to those who pay for sex. The sexual partners of trans women who do not need to pay are referred to as *cicilik*—in fact, trans women usually pay for various expenses of their cicilik, including food, alcohol, drugs, and so on. At times this situation emerges as a point of criticism, particularly if a trans woman is found to be spending too much money on a cicilik. While this setup somewhat resembles the one between travestis and their boyfriends in Brazil, as discussed by Don Kulick, it has significant differences, especially because cicilik are not seen as relationship material but only as cute (and usually young) boys to have a good time with. Some trans women have long-term boyfriends whom they refer to as husbands, but there is no similar continuity of these men and cicilik. Kulick, "A Man in the House."

68. Another reason this system did not always work for trans women was that some did not want to show their faces on their websites. Ayşin's webite did not feature any photos exposing her face either, but Esra explained that trans women had to have headshots on their pages, as clients wanted to be assured that they presented as feminine enough.

69. I place "pass" in quotation marks in order to indicate and reject the economies of normalcy that determine the contours of acceptable manhood and womanhood.

70. Gregory Mitchell discusses what he refers to as "whore's ontology" in the context of Brazilian sex workers, which has some overlaps with and some differences from gacı ontology in the case of Turkey. Mitchell, "Evangelical Ecstasy Meets Feminist Fury."

71. On this occasion the hairdresser had come to Mother Ezgi's house to do everyone's hair. It is important to note that hairdressers (almost exclusively a male occupation in Turkey) as well as cab drivers are (cis, hetero) men who participate regularly in trans women's lives. A number of trans women sex workers I spoke with had their trusted cab drivers whom they would call when they needed a ride. I mention these relationships to underline that transfeminine sex workers had an array of relationships with cis and presumably straight men, not all of which can be located in a desire-hate matrix.

72. Svati Shah notes a similar system among sex workers in Mumbai, where they would accompany each other to a client's place or a room he would rent and wait outside. Shah, *Street Corner Secrets*.

73. At the time this corresponded to between $55 and $85.

74. While the existence of other trans women offering transactional sex might read as competition, they all knew each other and operated with an informal union logic of not lowering prices.

75. Here I want to be clear that life for trans women in Ankara was not a utopian socialist existence in which everyone always got along (if there could ever be such a thing). Of course there were fights and competition, and people lied and cheated and stole from each other. Yet collective and cooperative behavior was what was *idealized* and reached out for. The underlying problem with Elif was not that she failed this ideal, but that she did not subscribe to it.

76. Berghan, "Patronsuz ve Pezevenksiz Bir Dünya!."

77. Although trans women were critical of the master status of sex work as well as its mandatory nature under the current labor conditions in Turkey, they were careful not to demonize sex work itself as a form of labor in their complaints. In fact, many trans women indicated that they likely would have chosen sex work as an occupation over other options but that they nevertheless wanted structural access to other forms of labor. One of the early protests organized by Pembe Hayat (Pink Life) consisted of a group of trans sex workers collectively filing applications for jobs at an İş ve İşçi Bulma Kurumu (Governmental Employment/Placement Agency) office.

78. Being a homeowner was necessary and desirable for most trans women, as renting was fairly difficult and problematic. Not only did most landlords not want trans women as tenants, but in cases where they did find rentals, they were at constant risk of complaints from neighbors, even though most trans women did not bring clients to their own homes but instead used koli houses for work.

79. Trans women often used *lubunya* and *gacı* interchangeably to refer to themselves and other trans women they knew, again indicating some flexibility and capaciousness of these terms.

80. Selek, *Maskeler, Süvariler, Gacılar*; LGBTT Hakları Platformu, "LGBTT Bireylerin İnsan Haklari Raporu 2007"; Öz, "Ahlaksızların Mekansal Dışlanması."

81. LGBTT Hakları Platformu, "LGBTT Bireylerin İnsan Haklari Raporu 2007," 16.

82. Like all concepts, deep state is also subject to travel, transformation, and co-optation. This use of the deep state in Turkey is very different from the recent alt-right uses of it in the United States. See Bobby Allyn, "'Deep, Dark Conspiracy Theories' Hound Some Civil Servants in Trump Era," *NPR*, November 14, 2019, https://www.npr.org/2019/11/14/779035797/deep-dark-conspiracy-theories-hound-some-civil-servants-in-trump-era.

83. The Mercedes was transporting a well-known mafia hitman, Abdullah Çatlı (INTERPOL had him on red alert at the time), and his girlfriend, Gonca Us, the former vice chief of the Istanbul police force (Hüseyin Kocadağ), as well as DYP (the Right Path Party) deputy Sedat Bucak. DYP was in power at the time of the accident and was led by Tansu Çiller, the first female prime minister of the Turkish Republic. The investigation undertaken by the attorney general of the national security court charged that some ex-convicts had been released on the order of then minister of the interior Mehmet Ağar and were then appointed as Bucak's bodyguards. Further, Ağar's signature was on the release orders of such figures as Yaşar Öz, an international drug trafficker.

84. In fact, public intellectuals have traced the formation of what came to be referred as the deep state to an earlier institution referred to as *kontrgerilla* (counterinsurgency), the Turkish arm of the CIA-supported anti-communist forces organized during the Cold War. Arcayürek, *Derin Devlet 1950–2007*. Unresolved murders of especially leftist politicians, intellectuals, and other public figures have been attributed to this formation, such as when, on May 1, 1977, labor union members and thousands of workers gathered at Taksim Square were fired upon and, on January 24, 1993,

when Left journalist Uğur Mumcu was murdered. While this initial formation was allegedly exclusively organized within the military, reports indicate that the reinforcement of nationalism in Turkey was a major device in the war against communism, and therefore patriotic citizens were imagined to be potential extensions of this formation. In fact, Bülent Ecevit, who was prime minister at the time, recounted finding out about Special Forces Command (Özel Kuvvetler Komutanlığı) for the first time in 1974, when the unit's exclusive funding from the CIA had been discontinued and it now needed funding from the Turkish state. He was also informed that a handful of "patriotic" volunteers, whose names were to remain anonymous, had been employed to work as the lifelong civilian extension of the Special War Unit (the earlier name of the Special Forces Command). Arcayürek, *Derin Devlet 1950–2007*, 40. Therefore, even in its early phases, the deep state was not confined to the military, and it mobilized civilian labor in its efforts to protect the nation. While Cüneyt Arcayürek recognizes that the Susurluk incident proves that the deep state involves more complex relationships between organized crime, the police, the army, and right-wing politics in Turkey as compared to the kontrgerilla, he nevertheless concludes the section of his book on the deep state with the suggestion that the deep state is, after all, the Turkish army. I disagree with this conclusion in the light of the reference to anonymous patriotic volunteers in the report to Bülent Ecevit mentioned above. The theory of deep citizenship I put forth emphasizes the utmost significance of the "civilian extension" of the deep state. In fact, I cannot help but wonder if such a formation ever consisted only of the military, even in its early phases.

85. This recognition by a state official that the boundaries of the state are porous is instructive in how we theorize the very institution of the state. Feminist scholars have long emphasized that the state is not a homogenous, bounded entity that can be spoken of in the singular. See Haney, "Homeboys, Babies, Men in Suits"; Navaro-Yashin, *Faces of the State*; Puri, *Sexual States*; Morgan and Orloff, eds., *Many Hands of the State*. While I agree with this scholarship and with ethnographers of the state who have shown that the state is by no means a monolithic entity, I also align with thinkers who have recognized that this is precisely why what Foucault refers to as state effect is necessary: States *present* themselves as coherent entities through various mechanisms, institutions, and discourses. Therefore, in my thinking through the deep state, I recognize that no matter how incoherent, messy, and nonhomogenous the state may be, it will be recognized by many subjects to be thing-like: reified, material, tangible, homogenous, and internally coherent. Foucault, *Security, Territory, Population*.

86. I would like to briefly consider the work of two scholars who have theorized deep state and similar formations and express how I diverge from them. Baskın Oran has defined the logic of the deep state as legitimizing the behavior of those who act according to state ideology and as the illegal outsourcing of state's needs and demands to third parties. See Oran, "Derin Devlet Nedir? Nasıl Oluşur?" Since legitimacy is a requirement of statehood, illegitimate acts that prove to be unlegitimizable become the domain of the deep state. In other words, if the state is an institution that monopolizes the means of "legitimate" violence, as Max Weber suggested, different agents' mobilization of illegitimate violence *on behalf of the state* is what constitutes

deep state. See Weber, *Theory of Social and Economic Organization*. This phenomenon is different from many documented cases in which states *legitimize illegitimate violence* under states of emergency, through discourses of terrorism or by instituting extraordinary renditions. In such cases, much of the violence in the hands of the state becomes codified before it is perpetuated. In the case of deep state, on the other hand, the perpetrators of illegitimate violence have no apparent relationship to the state. Oran keeps the definition of deep state narrow, leaving out (a) any actions that do not involve violence, such as money laundering, (b) actions that are undertaken by those who are not state officials, and (c) actions by those who are not acting according to a particular plan. However, I argue that (a) the violence of the totality of deep state cannot be measured by/limited to individual moments of violence and that, in fact, violence as an entity is not easily defined and measured (and therefore might not be the most apt term for defining the damage being done) and (b) the effects of ideology extend beyond proper recognizable orders being followed. This also means that those who feel appointed to act on behalf of the state might not always be state officials. I also agree with Haldun Gülalp's critique of Oran: Oran seems to take the legitimate/ illegitimate distinction that is produced by and follows the state logic at face value. Gülalp, "Derin Devlet Nerededir?" I agree that this would be a mistake, yet I also think that one can point out the contradictory state logics without endorsing state definitions of legitimacy and illegitimacy. Gülalp's definition of deep state as the container of our collectively held sins is enticing, yet I find that not all citizens are equally hailed as keepers of such sins.

The reliance of states on vigilante violence has also been documented by Paul Amar, who discusses the prerevolution Egyptian state's employment of gangs of thugs (*baltagiya*) either to mix in with protesters and shout extremist slogans in order to undermine the demonstrations or simply to create unrest and brutalize the protesters. While these thug groups were not initiated by the Egyptian state, as they had existed in the 1990s as "networks of violent extortion rackets seen as emanating from the informal settlements surrounding downtown Cairo . . . [and] were identified as terrorist enemies of the security state," by the 2000s they were appropriated as useful tools of the police to delegitimize protest groups as crazy extremists or simply to pacify them through the fear of facing violence. Amar, *Security Archipelago*, 211. While this is one of the key ways in which deep state operates, with the needs of the state being met by outsourcing illegitimate violence, I suggest that it is not the only one. Another mode consists of various agents who, if not legitimize, at least render intelligible their actions through the logic of acting on behalf of the state.

87. I am very grateful to the great questions of audience members at the Citizenship and Sexuality conference held in Istanbul in November 2018 and organized by kiss (Küresel İncelemeler ve Sınıfsal Stratejiler Araştırma Grubu); their points helped me improve my articulation of these connections.

88. The September 6–7 events were fueled by the Menderes government: News reports about possible violence against Turks on the island of Cyprus perpetuated by Greek Cypriots, as well as news that Atatürk's childhood home in Thessaloniki had been bombed, were used as excuses to incite the masses to violence. Bali, *6–7*

Eylül 1955 Olayları; Güven, *Cumhuriyet Dönemi Azınlık Politikaları ve Stratejileri Bağlamında 6–7 Eylül Olayları*.

89. Güllapoğlu, "Türk Gladio'su İçin Bazı İpuçları."

90. Of the 26 lawyers, 23 have been directly affiliated with AKP as ministers, deputies, lawyers, or directors of various offices under AKP district municipalities. For a list of each lawyer and their position in 2012 (in Turkish) see Mesut Karip, "Sivas Katliamında Sanıkları Savunan Avukatlar Şimdi Ne Yapıyor?" [What are the defense lawyers of the accused in the Sivas massacre currently doing?], *Milliyet Blog*, March 14, 2012, http://blog.milliyet.com.tr/sivas-katliami-nda-saniklari-savunan -avukatlar-simdi-ne-yapiyor-/Blog/?BlogNo=353491.

91. Ergut, *Modern Devlet ve Polis*; Reiner, *Politics of the Police*.

92. Habip Atam, Eray Erollu, and Serhat Alaattinoğlu, "Sanat Galerilerine 'İçki' Saldırısı"; "Tophane'de Güncel Sanata Saldırı" [Attack on contemporary art at Tophane], *Radikal*, September 22, 2010, http://www.radikal.com.tr/turkiye /tophanede-guncel-sanata-saldiri-1020180.

93. Evren Savcı, "What Does Public Security Exactly Secure?," *Jadaliyya*, January 3, 2018, http://jadaliyya.com/Details/34951/A-Critical-Forum-About-LGBTI -Prohibitions. Similar to the Ülker Street incident, the neighborhood in the Tophane incidents was constructed as a family-friendly place even though the area is centrally located and only a few minutes' walk from the long-standing entertainment districts of Taksim and Beyoğlu. Attacks on gallery openings continued. See, for instance, the attack on an exhibit in October 2016 with the excuse given that men and women were drinking wine together. See "Tophane'de kadınların sergisine saldırı" [Attack on women's exhibition in Tophane], *Evrensel*, October 2, 2016, https://www.evrensel .net/haber/291856/tophanede-kadinlarin-sergisine-saldiri.

94. See "Kanun Hükmünde Kararname" [Legislative Decree], *Resmî Gazete*, December 24, 2017, http://www.resmigazete.gov.tr/eskiler/2017/12/20171224-22.htm; emphasis added.

95. Emphasis added.

96. Esra also did not need a uniform LGBT subject who agreed with her on all political fronts: "We say we are against gay marriage. But we say this without considering the priorities of someone who wants to get married. . . . Everyone is imposing things on each other" (*herkes birbirine birşeyler dayatıyor*). Here Esra clearly identifies herself with the we who are against gay marriage but frames anti-gay-marriage politics as an imposition—and thus not necessarily any different from impositions of the state.

97. Ahmed, *Cultural Politics of Emotion*.

98. Hong, *Death beyond Disavowal*, 7.

99. Hong, *Death beyond Disavowal*, 15.

100. For an overview of the antisocial turn in queer studies, see Halberstam, "The Anti-Social Turn in Queer Studies."

101. Haritaworn, *Queer Lovers and Hateful Others*; Spade, *Normal Life*. According to this argument, privileged gays and lesbians, who can (only) imagine protection by law and law enforcement, demand liberal guarantees for their safety, but this will only serve the criminal system's disproportionate incarceration of the poor, the work-

ing classes, and people of color. This argument has special salience for the privatized US carceral system, which now has direct financial incentive to jail larger numbers of people. Hallett, *Private Prisons in America*. Yet, regardless of whether the carceral system in question is privatized, the imagined privileged subjects of the hate crime law demands are middle-class gays and lesbians who are trusting of the criminal system and who imagine themselves as deserving subjects of protection and not subjects of persecution.

102. The initial form of this chant was "Polis, simit sat, onurlu yaşa" (Police, sell *simit* [a Turkish pastry sold by street vendors], live honorably) and was formatted by LGBT activists.

103. Ahmed, *Cultural Politics of Emotion*, 57.

Chapter Four. Critique and Commons

Portions of this chapter previously appeared in "Who Speaks the Language of Queer Politics? Western Knowledge, Politico-cultural Capital and Belonging among Urban Queers in Turkey," *Sexualities* 19, no. 3 (2016): 369–87, and Cenk Özbay and Evren Savcı, "Queering Commons in Turkey," GLQ: *A Journal of Gay and Lesbian Studies* 24, no. 4 (2018): 516–21.

1. #*direnayol* (2016), directed by Rüzgâr Buşki.

2. Millnet-Larsen and Butt, "Introduction."

3. Federici, *Re-Enchanting the World*, 2; Curcio and Özselçuk, "On the Common, Universality, and Communism"; Özbay and Savcı, "Queering Commons in Turkey."

4. Özbay and Savcı, "Queering Commons in Turkey." In offering Gezi as a "queer commons," I am also inspired by José Muñoz's reflections on queer utopia as a "challenge to approach queer critique from a renewed and newly animated sense of the social." Muñoz, *Cruising Utopia*, 18. Directly countering the anti-social turn in queer theory that understands all of the social and the political as normative, Muñoz's work recuperated hope and utopia as sites of queer possibility instead of queer critique (and at times dismissal). While his emphasis is on the aesthetic in conceptualizing queer as utopia, and while I recognize the significance of the aesthetic to the Gezi protests, I underline the importance of developing a *collective vernacular* that was part of the Gezi spirit. The particular humor of the various slogans on banners, signs, and stencils did not go unnoticed by other scholars, and what I would like to add to those analyses is the important juxtaposition between humorous creativity and jaded critique—not only in terms of their tenor but also in terms of which subjects felt encouraged and entitled to participate. Dağtaş, "Down with Some Things!"; Gürel, "Bilingual Humor, Authentic Aunties, and the Transnational Vernacular at Gezi Park."

5. For instance, despite many scholars in the field subscribing to critiques of the modernist, linear, and progressive understanding of history, and despite the field's epistemic commitment to questioning normative categories of thought, both the scholarship as well as activism that focuses on gender and sexual politics often operate with a modernist historicity that is predicated on self-correction regarding the conceptual apparatus and the practices of naming—the change from *transgendered*

to *transgender*, from *trans* to *trans**, and the expansion of additional changes and abbreviations of LG(BT)(Q)(I)(A) are cases in point.

6. Ghassan Moussawi similarly reports that the two Lebanese LGBT organizations he researched, Helem and Meem, had deeply intersectional politics, including anti-war activism and participation in the BDS movement. Moussawi, "(Un)Critically Queer Organizing."

7. Gürel, *Limits of Westernization.*

8. I speak to some of these concerns in Savcı, "The LGBTI+ Movement."

9. Duggan, *Twilight of Equality?*; Eng, *Feeling of Kinship*; Puar, *Terrorist Assemblages*; Spade, *Normal Life*; Ward, *Respectably Queer.*

10. On single-issue identity movements see Ferguson, *One-Dimensional Queer*, and Hong, *Death beyond Disavowal.* On diversity culture see Ward, *Respectably Queer.*

11. I have changed the club's name in order to respect the privacy that its owners and managers tried to maintain for their clientele. During the period I worked at the bar, the management took great care in helping their clients remain anonymous by not allowing any cameras or video recording inside the bar. The bartender told me that while the club had an active Facebook page that they used to advertise the various events and parties, they also had a separate phone list for clients who did not want to have their Facebook profiles affiliated with the club but did want to receive text messages about the programming. In addition, the club was located on the fourth and fifth floors of a building that featured a different bar on each floor. Because this building was in an entertainment district full of similar establishments, there was really no way to know where Kadınca club was unless one had access to its address (or unless one knew to look out for the double-Venus sign at the entrance of the building).

12. Some of the women used *baç* (read: botch), and others said *buç* (read: butch), both seemingly referring to the English word *butch*. I prefer *baç* here because it was more commonly used among my interlocutors.

13. The structure of the Turkish education system, where the majority of the universities are public and the tuition and fees are affordable, enables some citizens to attain this particular form of cultural capital even if they are from working-class backgrounds. This access is not equally distributed, though, as oftentimes the (mostly public) high school system does not adequately prepare students for the central university placement exam. Those with financial means seek private tutors or prep schools (*dershane*) in order to attain a better score on the test. Nonetheless, in cases when students do well on the test and are placed in institutions of higher education, they gain access to learning English and computer skills among other things. I still contend that many of the dispositions Bourdieu discusses in his work cannot be simply learned in college; therefore, my argument pertains to only particular knowledges and skills that have value in LGBT activist circles. See Bourdieu, *Distinction.*

14. I admittedly take a particular approach to class, which cannot be reduced to simply annual income or employment but is very much informed by education as well as dispositions, some of which come in the form of taste and others in the form of manners, as discussed by Bourdieu. Bourdieu, *Distinction.* The Turkish Republic's foundational narrative is laden with civilizational discourses, as the goal of the

country as set by Mustafa Kemal Atatürk was to attain parity with other contemporary civilizations. While the national ideology included a rhetoric of class equality, infamously expressed in Atatürk's phrase "the peasants are the masters of the people," feminist scholars have challenged this by pointing out the pragmatic nature of such a proclamation, given the need to mobilize all bodies toward the building of the nation. They have also theorized the entry of the middle-class women into the workforce in high numbers as stemming from class anxieties. Öncü, "Turkish Women in the Professions." Further, the civilizational national rhetoric worked through notions of appropriate culture (understood as Westernized ways of dressing, speaking, and acting), which ultimately combined the racial othering of especially Kurdish citizens from rural areas with classed notions of being acculturated versus being attached to backward traditions. Islam also played a significant role in this national narrative (which I discuss in greater detail in chapter 1). In this chapter, the reason I categorize retail work as working class is because, differently from a career, retail work requires no college education or special training.

15. Bourdieu, *Distinction*.

16. I am by no means suggesting that subjects assigned female at birth who identify as men was new, but that the category of trans man was. The first trans men's association, Voltrans, was founded in the summer of 2008 by three trans men who identified as activists, one of whom was Eren.

17. Here it is worth underlining that given the Lambda activists' embrace of trans men, their critique of Kadınca clients was not based on the baç/feminen dynamic (presumably) reproducing heteronormativity or on masculinity performed by people assigned female at birth. It was a particular form of masculinity that they viewed as unsophisticated and as lacking a proper language to defend it that contributed to its lack of acceptance by the activists. This distinguishes my case from two sets of scholarship that have talked about dynamics in the US past that may seem similar at first sight. First, this case differs from the feminist backlash against butch-femme couples in the United States in the 1970s, as discussed by Halberstam among others. We also see a different articulation of Halberstam's analysis of the "butch-FTM border wars" here: Borders drawn in this case are not those between more or less fluidity, more or less realness, or more or less conformity, but those between having access to particular articulations of one's gendered being in the world. Halberstam, *Female Masculinity*.

This story also differs from the lesbian bar scene in Buffalo, New York, from the 1940s to 1960s discussed in Kennedy and Davis's classic *Boots of Leather, Slippers of Gold*, which details the evolving class divisions among queer women over time and emphasizes the role of bar socializing in the emergence of lesbian as a political identity. While there are similarities between this story and mine, the bar scene Kennedy and Davis detail through oral histories does not take place simultaneously with political LGBT formations. Therefore, unlike Kadınca women, the "rough and tough lesbians" who socialized in Buffalo bars did not openly reject a political existence represented by LGBT activists. Further, Lambdaistanbul activists are unlike the "elite lesbians" that Kennedy and Davis discuss in that their gender presentation, which is neither butch nor femme, is not due to an investment on their part to remain invisible as queers. In fact, as LGBT activists, many of these women believed in and practiced visibility politics, unlike the "elite lesbians" of Buffalo who were concerned with looking respectable in order to hold onto their respectable jobs. The concerns with respectable behavior in this case are not about queer visibility, but a particular middle-class disposition.

18. Savcı, "Who Speaks the Language of Queer Politics?"

19. It is my conviction that while this does not constitute the entire story, part of what hides the exclusions that can be produced by being political is an assumed politics/market (political/commercial) dichotomy built into most scholarship on neo-liberalism. For limitations of this dichotomy that were illustrated by the Kadınca club example, see Savcı, "On Putting Down and Destroying."

20. Kadınca management and clients did not distinguish between Lambdaistan-bul and Voltrans members or, for that matter, members of any other group that criticized them, as they all were placed under the rubric of being political queers.

21. Savcı, "Who Speaks the Language of Queer Politics?"

22. There are no gender pronouns in Turkish. The one pronoun "o" is used for all genders and things. My choice of *they* for Heval is due to them feeling like neither manhood nor womanhood properly captures their gender.

23. Felski, *Limits of Critique*; Latour, "Why Has Critique Run Out of Steam?"

24. Sedgwick, "Paranoid Reading and Reparative Reading"; Felski, *Limits of Critique*, 7.

25. Felski, *Limits of Critique*, 2.

26. Latour, "Why Has Critique Run Out of Steam?"

27. I am employing *Left* and *Right* as imperfect approximations of political positions, fully aware that neither of these terms properly captures the various subjects I am imagining to broadly fall under each.

28. This is of course also true for those who consider themselves not objects, but subjects, of progressive critique. As Latour notes, this is what makes it possible for anyone to be "at once and without sensing a contradiction (1) an antifetishist for everything you don't believe in" and "(2) an unrepentant positivist for all the sciences you believe in." Latour, "Why Has Critique Run Out of Steam?," 241.

29. Ahmed, *The Promise of Happiness*.

30. Sedgwick, "Paranoid Reading and Reparative Reading," 7.

31. Latour, "Why Has Critique Run Out of Steam?," 246.

32. Sedgwick, "Paranoid Reading and Reparative Reading."

33. Such large-scale celebrations of British or French imperial pasts, for instance, are unthinkable today. The Ottoman exceptionalism in question is most likely enabled due to the ongoing myth of the Ottoman tolerance of ethnic minorities, the empire's status as a past Muslim empire in a world of rising Islamophobia, and the fact that Turkey does not constitute a contemporary locus of economic or military power. Mahmood, *Religious Difference in a Secular Age*. While Saba Mahmood's discussion of how secularism structures contemporary understandings of religion, especially its relationship to gender and the family, is full of important insights, I have found her treatment of the Ottoman Empire as if it had been a Muslim empire

all along, and her romanticizing of the multiethnic and multireligious coexistence within it striking.

34. See "Erdoğan: Kürtaj bir cinayettir" [Erdoğan: Abortion is murder], *Milliyet*, May 26, 2012, http://www.milliyet.com.tr/erdogan-kurtaj-bir-cinayettir/siyaset /siyasetdetay/26.05.2012/1545254/default.htm.

35. Indeed, EU members seem happy to let Turkey host the refugees and have committed to paying Turkey €3 billion to support its accommodation of Syrians and help deal with European migration as a surrogate humanitarian host. See Leo Cendrowicz, "Refugee Crisis: EU Pays €3bn to Turkey in Exchange for Help on Dealing with European Migration," *Independent*, November 29, 2015, http://www.independent.co.uk /news/world/europe/refugee-crisis-eu-pays-3bn-to-turkey-in-exchange-for-help-on -dealing-with-european-migration-a6753861.html.

36. The 3.5 million number was reported in May 2019 by the Turkish Refugee Association (https://multeciler.org.tr/turkiyedeki-suriyeli-sayisi). Erdoğan's popularity as a supposed figure who stands up against human rights violations by Western countries dates back to his comments to then Israeli president Shimon Peres at the 2009 meetings in Davos that "when it comes to killing, you know well how to kill." Katrin Bennhold, "Leaders of Turkey and Israel Clash at Davos Panel," *New York Times*, January 29, 2009, https://www.nytimes.com/2009/01/30/world/europe/30clash .html.

37. Calling out so-called developed countries for not acting in accordance with civilizational standards not only hides the fact that the AKP itself employs its own pragmatic standards in order to serve its own interests and own people, but it also homogenizes the West by overlooking deep histories of racist, classist, gendered, sexual, and ableist exclusions *within* Europe and/or the United States, where citizens and residents continue to have differential access to resources and rights. For an example of Erdoğan presented as the voice of the oppressed, see "Malcolm X's Daughter Says Erdoğan 'Represents' Legacy of Her Father," *Daily Sabah*, September 25, 2018, https:// www.dailysabah.com/politics/2018/09/25/malcolm-xs-daughter-says-erdogan -represents-legacy-of-her-father.

38. Ahıska, "Occidentalism." Official Turkish history published in ministry of education–produced primary and secondary school textbooks also presents the fall of the Ottoman Empire, the war of independence, and the subsequent forming of the Turkish Republic in terms of foreign envy of Ottoman glory, Western attempts to colonize the remainders of the empire following World War I, and the successful battling of colonizers who had had their eyes on precious Turkish land.

39. See "Erdoğan: O banka zaten batmış … " [Erdoğan: That bank is already underwater], *Hürriyet*, September 18, 2014, http://www.hurriyet.com.tr/ekonomi /27227996.asp.

40. Menderes's term had indeed ended with a military coup as well as his execution. Özal, however, had come to power following the 1980 military coup, and as mentioned in introduction, while he had run and won against the junta's candidate in the 1983 general elections, he had also been appointed as deputy prime minister during the postcoup military regime. His early death as president has been the subject

of conspiracy theories claiming he was poisoned, which resulted in an investigation almost two decades after his passing. In Erdoğan's narrative, these important distinctions disappear, and the right-wing history of economic liberalization becomes the distinguishing feature of successful governments as well as reasons why they have been targets of international plots backed by the Turkish military.

41. "Erdoğan: O banka zaten batmış . . . ."

42. Keyder et al., *New Poverty and the Changing Welfare Regime of Turkey*; Kiliç, "Gender Dimension of Social Policy Reform in Turkey"; Potuoğlu-Cook, "Hope with Qualms"; Yoltar, "When the Poor Need Healthcare."

43. Candan and Kolluoğlu, "Emerging Spaces of Neoliberalism"; Erman, *Mış Gibi Site.*

44. In the first three years following the AKP coming to power, the nation saw growth rates of 5.6 percent, 9.6 percent, and 9 percent, respectively. See the IMF World Economic Outlook Database, "5. Report for Selected Countries and Subjects," April 2018, https://www.imf.org/external/pubs/ft/weo/2018/01/weodata/weorept .aspx?sy=1980&ey=2023&scsm=1&ssd=1&sort=country&ds=.&br=1&c=186&s =NGDP_RPCH%2CPPPGDP%2CPPPPC%2CPCPIPCH%2CLUR%2CGGX WDG_NGDP&grp=0&a=&pr.x=17&pr.y=7.

45. Kus, "Financial Citizenship and the Hidden Crisis of the Working Class in the 'New Turkey.'"

46. Çavuşoğlu, "İslâmcı Neo-Liberalizmde İnşaat Fetişi ve Mülkiyet Üzerindeki Simgesel Hâle." For various projects that connect the government to big business see the Networks of Dispossession (Mülksüzleştirme Ağları) maps produced after the Gezi Park protests at http://mulksuzlestirme.org.

47. These included the hydroelectric dam projects on various rivers in the country; the third bridge project over the Bosporus, which has led to significant deforestation in the north of Istanbul; the dam project over the river Tigris, which will flood and destroy the twelve-thousand-year-old historic town of Hasankeyf; and what then prime minister Erdoğan referred to as his *çılgın proje* (wild project) prior to the 2011 elections: digging an additional canal through the European part of Istanbul to provide an alternative connection between the Black Sea and the Marmara Sea to reroute tanker traffic. Çavuşoğlu, "İslâmcı Neo-Liberalizmde İnşaat Fetişi ve Mülkiyet Üzerindeki Simgesel Hâle"; Sarah El-Kazaz, "It Is about the Park: A Struggle for Turkey's Cities," *Jadaliyya*, June 16, 2013, http://www.jadaliyya.com/Details/28789/It-Is -About-the-Park-A-Struggle-for-Turkey's-Cities. Despite much controversy and protests in some of these cases, by September 2018 the government had either completed or passed legislation to permit many of these projects, portrayed by the president as signs of the grandeur of the Turkish nation.

48. See "TEKEL işçileri açlık grevine başladı" [TEKEL workers go on hunger strike], *Hürriyet*, January 19, 2010, http://www.hurriyet.com.tr/gundem/tekel -iscileri-aclik-grevine-basladi-13523941.

49. Yet, neither the government's international humanitarian discourse nor its maltreatment of laborers was curbed. In 2012, during a Turkish Airlines work stop-

page, parliament outlawed strikes for airline workers, and 305 employees were sacked for protesting this decision. While the strike ban was annulled in November 2012, the workers who were let go were not rehired. See Aziz Çelik, "Bir grevfobi öyküsü: Bütün yönleriyle THY grevi" [A story of strike phobia: THY [Turkish Airlines] strike in all its aspects], *T24*, July 9, 2013, http://t24.com.tr/yazarlar/bilinmeyen/bir -grevfobi-oykusu-butun-yonleriyle-thy-grevi,7030.

50. See "Başbakan: Ölüm Madencinin kaderi (kapitalizmin Kurbanları)" [Prime minister: Death miners' fate: Victims of capitalism], YouTube video, posted May 19, 2010, https://www.youtube.com/watch?v=-t7z6dyKwtE.

51. See "Erdoğan: Senin kadere imanın yoksa . . ." [Erdoğan: If you don't have faith in fate . . .], *NTV*, May 21, 2010, http://www.ntv.com.tr/turkiye/erdogan -senin-kadere-imanin-yoksa,93JK2SbdQk6SS7a27qsImQ.

52. See "Erdoğan: İş işten geçmeden en az üç çocuk" [Erdoğan: At least three children before it is too late], *NTV*, October 10, 2009, https://www.ntv.com.tr/turkiye /erdogan-is-isten-gecmeden-en-az-3-cocuk,ZEQhCeWHVkSo6lEDhd72Ng.

53. Akkaya, "AKP versus Women"; Potuoğlu-Cook, "Hope with Qualms"; Yücesan-Özdemir, "Social Policy Regime in the AKP Years."

54. Such neoliberal states of exception are not unique to Turkey of course. The neoliberal refusal of state intervention in the market mostly applies to regulation but not so much to bailouts. The United States experienced a significant moment of bailouts during the financial crisis of 2007–2008, the most important being the proposal of the Emergency Economic Stabilization Act in October 2008. Even though the most bank-friendly version of the act was ultimately voted down at the House of Representatives, the very fact that the government understands itself as in charge of setting the economy back on its track is the logic of the neoliberal state of exception.

55. For an in-faith feminist critique of Islamic interpretations of women being "entrusted" to men or of men and women's complementarity (an argument often used by Erdoğan and his daughter Sümeyye Erdoğan) see Wadud, *Inside the Gender Jihad*.

56. See "Erdoğan: Kadın-erkek eşitliği fıtrata ters" [Erdoğan: Equality between women and men is contrary to fıtrat], *BBC News*, November 24, 2014, https://www .bbc.com/turkce/haberler/2014/11/141124_kadininfitrati_erdogan.

57. Korkman, "Blessing Neoliberalism"; Potuoğlu-Cook, "Hope with Qualms"; Savcı, "Turkey's AKP and Public Morality." Despite these talks about a ban, abortion remained legal in Turkey up to ten weeks after conception, as it has been since 1983. But the president's denunciations have resulted in unofficial social controls: Numerous hospitals were reported to have turned away patients seeking abortions, variously claiming the procedure to be illegal or allowable only with spousal consent. See "Yasa yok ama kürtaj yasak" [No law but abortion is forbidden], *Milliyet*, February 19, 2014, http://www.milliyet.com.tr/yasa-yok-ama-kurtaj-yasak/gundem/detay/1838845 /default.htm. In other words, Erdoğan's moral discourses either turned into legislation, or they had such power that they left the impression of legal change and were followed as if they had actually been enacted. Another example for this are accounts that surfaced in the news regarding the Aile Sağlığı Merkezleri (Family Health Cen-

ters), which operate under the Ministry of Health and have been standardized under the AKP regime's health care bill. News covered women's accounts of phone calls their husbands and fathers had received from these centers informing them of their visits for pregnancy tests—in case, it seemed, they were pregnant unbeknownst to their male kin and might seek to terminate the pregnancy without their consent. See Ayşe Arman, "Yeter artık, kesin kadınlara düşmanlık etmeyi!" [Enough with your hostility towards women!], *Hürriyet*, May 28, 2013, http://www.hurriyet.com.tr/yeter-artik -kesin-kadinlara-dusmanlik-etmeyi-23379489. For more on the larger neoliberal impacts on family health centers see Ağartan, "Gender and Health Sector Reform." C-sections were targeted in the same breath during this speech, and elective C-sections ultimately became punishable by law. See Constanze Letsch, "Turkish Doctors Face Fines for Elective Caesareans, *Guardian*, July 13, 2012, https://www .theguardian.com/world/2012/jul/13/turkish-doctors-fines-elective-caesareans ?newsfeed=true.

58. See "Erdoğan: Alkol yerine meyve yiyin" [Erdoğan: Eat fruit instead of alcohol], *NTV*, July 19, 2010, http://www.ntv.com.tr/turkiye/erdogan-alkol-yerine -meyve-yiyin,QyzXgIWVQEKOORA49Etu6Q.

59. See "Erdoğan: Gezi olaylarındaki gibi, gençlerimize bedava alkol dağıtmaktan geri durmuyorlar!" [Erdoğan: As in the Gezi events, they do not hesitate to distribute free alcohol to our young people], *T24*, March 3, 2017, http://t24.com.tr/haber /erdogan-gezi-olaylarindaki-gibi-genclerimize-bedava-alkol-dagitmaktan-geri -durmuyorlar,391914.

60. Grewal, *Saving the Security State*.

61. See Tülay Çetingüleç, "Turkey's Family Ministry Shames Singles in New Ad," *Al-Monitor*, September 19, 2014, http://www.al-monitor.com/pulse/originals /2014/09/turkey-family-ministry-battle-aloneness.html.

62. Çelik, "Bir grevfobi öyküsü."

63. I was in Istanbul the night of the July 15, 2016, coup attempt and heard the announcements made from the mosques firsthand.

64. These new terrorism-related charges were brought forth against citizens for being allegedly affiliated with what was termed the Fethullah Gülen Terrorist Organization (FETÖ). Much ink has been spilled on the reasons and implications of the fallout between Erdoğan and Gülen, two former friends and allies. Yet for my purposes the significance of the event resides in the addition of yet another category of terrorism under which a variety of subjects were detained, laid off, and tried. A number of those tried and sentenced for being allegedly FETÖ members have in the past openly criticized the Gülen organization as well as the AKP government's relationship with it.

65. GIT (Group Intellectuel du Travail) was founded first in France and then in North America by academics from Turkey as well as some international academics who study Turkey or the Ottoman Empire precisely because of the lack of international coverage of these unfolding events and to publicize what was happening in Turkey to the international community by writing op-eds and translating Turkish news accounts. GIT-North America's blog can be found at http://gitamerica.blogspot .co.uk.

66. According to a report by the Organization for Security and Co-operation in Europe (OSCE), Turkey was the world's leading jailer of journalists in 2011. Ellis, "OSCE Report Finds Turkey Is Holding 57 Journalists in Prison."

67. Özbay and Savcı, "Queering Commons in Turkey."

68. Hikmet Kocamaner, "Delinquent Kids, Revolutionary Mothers, Uncle Governor, and Erdogan the Patriarch (Part One)," *Jadaliyya*, August 5, 2013, http://www.jadaliyya.com/Details/29244/Delinquent-Kids,-Revolutionary-Mothers,-Uncle-Governor,-and-Erdogan-the-Patriarch-Part-One; Potuoğlu-Cook, "Hope with Qualms."

69. Zengin, "What Is Queer about Gezi?"

70. Savcı, "Why Every City Needs a Center Square"; Bieberstein and Tataryan, "The What of Occupation."

71. Ayfer Karakaya-Stump analyzes the significance of Alevis to Gezi, including government media claims that Gezi was an Alevi-led revolt and the fact that seven of the eight youth killed during the protests were Alevi. Ayfer Karakaya-Stumpf, "Alevizing Gezi," *Jadaliyya*, March 26, 2014, http://www.jadaliyya.com/Details/30456/Alevizing-Gezi.

72. Potuoğlu-Cook, "Hope with Qualms."

73. Associated Press in Ankara, "Recep Tayyip Erdoğan Dismisses Turkey Protestors as Vandals," *Guardian*, June 9, 2013, https://www.theguardian.com/world/2013/jun/09/recep-tayyip-erdogan-turkey-protesters-looters-vandals.

74. "I Did Not See Anyone Consume Alcohol in Mosque during Gezi Protests, Muezzin Says," *Hürriyet*, June 27, 2013, https://www.hurriyetdailynews.com/i-did-not-see-anyone-consume-alcohol-in-mosque-during-gezi-protests-muezzin-says-49573.

75. Hong, *Death beyond Disavowal*.

76. Kandiyoti, "No Laughing Matter."

77. Arslanalp, "Yerinde Duramamak."

78. It is interesting and telling that Erdoğan linked "loot" with resistance symbolically, since no looting took place during Gezi Park protests.

79. "'Gezi'nin Ramazana Yansıması: Yeryüzü İftarları" [The reflection of Gezi on Ramadan: Iftars of the Earth], *BBC Türkçe*, July 9, 2013, https://www.bbc.com/turkce/haberler/2013/07/130709_yeryuzu_iftari.

80. #direnayol.

81. Arslanalp, "Yerinde Duramamak."

82. Kurtulus Korkman and Açıksöz, "Erdogan's Masculinity and the Language of the Gezi Resistance"; Zengin, "What Is Queer about Gezi?"

83. #direnayol.

84. #direnayol.

85. See Berkant Çağlar, "LGBT'lerin Gözünden Gezi Direnişi" [Gezi resistance through the eyes of LGBTs], *Bianet*, June 26, 2013, https://bianet.org/bianet/lgbti/147965-lgbt-lerin-gozunden-gezi-direnisi.

86. Tüfekçi, *Twitter and Teargas*. This popular slogan also lent itself to the title of Buşki's documentary *#direnayol*.

87. Hong, *Death beyond Disavowal*.

88. Gürel, "Bilingual Humor, Authentic Aunties, and the Transnational Vernacular at Gezi Park"; Dağtaş, "Down with Some Things!"

89. Arslanalp, "Yerinde Duramamak," 56.

90. Tuğal, "'Resistance Everywhere.'"

91. Potuoğlu-Cook, "Hope with Qualms"; Parla, "Protest and the Limits of the Body."

92. "AKP'li vekil 'Adalet Yürüyüşü'nün sırrını 'çözdü': Gezi olaylarını hortlatmak" [AKP deputy has "solved" the mystery of the "March for Justice": To resurrect the Gezi events], *Diken*, July 2, 2017, http://www.diken.com.tr/akpli-vekil-adalet -yuruyusunun-sirrini-cozdu-gezi-olaylarini-hortlatmak/; "İkinci Gezi'ye izin vermeyiz" [We will not allow a second Gezi], *Aksam*, October 23, 2013, https://www .aksam.com.tr/siyaset/ikinci-geziye-izin-vermeyiz/haber-254912?fbclid=IwAR126LYf OidIt8gizpfFrXdpjpbbqIu-TZeUazKnhDvAe7wgS5RoMPnpo6s.

Conclusion

1. I do not mean to undermine the importance of representation, especially its contribution to the very historical context in which religion is experienced by pious and secular subjects alike. Yet we need to remember that it is not easy to stand outside of representational paradigms as scholars who produce knowledge and that critiques of representation can themselves become representations of that very thing. Saba Mahmood's *Politics of Piety* is a case in point: As she insightfully stated that representation is only one issue among many in the ethical relationship of the body to the self and others and that it does not by any means "determine the form this relationship takes," she nevertheless produced a seemingly unified/homogenous model of female piety in Islam and the model of the relationship of the body to the self. Mahmood, *Politics of Piety*, 159.

2. Clifford, *Predicament of Culture*, 272. Also see Ahıska, "Occidentalism."

3. Butler, "Against Proper Objects."

4. Eng, Halberstam, and Muñoz, "Introduction."

5. Amin, "Haunted by the 1990s."

6. Edelman, *No Future*; Eng, *Racial Castration*.

7. Al-Kassim, "Psychoanalysis and the Postcolonial Genealogy of Queer Theory"; Liu, *Queer Marxism in Two Chinas*; Najmabadi, "Beyond the Americas"; Najmabadi, "Types, Acts, or What?"

8. Stoler, *Race and the Education of Desire*.

9. Rosenberg and Villarejo, eds., "Queer Studies and the Crises of Capitalism."

10. Gayatri Chakravorty Spivak has infamously pointed out that untethering analyses that center desire from those that center interest is made possible precisely by overlooking the question of the colonies. See Spivak, "Can the Subaltern Speak?" Also see Kaplan and Grewal, "Transnational Feminist Cultural Studies," for a discussion of how masculinist Marxist texts often ignore Spivak's contributions.

11. D'Emilio, "Capitalism and Gay Identity."

12. Altman, "Global Gaze/Global Gays." Dennis Altman himself revised his position over time. See Altman, "Rupture or Continuity?"

13. Jackson, "Capitalism and Global Queering," 361.

14. Liu, *Queer Marxism in Two Chinas*.

15. Liu, *Queer Marxism in Two Chinas*, 23.

16. Liu, *Queer Marxism in Two Chinas*, 24.

17. Dirlik, "Thinking Modernity Historically."

18. As underlined by Dirlik, and as mentioned in the introduction, Islamic civilization has been proposed as a true alternative to Western civilization by Ahmet Davutoğlu, one of the masterminds behind the AKP, who has served in various higher ranking positions, including as chief advisor to Erdoğan (then prime minister), minister of foreign affairs, and prime minister of the party. See Davutoğlu, *Alternative Paradigms*. In 2007 AKP's neoliberal branding project Alliance of Civilizations, a turning inside out of the Clash of Civilizations thesis, rested on the same neat distinctions between East and West that reify an ahistorical culture of each civilization. Iğsız, "Brand Turkey and the Gezi Protests." Such a reification of difference makes it easy to package and sell nations worldwide via neoliberal branding projects. For a similar neoliberal branding project by India, see Puri, "Sculpting the Saffron Body."

19. Notable exceptions to this are Özbay, *Queering Sexualities in Turkey*; Ozyegin, *New Desires, New Selves*.

20. In fact, Saba Mahmood's *Politics of Piety*, which has been welcomed as a critical intervention in feminist studies, is predicated on a similar radical alterity of Islam and the relationship between norms and the making of the Islamic pious self. As various critics have pointed out, Mahmood leaves out the political economic context of the Egyptian mosque movement she studies, which includes funding flows from Saudi Arabia for Salafist publications and infrastructure. Bangstad, "Saba Mahmood and Anthropological Feminism after Virtue." I read Talal Asad's work as also arguing for a radical difference of Islam as tradition that exceeds the category of religion. For the significance of the Western/non-Western binary in Asad's work and the alterity of Islam see Bangstad, "Contesting Secularism/s."

21. Blackwood, "Sexuality and Gender in Certain Native American Tribes"; Gay, "'Mummies and Babies' and Friends and Lovers in Lesotho"; Nanda, *Neither Man nor Woman*; Oboler, "Is the Female Husband a Man?"; Roscoe, *Zuni Man–Woman*; Wikan, *Behind the Veil in Arabia*.

22. For some examples of work that has purposefully tried to open the discussion to other aspects of modernity, such as the nation-state or neoliberalism, see Boellstorff, *Gay Archipelago;* Rofel, *Desiring China*.

23. Tom Boellstorff's careful analysis of the emergence of *gay* and *lesbi* subjectivities in the context of the Indonesian nation-state, while not directly stating it, implies that *gay* and *lesbi* subjectivities (experienced differently from US gay and lesbian subjectivity) are no less authentic to Indonesia than is the nation-state form. Boellstorff, *Gay Archipelago*. It is unfortunate that this creative account does not engage with Islam at all, except in a separate article (not included in the book) in which Boellstorff

positions Islam and *gay* identity in Indonesia as an inhabitable incommensurability. Boellstorff, "Between Religion and Desire."

24. Gal, "Migration, Minorities, and Multilingualism: Language Ideologies in Europe"; Gramling, *The Invention of Monolingualism*; Makoni and Pennycook, *Disinventing and Reconstituting Languages*; Mezzadra and Sakai, introduction; Rafael, *Motherless Tongues*; Sakai, *Translation and Subjectivity*.

25. Asad, *Genealogies of Religion*, 171–99.

26. Asad, *Genealogies of Religion*, 179, 199.

27. While Massad has kept his discussion limited to the Arab world and therefore in theory has exempted Turkey from the effects of the gay international, his work has been very influential in framing the workings of queer activism. Massad, *Desiring Arabs*.

28. Massad, *Desiring Arabs*, 80.

29. Massad, *Desiring Arabs*, 80.

30. Massad, *Desiring Arabs*, 80. This is particularly striking because elsewhere Massad is attuned to historical shifts that language undergoes. A case in point is his discussion of the changed meaning of *turath* from financial inheritance and legacy to heritage in the nineteenth century, which as a result simplified and consolidated culture understood as civilization.

31. I am using *citational* here to mean two things: First, Erdoğan continually cites the Menderes and Özal governments as his predecessors and puts the AKP regime in a genealogy with Menderes and Özal regimes (as recounted in chapter 4). Therefore, a relationship is intentionally established between the AKP and this history. Second, I use the term to mean that the AKP regime is a product of the history of the Turkish-Islamic synthesis—it is, at once, made possible by it and yet is another iteration of it. This second use I owe to Judith Butler's use of *citationality*; Butler borrows the term from J. L. Austin. Butler, *Gender Trouble*; Austin, *How to Do Things with Words*.

32. Mezzadra and Sakai, introduction, 11.

Bibliography

Abu-Lughod, Lila. "Do Muslim Women Really Need Saving? Anthropological Reflections on Cultural Relativism and Its Others." *American Anthropologist* 104, no. 3 (2002): 783–90. https://doi.org/10.1525/aa.2002.104.3.783.

Abu-Lughod, Lila, ed. *Remaking Women: Feminism and Modernity in the Middle East*. Princeton, NJ: Princeton University Press, 1998.

Abu-Lughod, Lila. "Seductions of the 'Honor Crime.'" *differences* 22, no. 1 (2011): 17–63. https://doi.org/10.1215/10407391-1218238.

Acar, Feride, and Gülbanu Altunok. "The 'Politics of Intimate' at the Intersection of Neo-liberalism and Neo-conservatism in Contemporary Turkey." *Women's Studies International Forum* 41, pt. 1 (2013): 14–23. https://doi.org/10.1016/j.wsif.2012.10.001.

Acar, Feride, and Gülbanu Altunok. "Understanding Gender Equality Demands in Turkey: Foundations and Boundaries of Women's Movements." In *Gender and Society in Turkey: The Impact of Neoliberal Policies, Political Islam and EU Accession*, edited by Saniye Dedeoglu and Adem Yavuz Elveren, 31–46. London: I. B. Tauris, 2012.

Ağartan, Tuba. "Gender and Health Sector Reform: Policies, Actions and Effects." In *Gender and Society in Turkey: The Impact of Neoliberal Policies, Political Islam and EU Accession*, edited by Saniye Dedeoğlu and Adem Yavuz Elveren, 155–72. London: I. B. Tauris, 2012.

Ahıska, Meltem. "Occidentalism: The Historical Fantasy of the Modern." *South Atlantic Quarterly* 102, nos. 2–3 (2003): 351–79. https://doi.org/10.1215/00382876-102-2-3-351.

Ahmad, Feroz. *The Making of Modern Turkey*. New York: Routledge, 1993.

Ahmed, Sara. *The Cultural Politics of Emotion*. 10th anniv. ed. New York: Routledge, 2013. https://doi.org/10.4324/9780203700372.

Ahmed, Sara. "Happy Objects." In *The Affect Theory Reader*, edited by Melissa Gregg and Gregory J. Seigworth, 1–30. Durham, NC: Duke University Press, 2010. https://doi.org/10.1215/9780822393047-001.

Ahmed, Sara. *The Promise of Happiness*. Durham, NC: Duke University Press, 2010.

Akın, Erkan, and Ömer Karasapan. "The 'Turkish-Islamic' Synthesis." *Middle East Report* 153 (July/August 1988): 18. https://merip.org/1988/07/the-turkish-islamic-synthesis.

Akkaya, Gülfer. "AKP versus Women." *Perspectives: Political Analysis and Commentary from Turkey*, no. 4 (2013): 52–56.

Alexander, M. Jacqui, and Chandra Talpade Mohanty, eds. *Feminist Genealogies, Colonial Legacies, Democratic Futures*. New York: Routledge, 1997.

Alkan, Ayten. *Cins Cins Mekan* [Queer space/place]. Istanbul: Varlık Yayınları, 2009.

Al-Kassim, Dina. "Psychoanalysis and the Postcolonial Genealogy of Queer Theory." *International Journal of Middle East Studies* 45, no. 2 (2013): 343–46.

Altınay, Ayşe Gül. *The Myth of the Military Nation: Militarism, Gender, and Education in Turkey*. New York: Palgrave Macmillan, 2004.

Altinay, Rustem Ertug. "Reconstructing the Transgendered Self as a Muslim, Nationalist, Upper-Class Woman: The Case of Bulent Ersoy." *WSQ: Women's Studies Quarterly* 36, nos. 3–4 (2008): 210–29. https://doi.org/10.1353/wsq.0.0090.

Altınordu, Ateş. "The Politicization of Religion: Political Catholicism and Political Islam in Comparative Perspective." *Politics and Society* 38, no. 4 (2010): 517–51. https://doi.org/10.1177/0032329210381238.

Altman, Dennis. "Global Gaze/Global Gays." *GLQ: A Journal of Gay and Lesbian Studies* 3, no. 4 (1997): 417–36.

Altman, Dennis. "Rupture or Continuity? The Internationalization of Gay Identities." *Social Text*, no. 48 (1996): 77–94.

Amar, Paul. *The Security Archipelago: Human-Security States, Sexuality Politics, and the End of Neoliberalism*. Durham, NC: Duke University Press, 2013.

Amar, Paul. "Turning the Gendered Politics of the Security State Inside Out? Charging the Police with Sexual Harassment in Egypt." *International Feminist Journal of Politics* 13, no. 3 (2011): 299–328. https://doi.org/10.1080/14616742.2011.587364.

Amar, Paul, and Omnia El Shakry. "Introduction: Curiosities of Middle East Studies in Queer Times." *International Journal of Middle East Studies*, no. 45 (2013): 331–35. https://doi.org/10.1017/S0020743813000068.

Amin, Kadji. "Haunted by the 1990s: Queer Theory's Affective Histories." *WSQ: Women's Studies Quarterly* 44, nos. 3–4 (2016): 173–89. https://doi.org/10.1353/wsq.2016.0041.

Arat, Yeşim. *Rethinking Islam and Liberal Democracy: Islamist Women in Turkish Politics*. Albany: State University of New York Press, 2005.

Arat, Yeşim. "The Project of Modernity and Women in Turkey." In *Rethinking Modernity and National Identity in Turkey*, edited by Sibel Bozdoğan and Reşat Kasaba, 95–112. Seattle: University of Washington Press, 1997.

Arcayürek, Cüneyt. *Derin Devlet 1950–2007: Darbeler ve Gizli Servisler* [Deep state 1950–2007: Military coups and secret services]. Istanbul: Detay Yayıncılık, 2007.

Arnold, David. "The Police and Colonial Control in South India." *Social Scientist* 4, no. 12 (1976): 3–16.

Arondekar, Anjali, and Geeta Patel. "Area Impossible: Notes toward an Introduction." *GLQ: A Journal of Gay and Lesbian Studies* 22, no. 2 (2016): 151–71. https://doi.org/10.1215/10642684-3428687.

Arslanalp, Mert. "Yerinde Duramamak: 'Apolitik' Üst-Orta Sınıf Gençlerin Gözünden Gezi ve Sokak Siyaseti" [Euphoria: Gezi and street politics from the eyes of "apolitical" upper-middle-class youths]. *Birikim Dergisi*, no. 302 (2014): 48–58.

Asad, Talal. *Formations of the Secular: Christianity, Islam, Modernity*. Stanford, CA: Stanford University Press, 2003.

Asad, Talal. *Genealogies of Religion: Discipline and Reason of Power in Christianity and Islam*. Baltimore: Johns Hopkins University Press, 1993.

Atanasoski, Neda. *Humanitarian Violence: The U.S. Deployment of Diversity*. Minneapolis: University of Minnesota Press, 2013.

Atasoy, Yıldız. *Islam's Marriage with Neoliberalism: State Transformation in Turkey*. New York: Palgrave Macmillan, 2009.

Austin, J. L. *How to Do Things with Words*. 1962; Cambridge, MA: Harvard University Press, 1975.

Baer, Brian James. "Russian Gays/Western Gaze: Mapping (Homo)Sexual Desire in Post-Soviet Russia." *GLQ: A Journal of Gay and Lesbian Studies* 8, no. 4 (2002): 499–521.

Baer, Brian James, and Klaus Kaindl, eds. *Queering Translation, Translating the Queer: Theory, Practice, Activism*. New York: Routledge, 2018.

Bali, Rıfat N. *6–7 Eylül 1955 Olayları: Tanıklar-Hatıralar* [6–7th September 1955 events: Witnesses-memories]. Istanbul: Libra Kitap, 2010.

Balkan, Neşecan, Erol M. Balkan, and Ahmet F. Öncü, eds. *The Neoliberal Landscape and the Rise of Islamist Capital in Turkey*. New York: Berghan, 2015.

Bangstad, Sindre. "Contesting Secularism/s: Secularism and Islam in the Work of Talal Asad." *Anthropological Theory* 9, no. 2 (2009): 188–208.

Bangstad, Sindre. "Saba Mahmood and Anthropological Feminism after Virtue." *Theory, Culture and Society* 28, no. 3 (2011): 28–54. https://doi.org/10.1177/0263276410396914.

Bargu, Banu. "Another Necropolitics." *Theory and Event* 19, no. 1 (suppl. 2016). https://www.muse.jhu.edu/article/610222.

Bargu, Banu. *Starve and Immolate: Politics of Human Weapons*. New York: Columbia University Press, 2014.

Bassi, Serena. "Displacing LGBT: Global Englishes, Activism and Translated Sexualities." In *Feminist Translation Studies: Local and Transnational Perspectives*, edited by Olga Castro and Emek Ergun, 235–248. New York: Routledge, 2017.

Bereket, Tarik, and Barry D. Adam. "The Emergence of Gay Identities in Turkey." *Sexualities* 9, no. 2 (2006): 131–51.

Bereket, Tarik, and Barry D. Adam. "Navigating Islam and Same-Sex Liaisons among Men in Turkey." *Journal of Homosexuality* 55, no. 2 (2008): 204–22. https://doi.org/10.1080/00918360802129428.

Berg, Heather. *Porn Work*. Chapel Hill: University of North Carolina Press, forthcoming.

Berghan, Selin. "Patronsuz ve Pezevenksiz Bir Dünya! Feminist Yaklaşımlar Açısından Seks İşçiliği" [A world without bosses and pimps! Sex work from a feminist perspective]. In *Başkaldıran Bedenler: Türkiye'de Transgender, Aktivism ve Altkültürel Pratikler* [Revolting bodies: Transgender, activism, and subcultural practices in Turkey], edited by Berfu Şeker, 90–99. Istanbul: Metis Yayınları, 2013.

Berlant, Lauren. *Cruel Optimism*. Durham, NC: Duke University Press, 2011.

Bernstein, Elizabeth, and Janet R. Jakobsen. Introduction to "Gender, Justice and Neoliberal Transformations" (special issue). *Scholar and Feminist Online*, nos. 11.1–11.2 (2012/2013). http://sfonline.barnard.edu/gender-justice-and-neoliberal-transformations/introduction.

Bieberstein, Alice von, and Nora Tataryan. "The What of Occupation: 'You Took Our Cemetery, You Won't Have Our Park!'" Hot Spots, October 13, 2013, *Cultural Anthropology* website. https://culanth.org/fieldsights/the-what-of-occupation-you-took-our-cemetery-you-wont-have-our-park.

Blackwood, Evelyn. "Sexuality and Gender in Certain Native American Tribes: The Case of Cross-Gender Females." *Signs* 10, no. 11 (1984): 27–42. https://www.journals.uchicago.edu/doi/10.1086/494112.

Blackwood, Evelyn. "Transnational Discourses and Circuits of Queer Knowledge in Indonesia." *GLQ: A Journal of Gay and Lesbian Studies* 14, no. 4 (2008): 481–507.

Blackwood, Evelyn. "Transnational Sexualities in One Place: Indonesian Readings." *Gender and Society* 19, no. 2 (2005): 221–42.

Boellstorff, Tom. *A Coincidence of Desires: Anthropology, Queer Studies, Indonesia*. Durham, NC: Duke University Press, 2007.

Boellstorff, Tom. "Between Religion and Desire: Being Muslim and Gay in Indonesia." *American Anthropologist* 107, no. 4 (2005): 575–85.

Boellstorff, Tom. *The Gay Archipelago: Sexuality and Nation in Indonesia*. Princeton, NJ: Princeton University Press, 2005.

Boltanski, Luc. *Distant Suffering: Morality, Media and Politics*. Cambridge: Cambridge University Press, 1999.

Bourdieu, Pierre. *Distinction: A Cultural Critique of the Judgment of Taste*. Cambridge, MA: Harvard University Press, 1984.

Boyd, Nan Alamilla. "San Francisco's Castro District: From Gay Liberation to Tourist Destination." *Journal of Tourism and Cultural Change* 9, no. 3 (2011): 237–48. https://doi.org/10.1080/14766825.2011.620122.

Bozçalı, Fırat V. "Türkiye'nin Kürt Sorunu: 1999–2007" [Turkey's Kurdish question: 1999–2007]. *Birikim*, no. 225 (2008): 9–19.

Bozkurt, İpek. "Bir Feminist Aktivizm Yöntemi Olarak Dava Takibi" [Legal advocacy as a feminist activist method]. Master's thesis, Bilgi University, 2019.

Bracke, Sarah. "From 'Saving Women' to 'Saving Gays': Rescue Narratives and Their Dis/Continuities." *European Journal of Women's Studies* 19, no. 2 (2012): 237–52.

Brown, Wendy. "American Nightmare: Neoliberalism, Neoconservatism, and De-Democratization." *Political Theory* 34, no. 6 (2006): 690–714.

Brown, Wendy. *Undoing the Demos: Neoliberalism's Stealth Revolution*. London: Zone, 2015.

Butler, Judith. "Against Proper Objects." *differences* 6, nos. 2–3 (1994): 1–26.

Butler, Judith. *Bodies That Matter: On the Discursive Limits of "Sex"*. New York: Routledge, 1993.

Butler, Judith. *Excitable Speech: The Politics of the Performative*. New York: Routledge, 1997.

Butler, Judith. *Gender Trouble: Feminism and the Subversion of Identity*. New York: Routledge, 1990.

Butler, Judith. *Precarious Life: The Powers of Mourning and Violence*. London: Verso, 2004.

Butler, Judith. *The Psychic Life of Power: Theories in Subjection*. Stanford, CA: Stanford University Press, 1997.

Butler, Judith, and Athena Athanasiou. *Dispossession: The Performative in the Political*. Cambridge: Polity, 2013.

Büyükkara, Mehmet Ali. "Ilımlı İslam Tartışmaları Zemininde Günümüz Türkiyesi'nde Laikliğin Anlam ve Sınırları" [Meanings and boundaries of secularism in contemporary Turkey in the context of current discussions on moderate Islam]. *Usûl: İslam Araştırmaları* 9 (January–June 2008): 173–200.

Çakır, Ruşen. *Mahalle Baskısı: Prof. Dr. Şerif Mardin'in Tezlerinden Hareketle Türkiye'de İslam, Cumhuriyet, Laiklik ve Demokrasi* [Neighborhood pressure: Islam, republic, secularism, and democracy in Turkey departing from Prof. Şerif Mardin's theses]. Istanbul: Doğan Kitap, 2008.

Çakırlar, Cüneyt, and Serkan Delice, eds. *Cinsellik Muamması: Türkiye'de Queer Kültür ve Muhalefet* [Sexual enigma: Queer culture and dissent in Turkey]. Istanbul: Metis Yayınları, 2012.

Camp, Jordan T., and Christina Heatherton, eds. *Policing the Planet: Why the Policing Crisis Led to Black Lives Matter*. London: Verso, 2016.

Candan, Ayfer Bartu, and Biray Kolluoğlu. "Emerging Spaces of Neoliberalism: A Gated Town and a Public Housing Project in İstanbul." *New Perspectives on Turkey* 39 (2008): 5–46. https://doi.org/10.1017/S0896634600005057.

Carrier, James G., ed. *Occidentalism: Images of the West*. Oxford: Oxford University Press, 1995.

Carrillo, Héctor. *The Night Is Young: Sexuality in Mexico in the Time of AIDS*. Chicago: University of Chicago Press, 2002.

Çavuşoğlu, Erbatur. "İslâmcı Neo-Liberalizmde İnşaat Fetişi ve Mülkiyet Üzerindeki Simgesel Hâle" [Construction fetishism and the symbolic halo on property in Islamist neoliberalism]. In *İnşaat Ya Resullullah*, edited by Tanıl Bora, 131–53. Istanbul: İletişim Yayınları, 2016.

Cindoglu, Dilek, and Didem Unal. "Gender and Sexuality in the Authoritarian Discursive Strategies of 'New Turkey.'" *European Journal of Women's Studies* 24, no. 1 (2017): 39–54. https://doi.org/10.1177/1350506816679003.

Civelek, Yaprak, and İsmet Koç. "Türkiye'de 'İmam Nikahı'" ["Islamic matrimony" in Turkey]. *Hacettepe Üniversitesi Sosyolojik Araştırmalar E-Dergi*, April 27, 2007. http://www.sdergi.hacettepe.edu.tr/makaleler/Yaprak_Civelek_Ismet _Koc-4-2007.pdf.

Cizre, Ümit. *Secular and Islamic Politics in Turkey: The Making of the Justice and Development Party*. Abingdon-on-Thames, UK: Routledge, 2008.

Clifford, James. *The Predicament of Culture: Twentieth-Century Ethnography, Literature, and Art*. Cambridge, MA: Harvard University Press, 1988.

Çolak, Saliha, and Abdullah Karakuş. "Eşcinseller de Eşitlik İstiyor, Verecek Miyiz?" [Homosexuals also are demanding equality; are we going to bestow it?]. *Milliyet*, January 28, 2008. http://www.milliyet.com.tr/2008/01/28/siyaset/asiy .html (accessed August 1, 2011; link discontinued).

Collins, Patricia Hill. "Black Women and Motherhood." In *Black Feminist Thought: Knowledge, Consciousness, and the Politics of Empowerment*, 187–215. New York: Routledge, 2000.

Connell, R. W. *Masculinities*. Berkeley: University of California Press, 2005.

Coşar, Simten. "The AKP's Hold on Power: Neoliberalism Meets the Turkish-Islamic Synthesis." In *Silent Violence: Neoliberalism, Islamist Politics, and the AKP Years in Turkey*, edited by Gamze Yücesan-Özdemir and Simten Coşar, 67–92. Ottawa: Red Quill Books, 2012.

Coşar, Simten, and Metin Yeğenoğlu. "New Grounds for Patriarchy in Turkey? Gender Policy in the Age of AKP." *South European Society and Politics* 16, no. 4 (2011): 555–73. https://doi.org/10.1080/13608746.2011.571919.

Cruz-Malave, Arnaldo, and Martin F. Manalansan IV. *Queer Globalizations: Citizenship and the Afterlife of Colonialism*. New York: New York University Press, 2002.

Curcio, Anna, and Ceren Özselçuk. "On the Common, Universality, and Communism." *Rethinking Marxism* 22, no. 3 (2010): 312–28.

Dağtaş, Seçil M. "'Down with Some Things!': The Politics of Humour and Humour as Politics in Turkey's Gezi Park Protests." *Etnofoor* 28, no. 1 (2013): 11–34.

Davis, Angela Y. *Racism, Birth Control and Reproductive Rights*. New York: Random House, 1981.

Davutoğlu, Ahmet. *Alternative Paradigms: Impact of Islamic and Western Weltanschauungs on Political Theory*. Lanham, MD: University Press of America, 1993.

Dedeoğlu, Saniye, and Adem Yavuz Elveren, eds. *Gender and Society in Turkey: The Impact of Neoliberal Policies, Political Islam and EU Accession*. London: I. B. Tauris, 2012.

D'Emilio, John. "Capitalism and Gay Identity." In *The Lesbian and Gay Studies Reader*, edited by Henry Abelove, Michèle Aina Barale, and David M. Halperin, 467–76. New York: Routledge, 1993.

Despentes, Virginie. *King Kong Theory*. New York: Feminist Press, 2010.

Dirlik, Arif. "Thinking Modernity Historically: Is 'Alternative Modernity' the Answer?" *Asian Review of World Histories* 1, no. 1 (2013): 5–44.

Duggan, Lisa. *The Twilight of Equality? Neoliberalism, Cultural Politics, and the Attack on Democracy*. Boston: Beacon, 2004.

Duran, Burhanettin. "The Justice and Development Party's 'New Politics': Steering toward Conservative Democracy, a Revised Islamic Agenda or Management of New Crises?" In *Secular and Islamic Politics in Turkey: The Making of the Justice and Development Party*, edited by Ümit Cizre, 80–106. New York: Routledge, 2008.

Edelman, Lee. *No Future: Queer Theory and the Death Drive*. Durham, NC: Duke University Press, 2004.

Ellis, Steven M. "OSCE Report Finds Turkey Is Holding 57 Journalists in Prison." International Press Institute newsroom, April 4, 2011. https://ipi.media/osce -report-finds-turkey-is-holding-57-journalists-in-prison.

El-Tayeb, Fatima. *European Others: Queering Ethnicity in Postnational Europe*. Minneapolis: University of Minnesota Press, 2011.

Eng, David L. *The Feeling of Kinship: Queer Liberalism and the Racialization of Intimacy*. Durham, NC: Duke University Press, 2010.

Eng, David L. *Racial Castration: Managing Masculinity in Asian America*. Durham, NC: Duke University Press, 2001.

Eng, David L., Judith Halberstam, and José Esteban Muñoz. "Introduction: What's Queer about Queer Studies Now?" *Social Text* 23, nos. 3–4 (2005): 1–17. https://doi.org/10.1017/CB09781107415324.004.

Erdem, Tuna, and Seda Ergül, eds. *Fetiş İkâme* [Fetish substitute]. Istanbul: Sel Yayıncılık, 2014.

Ergut, Ferdan. *Modern Devlet ve Polis: Osmanlı'dan Cumhuriyet'e Toplumsal Denetimin Diyalektiği* [Modern state and police: The dialectic of social control from Ottomans to republic]. Istanbul: İletişim Yayınları, 2004.

Ergut, Ferdan. "Policing the Poor in the Late Ottoman Empire." *Middle Eastern Studies* 38, no. 2 (2002): 149–64.

Erman, Tahire. *Mış Gibi Site: Ankara'da Bir TOKİ-Gecekondu Dönüşüm Sitesi* [As if housing development: A TOKİ-squatter home housing complex in Ankara]. Istanbul: İletişim Yayınları, 2016.

Ertür, Başak, and Alisa Lebow. "Coup de Genre : The Trials and Tribulations of Bülent Ersoy." *Theory and Event* 17, no. 1 (2014). https://muse.jhu.edu/issue/29541.

Ertürk, Yakın. "State Responses to Honour Killing." In *Violence in the Name of Honour: Theoretical and Political Challenges*, edited by Shahrzad Mojab and Nahla Abdo-Zubi, 165–76. Istanbul: İstanbul Bilgi Üniversitesi Yayınları, 2004.

Esmeir, Samera. *Juridical Humanity: A Colonial History*. Stanford, CA: Stanford University Press, 2012.

Federici, Silvia. *Re-Enchanting the World: Feminism and the Politics of the Commons.* Oakland, CA: PM Press, 2019.

Felski, Rita. *The Limits of Critique.* Chicago: University of Chicago Press, 2015.

Ferguson, Roderick A. *One-Dimensional Queer.* Minneapolis: University of Minnesota Press, 2018.

Ferguson, Roderick A., and Grace Kyungwon Hong. "The Sexual and Racial Contradictions of Neoliberalism." *Journal of Homosexuality* 59, no. 7 (2012): 1057–64.

Finkel, Andrew, and Nükhet Sirman. Introduction to *Turkish State, Turkish Society*, edited by Andrew Finkel and Nükhet Sirman, 1–20. New York: Routledge, 1990.

Foucault, Michel. *Abnormal: Lectures at the Collège de France, 1974–1975.* Translated by Graham Burchell. New York: Picador, 2003.

Foucault, Michel. *The Archaeology of Knowledge: And the Discourse on Language.* Translated by A. M. Sheridan Smith. New York: Pantheon, 1972.

Foucault, Michel. *The Birth of the Clinic: An Archaeology of Medical Perception.* Translated by Alan Sheridan. New York: Vintage, 1973.

Foucault, Michel. *Discipline and Punish: The Birth of the Prison.* Translated by Alan Sheridan. New York: Vintage, 1977.

Foucault, Michel. *The History of Sexuality.* Vol. 1, *An Introduction.* Translated by Robert Hurley. New York: Pantheon, 1978.

Foucault, Michel. *Security, Territory, Population: Lectures at the Collège de France, 1977–1978.* Translated by Graham Burchell. New York: Picador, 2007.

Foucault, Michel. *"Society Must Be Defended": Lectures at the Collège de France, 1975–1976.* Translated by David Macey. New York: Picador, 2008.

Gal, Susan. "Migration, Minorities, and Multilingualism: Language Ideologies in Europe." In *Language Ideologies, Policies and Practices: Language and the Future of Europe*, edited by Clare Mar-Molinero and Patrick Stevenson, 13–27. Basingstoke, UK: Palgrave, 2006.

Gay, Judith. "'Mummies and Babies' and Friends and Lovers in Lesotho." In *The Many Faces of Homosexuality*, edited by Evelyn Blackwood, 97–116. New York: Haworth, 1986.

Göle, Nilüfer. "The Quest for the Islamic Self." In *Rethinking Modernity and National Identity in Turkey*, edited by Sibel Bozdoğan and Reşat Kasaba, 81–94. Seattle: University of Washington Press, 1997.

Gopinath, Gayatri. *Impossible Desires: Queer Diasporas and South Asian Public Cultures.* Durham, NC: Duke University Press, 2005.

Gordon, Avery. *Ghostly Matters: Haunting and the Sociological Imagination.* Minneapolis: University of Minnesota Press, 1997.

Gorkemli, Serkan. "'Coming Out of the Internet': Lesbian and Gay Activism and the Internet as a 'Digital Closet' in Turkey." *Journal of Middle East Women's Studies* 8, no. 3 (2012): 63–88. https://doi.org/10.2979/jmiddeastwomstud.8.3.63.

Gorkemli, Serkan. *Grassroots Literacies: Lesbian and Gay Activism and the Internet in Turkey.* Albany: State University of New York Press, 2014.

Gramling, David. *The Invention of Monolingualism.* New York: Bloomsbury, 2016.

Gramling, David, and Aniruddha Dutta, eds. "Translating Transgender" (special issue). *TSQ: Transgender Studies Quarterly* 3, nos. 3–4, 2016.

Grewal, Inderpal. "Outsourcing Patriarchy: Feminist Encounters, Transnational Mediations and the Crime of Honour Killings." *International Feminist Journal of Politics* 15, no. 1 (2013): 1–19. https://doi.org/10.1080/14616742.2012.755352.

Grewal, Inderpal. *Saving the Security State: Exceptional Citizens in Twenty-First-Century America*. Durham, NC: Duke University Press, 2017.

Grewal, Inderpal, and Caren Kaplan. "Global Identities: Theorizing Transnational Theories of Sexuality." *GLQ: A Journal of Gay and Lesbian Studies* 7, no. 4 (2001): 663–79.

Grewal, Inderpal, and Caren Kaplan, eds. *Scattered Hegemonies: Postmodernity and Transnational Feminist Practices*. Minneapolis: University of Minnesota Press, 1994.

Grewal, Inderpal, and Caren Kaplan. "Warrior Marks: Global Womanism's Neo-Colonial Discourse in a Multicultural Context." *Camera Obscura* 13, no. 3 (1996): 4–33.

Gülalp, Haldun. "Derin Devlet Nerededir?" [Where is the deep state?]. *Birikim Dergisi*, February 3, 2012. https://www.birikimdergisi.com/guncel/394/derin-devlet-nerededir.

Güllapoğlu, Fatih. "Türk Gladio'su İçin Bazı İpuçları" [Some clues for the Turkish gladio]. *Tempo Dergisi*, June 1991.

Güneş, Ahmet. *Göğe Kuşak Lazım* [The sky needs a rainbow belt]. Istanbul: Sel Yayıncılık, 2016.

Güngör, Aras. *Öteki Erkekler* [Other men]. Istanbul: Sel Yayıncılık, 2013.

Gürel, Perin. "Bilingual Humor, Authentic Aunties, and the Transnational Vernacular at Gezi Park." *Journal of Transnational American Studies* 6, no. 1 (2015): 1–30. https://escholarship.org/uc/item/2md6f6fr.

Gürel, Perin E. *The Limits of Westernization: A Cultural History of America in Turkey*. New York: Columbia University Press, 2017.

Gürsu, Erdem, and Sinan Elitemiz, eds. *80'lerde Lubunya Olmak* [Being "Lubunya" in the 1980s]. Izmir: Siyah Pembe Üçgen, 2012.

Güven, Dilek. *Cumhuriyet Dönemi Azınlık Politikaları ve Stratejileri Bağlamında 6–7 Eylül Olayları* [September 6–7 events in the context of republican era minority politics and strategies]. Istanbul: İletişim Yayınları, 2006.

Halberstam, Jack. "The Anti-Social Turn in Queer Studies." *Graduate Journal of Social Science* 5, no. 2 (2008): 140–56.

Halberstam, Jack. *Female Masculinity*. Durham, NC: Duke University Press, 1998.

Halberstam, Jack. *The Queer Art of Failure*. Durham, NC: Duke University Press, 2011.

Hall, Stuart. "The Neo-liberal Revolution." *Cultural Studies* 25, no. 6 (2011): 705–28. https://doi.org/10.1080/09502386.2011.619886.

Hallett, Michael A. *Private Prisons in America: A Critical Race Perspective*. Urbana: University of Illinois Press, 2006.

Haney, Lynn. "Homeboys, Babies, Men in Suits: The State and the Reproduction of Male Dominance." *American Sociological Review* 61, no. 5 (1996): 759–78.

Hanhardt, Christina B. *Safe Space: Gay Neighborhood History and the Politics of Violence.* Durham, NC: Duke University Press, 2013.

Haritaworn, Jinthana. *Queer Lovers and Hateful Others: Regenerating Violent Times and Places.* London: Pluto, 2015.

Haritaworn, Jinthana, and Jennifer Petzen. "Invented Traditions and New Intimate Publics: Tracing the German 'Muslim Homophobia' Discourse." In *Islam in Its International Context: Comparative Perspectives,* edited by Stephen Hutchings, Chris Flood, Galina Miazhevich, and Henri Nickels, 48–64. Newcastle, UK: Cambridge Scholars, 2011.

Harkins, Gillian. *Everybody's Family Romance: Reading Incest in Neoliberal America.* Minneapolis: University of Minnesota Press, 2009.

Harvey, David. *A Brief History of Neoliberalism.* New York: Oxford University Press, 2005.

Harvey, David. "Neoliberalism as Creative Destruction." *Annals of the American Academy of Political and Social Science* 610, no. 1 (2007): 21–44. https://doi.org /10.1177/0002716206296780.

Hoang, Kimberly Kay. *Dealing in Desire: Asian Ascendancy, Western Decline, and the Hidden Currencies of Global Sex Work.* Berkeley: University of California Press, 2015.

Hocaoğlu, Murat. *Eşcinsel Erkekler: Yirmi Beş Tanıklık* [Homosexual men: Twenty-five testimonies]. Istanbul: Metis Yayıncılık, 2002.

Hochberg, Gil Z. "Introduction: Israelis, Palestinians, Queers: Points of Departure." *GLQ: A Journal of Gay and Lesbian Studies* 16, no. 4 (2010): 493–516. https:// doi.org/10.1215/10642684-2010-001.

Hong, Grace Kyungwon. *Death beyond Disavowal: The Impossible Politics of Difference.* Minneapolis: University of Minnesota Press, 2015.

Hua, Julietta. *Trafficking Women's Human Rights.* Minneapolis: University of Minnesota Press, 2011.

İflazoğlu, Evrim C., and A. Aslı Demir, eds. *Öteki Olarak Ölmek* [Dying as the other]. Ankara: Dipnot Yayınları, 2016.

Iğsız, Aslı. "Brand Turkey and the Gezi Protests: Authoritarianism in Flux, Law and Neoliberalism." In *The Making of a Protest Movement in Turkey: #occupygezi,* edited by Umut Özkırımlı, 25–49. New York: Palgrave Macmillan, 2014.

Iğsız, Aslı. "From Alliance of Civilizations to Branding the Nation: Turkish Studies, Image Wars and Politics of Comparison in an Age of Neoliberalism." *Turkish Studies* 15, no. 4 (2014): 689–704. https://doi.org/10.1080/14683849.2014 .983689.

Jackson, Peter A. "Capitalism and Global Queering: National Markets, Parallels among Sexual Cultures, and Multiple Queer Modernities." *GLQ: A Journal of Gay and Lesbian Studies* 15, no. 3 (2009): 357–95.

Jackson, Peter A. *Queer Bangkok: Twenty-First-Century Markets, Media, and Rights.* Hong Kong: Hong Kong University Press, 2011.

Joseph, Miranda. *Against the Romance of Community*. Minneapolis: University of Minnesota Press, 2002.

Kandiyoti, Deniz. "End of Empire: Islam, Nationalism and Women in Turkey." In *Women, Islam and the State*, edited by Deniz Kandiyoti, 22–48. Philadelphia: Temple University Press, 1991.

Kandiyoti, Deniz. "No Laughing Matter: Women and the New Populism in Turkey." *OpenDemocracy*, September 1, 2014. https://www.opendemocracy.net/5050 /deniz-kandiyoti/no-laughing-matter-women-and-new-populism-in-turkey.

Kandiyoti, Deniz. "Pink Card Blues: Trouble and Strife at the Crossroads of Gender." In *Fragments of Culture: The Everyday of Modern Turkey*, edited by Deniz Kandiyoti and Ayşe Saktanber, 277–94. New Brunswick, NJ: Rutgers University Press, 2002.

Kaplan, Caren, and Inderpal Grewal. "Transnational Feminist Cultural Studies." In *Between Woman and Nation: Nationalisms, Transnational Feminisms, and the State*, edited by Caren Kaplan, Norma Alarcón, and Minoo Moallem, 349–63. Durham, NC: Duke University Press, 1999.

Kauanui, Kēhaulani J. "Native Hawaiian Decolonization and the Politics of Gender." *American Quarterly* 60, no. 2 (2008): 81–87.

Kelley, Robin D. G. "Thug Nation: On State Violence and Disposability." In *Policing the Planet: Why the Policing Crisis Led to Black Lives Matter*, edited by Jordan T. Camp and Christina Heatherton, 15–33. London: Verso, 2016.

Keniş, Şebnem. "Islam and Homosexuality Debates in Turkey: Discursive Contestation among Muslims over LGBTQ Rights." Master's thesis, Koç University, 2012.

Kennedy, Elizabeth Lapovsky, and Madeline D. Davis. *Boots of Leather, Slippers of Gold: The History of a Lesbian Community*. New York: Routledge, 1993.

Keyder, Çağlar, Ayşe Buğra, Utku B. Balaban, and Burcu Yakut. *New Poverty and the Changing Welfare Regime of Turkey*. Report prepared for the UN Development Programme. Ankara: UNDP, 2003. http://www.tr.undp.org/content/dam /turkey/docs/povreddoc/UNDP-TR-new_poverty.pdf.

Kılıç, Azer. "The Gender Dimension of Social Policy Reform in Turkey: Towards Equal Citizenship?" *Social Policy and Administration* 42, no. 5 (2008): 487–503. https://doi.org/10.1111/j.1467-9515.2008.00620.x.

Kocamaner, Hikmet. "How New Is Erdoğan's 'New Turkey'?" *Middle East Brief*, no. 91 (2015). https://www.brandeis.edu/crown/publications/middle-east-briefs /pdfs/1-100/meb91.pdf.

Koğacıoğlu, Dicle. "Law in Context: Citizenship and Reproduction of Inequality in an İstanbul Courthouse." PhD diss., State University of New York at Stony Brook, 2003.

Koğacıoğlu, Dicle. "The Tradition Effect: Framing Honor Crimes in Turkey." *differences* 15, no. 2 (2004): 118–51. https://doi.org/10.1215/10407391-15-2-118.

Kontavas, Nicholas. "Lubunca: The Historical Development of Turkish Queer Slang and a Socio-Functional Approach to Diachronic Processes in Language." Master's thesis, Indiana University, 2012.

Kotiswaran, Prabha. *Dangerous Sex, Invisible Labor: Sex Work and the Law in India.* Princeton, NJ: Princeton University Press, 2011.

Kulick, Don. "A Man in the House: The Boyfriends of Brazilian *Travesti* Prostitutes." *Social Text*, nos. 52–53 (1997): 133–60.

Kurtoğlu, Ayça. "Cinsiyet ve Cinselliğin İnşası: Türk Medeni Kanunu'nda Cinsiyet Değiştirme ve Cinsel Vatandaşlık" [The construction of sex and sexuality: sex change in Turkish civil code and sexual citizenship]. In *Başkaldıran Bedenler: Türkiye'de Transgender, Aktivism ve Altkültürel Pratikler* [Revolting bodies: Transgender, activism, and subcultural practices in Turkey], edited by Berfu Şeker, 116–137. Istanbul: İletişim Yayınları, 2013.

Kurtulus Korkman, Zeynep. "Blessing Neoliberalism: Economy, Family, and the Occult in Millennial Turkey." *Journal of the Ottoman and Turkish Studies Association* 2, no. 2 (2015): 335–57.

Kurtulus Korkman, Zeynep, and Can Açıksöz. "Erdogan's Masculinity and the Language of the Gezi Resistance." *Jadaliyya*, June 22, 2013. http://www.jadaliyya.com/Details/28822/Erdogan's-Masculinity-and-the-Language-of-the-Gezi-Resistance.

Kus, Basak. "Financial Citizenship and the Hidden Crisis of the Working Class in the 'New Turkey.'" *Middle East Report* 278 (Spring 2016): 40–48. https://merip.org/2016/04/financial-citizenship-in-the-new-turkey.

Latour, Bruno. "Why Has Critique Run Out of Steam? From Matters of Fact to Matters of Concern." *Critical Inquiry*, no. 30 (2004): 225–48.

LGBTT Hakları Platformu. "LGBTT Bireylerin İnsan Hakları Raporu 2007" [LGBTT people's human rights report 2007], Kaosgl.org, December 31, 2008. http://www.kaosgldernegi.org/yayindetay.php?id=40.

Long, Scott. "Unbearable Witness: How Western Activists (Mis)Recognize Sexuality in Iran." *Contemporary Politics* 15, no. 1 (2009): 119–36.

Liu, Petrus. *Queer Marxism in Two Chinas.* Durham, NC: Duke University Press, 2015.

Macit, Nadim. *Küresel Güç Politikaları: Türkiye ve İslam* [Global politics of power: Turkey and Islam]. Istanbul: Sarkaç Yayınları, 2011.

Mahmood, Saba. *Politics of Piety: The Islamic Revival and the Feminist Subject.* Princeton, NJ: Princeton University Press, 2005.

Mahmood, Saba. *Religious Difference in a Secular Age: A Minority Report.* Princeton, NJ: Princeton University Press, 2016.

Makoni, Sinfree, and Alastair Pennycook, eds. *Disinventing and Reconstituting Languages.* Bristol, UK: Multilingual Matters, 2007.

Manalansan, Martin F. *Global Divas: Filipino Gay Men in the Diaspora.* Durham, NC: Duke University Press, 2003.

Manalansan, Martin F. "In the Shadows of Stonewall: Examining Gay Transnational Politics and the Diasporic Dilemma." *GLQ: A Journal of Gay and Lesbian Studies* 2, no. 4 (1995): 425–38. https://doi.org/10.1215/10642684-2-4-425.

Manalansan, Martin F. "Race, Violence, and Neoliberal Spatial Politics in the Global City." *Social Text* 23, nos. 3–4 (2005): 141–55. https://doi.org/10.1215/01642472-23-3-4_84-85-141.

Margulies, Ronnie, and Ergin Yildizoglu. "The Political Uses of Islam in Turkey." *Middle East Report* 153 (July/August 1988): 12–17.

Martel, James R. *The Misinterpellated Subject*. Durham, NC: Duke University Press, 2017.

Massad, Joseph A. "Re-orienting Desire: The Gay International and the Arab World." *Public Culture* 14, no. 2 (2002): 361–85.

Massad, Joseph A. *Desiring Arabs*. Chicago: University of Chicago Press, 2007.

Mezzadra, Sandro, and Naoki Sakai. Introduction to "Politics" (special issue). *Translation: A Transdisciplinary Journal*, no. 4 (2014): 9–27.

Mikdashi, Maya, and Jasbir K. Puar. "Queer Theory and Permanent War." *GLQ: A Journal of Gay and Lesbian Studies* 22, no. 2 (2016): 215–22. https://doi .org/10.1215/10642684-3428747.

Millnet-Larsen, Nadja, and Gavin Butt. "Introduction: The Queer Commons." *GLQ: A Journal of Gay and Lesbian Studies* 24, no. 4 (2018): 399–419.

Mitchell, Gregory. "Evangelical Ecstasy Meets Feminist Fury: Sex Trafficking, Moral Panics, and Homonationalism during Global Sporting Events." *GLQ: A Journal of Gay and Lesbian Studies* 22, no. 3 (2016): 325–57.

Moallem, Minoo. *Between Warrior Brother and Veiled Sister: Islamic Fundamentalism and the Politics of Patriarchy in Iran*. Berkeley: University of California Press, 2005.

Mohanty, Chandra Talpade. "Under Western Eyes: Feminist Scholarship and Colonial Discourses." *Feminist Review*, no. 30 (1988): 60–88. https://www.jstor.org /stable/1395054?seq=1.

Mojab, Shahrzad, and Nahla Abdo-Zubi. *Violence in the Name of Honour: Theoretical and Political Challenges*. Istanbul: Bilgi University Press, 2004.

Morgan, Kimberly J., and Ann Shola Orloff, eds. *The Many Hands of the State: Theorizing Political Authority and Social Control*. Cambridge: Cambridge University Press, 2017.

Mourad, Sara. "Queering the Mother Tongue." *International Journal of Communication: Sexuality Research in Communication* 7 (2013): 2533–46.

Moussawi, Ghassan. "(Un)Critically Queer Organizing: Towards a More Complex Analysis of LGBTQ Organizing in Lebanon." *Sexualities* 18, nos. 5–6 (2015): 593–617.

Muñoz, José Esteban. *Cruising Utopia: The Then and There of Queer Futurity*. New York: New York University Press, 2009.

Murphy, Michelle. "The Girl: Mergers of Feminism and Finance in Neoliberal Times." *Scholar and Feminist Online*, 11.1–11.2 (2012/2013). http://sfonline .barnard.edu/gender-justice-and-neoliberal-transformations/the-girl-mergers -of-feminism-and-finance-in-neoliberal-times.

Mutluer, Nil, ed. *Cinsiyet Halleri: Türkiye'de Toplumsal Cinsiyetin Kesişim Sınırları* [States of gender: The intersectional limits of gender in Turkey]. Istanbul: Varlık Yayınları, 2008.

Mutluer, Nil. "Kemalist Feminists in the Era of the AK Party." In *The Turkish AK Party and Its Leader: Criticism, Opposition and Dissent*, edited by Ümit Cizre, 40–75. New York: Routledge, 2016.

Nagar, Richa, and Amanda Lock Swarr, eds. *Critical Transnational Feminist Praxis*. Albany: State University of New York Press, 2010.

Najmabadi, Afsaneh. "Beyond the Americas: Are Gender and Sexuality Useful Categories of Analysis?" *Journal of Women's History* 18, no. 1 (2006): 11–21. https://doi.org/10.1353/jowh.2006.0022.

Najmabadi, Afsaneh. *Professing Selves: Transsexuality and Same-Sex Desire in Contemporary Iran*. Durham, NC: Duke University Press, 2013.

Najmabadi, Afsaneh. "Transing and Transpassing across Sex-Gender Walls in Iran." *WSQ: Women's Studies Quarterly* 36, nos. 3–4 (2008): 23–42. https://doi.org/10.1353/wsq.0.0117.

Najmabadi, Afsaneh. "Types, Acts, or What? Regulation of Sexuality in Nineteenth-Century Iran." In *Islamicate Sexualities: Translations across Temporal Geographies of Desire*, edited by Kathryn Babayan and Afsaneh Najmabadi, 275–98. Cambridge, MA: Harvard University Press, 2008.

Najmabadi, Afsaneh. *Women with Mustaches and Men without Beards: Gender and Sexual Anxieties of Iranian Modernity*. Berkeley: University of California Press, 2005.

Nanda, Serena. *Neither Man nor Woman: The Hijras of India*. Belmont, CA: Wadsworth, 1990.

Navaro-Yashin, Yael. *Faces of the State: Secularism and Public Life in Turkey*. Princeton, NJ: Princeton University Press, 2002.

Oboler, Regine Smith. "Is the Female Husband a Man? Woman/Woman Marriage among the Nandi in Kenya." *Ethnology* 19, no. 1 (1980): 69–88.

Öncü, Ayşe. "Turkish Women in the Professions: Why So Many?" In *Women in Turkish Society*, edited by Nermin Abandan-Unat, 181–93. Leiden: E. J. Brill, 1981.

Oran, Baskın. "Derin Devlet Nedir? Nasıl Oluşur?" [What is deep state? How is it formed?]. *Birgün*, June 9, 1996. https://baskinoran.com/yazilar-2006.php (click on #312 to access).

Öz, Yasemin. "Ahlaksızların Mekansal Dışlanması" [The spatial exclusion of the immorals]. In *Cins Cins Mekan*, edited by Ayten Alkan, 284–302. Istanbul: Varlık Yayınları, 2009.

Özbay, Cenk. "Nocturnal Queers: Rent Boys' Masculinity in Istanbul." *Sexualities* 13, no. 5 (2010): 645–63. https://doi.org.10.1177/1363460710376489.

Özbay, Cenk. *Queering Sexualities in Turkey: Gay Men, Male Prostitutes and the City*. London: I. B. Tauris, 2017.

Özbay, Cenk, and Evren Savcı. "Queering Commons in Turkey." *GLQ: A Journal of Gay and Lesbian Studies* 24, no. 4 (2018): 516–21.

Özbay, Cenk, and Serdar Soydan. *Eşcinsel Kadınlar: Yirmi Dört Tanıklık* [Homosexual women: Twenty-four testimonies]. Istanbul: Metis Yayınları, 2002.

Özbay, Cenk, Maral Erol, Aysecan Terzioglu, and Z. Umut Turem. *The Making of Neoliberal Turkey*. New York: Routledge, 2016.

Özkırımlı, Umut, ed. *The Making of a Protest Movement in Turkey: #occupygezi*. New York: Palgrave Macmillan, 2014.

Ozyegin, Gul. *New Desires, New Selves: Sex, Love, and Piety among Turkish Youth.* New York: New York University Press, 2015.

Ozyegin, Gul. "Reading the Closet through Connectivity." *Social Identities* 18, no. 2 (2012): 201–22. https://doi.org/10.1080/13504630.2012.652845.

Parla, Ayşe. "Protest and the Limits of the Body." Hot Spots, October 31, 2013. *Cultural Anthropology* website. https://culanth.org/fieldsights/protest-and-the-limits-of-the-body.

Parla, Ayse. "The 'Honor' of the State: Virginity Examinations in Turkey." *Feminist Studies* 27, no. 1 (2001): 65–88. https://doi.org/10.2307/3178449.

Pervizat, Leyla. "In the Name of Honour." In *Violence in the Name of Honour: Theoretical and Political Challenges*, edited by Sharzad Mojab and Nahla Abdo, 137–41. Istanbul: Bilgi University Press, 2004.

Potuoğlu-Cook, Öykü. "Hope with Qualms: A Feminist Analysis of the 2013 Gezi Protests." *Feminist Review* 109, no. 1 (2015): 96–123. https://doi.org/10.1057/fr.2014.56.

Puar, Jasbir K. "Circuits of Queer Mobility: Tourism, Travel, and Globalization." *GLQ: A Journal of Gay and Lesbian Studies* 8, no. 1–2 (2002): 101–37. https://doi.org/10.1215/10642684-8-1-2-101.

Puar, Jasbir K. *Terrorist Assemblages: Homonationalism in Queer Times.* Durham, NC: Duke University Press, 2007.

Puar, Jasbir K., and A. S. Rai. "Monster, Terrorist, Fag: The War on Terrorism and the Production of Docile Patriots." *Social Text* 20, no. 3 (2002): 117–48.

Puri, Jyoti. "Sculpting the Saffron Body: Yoga, Hindutva, and the International Marketplace." In *Majoritarian State: How Hindu Nationalism Is Changing India*, edited by Angana P. Chatterji, Thomas Blom Hansen, and Christophe Jaffrelot, 317–31. London: Hurst, 2019.

Puri, Jyoti. *Sexual States: Governance and the Struggle over the Antisodomy Law in India.* Durham, NC: Duke University Press, 2016.

Rafael, Vicente L. *Motherless Tongues: The Insurgency of Language amid Wars of Translation.* Durham, NC: Duke University Press, 2016.

Reddy, Chandan. *Freedom with Violence: Race, Sexuality, and the US State.* Durham, NC: Duke University Press, 2011.

Reddy, Chandan. "Homes, Houses, Non-Identity: Paris Is Burning." In *Burning Down the House: Recycling Domesticity*, edited by Rosemary Marangoly George, 355–79. Boulder, CO: Westview, 1998.

Reddy, Gayatri. *With Respect to Sex: Negotiating Hijra Identity in South India.* Chicago: University of Chicago Press, 2005.

Reiner, Robert. *The Politics of the Police.* New York: St. Martin's, 1985.

Ritchie, Jason. "How Do You Say 'Come Out of the Closet' in Arabic? Queer Activism and the Politics of Visibility in Israel-Palestine." *GLQ: A Journal of Gay and Lesbian Studies* 16, no. 4 (2010): 557–75. https://doi.org/10.1215/10642684-2010-004.

Ritchie, Jason. "Pinkwashing, Homonationalism, and Israel-Palestine: The Conceits of Queer Theory and the Politics of the Ordinary." *Antipode* 47, no. 3 (2015): 616–34. https://doi.org/10.1111/anti.12100.

Rofel, Lisa. *Desiring China: Experiments in Neoliberalism, Sexuality, and Public Culture*. Durham, NC: Duke University Press, 2007.

Roscoe, Will. *The Zuni Man–Woman*. Albuquerque: University of New Mexico Press, 1991.

Rosenberg, Jordana, and Amy Villarejo, eds. "Queer Studies and the Crises of Capitalism" (special issue). *GLQ: A Journal of Gay and Lesbian Studies* 18, no. 1 (2012).

Sakai, Naoki. *Translation and Subjectivity: On "Japan" and Cultural Nationalism*. Minneapolis: University of Minnesota Press, 1997.

Sanchez, Lisa E. "The Global E-rotic Subject, the Ban, and the Prostitute-Free Zone: Sex Work and the Theory of Differential Exclusion." *Environment and Planning D: Society and Space* 22, no. 6 (2004): 861–83. https://doi.org/10.1068 /d413.

Savcı, Evren. "On Putting Down and Destroying: Affective Economies of a Woman-only Club in İstanbul." In *Mapping Intimacies: Relations, Exchanges, Affects*, edited by Tam Sanger and Yvette Taylor, 95–111. New York: Palgrave Macmillan, 2013.

Savcı, Evren. "Queer in Translation: Paradoxes of Westernization and Sexual Others in the Turkish Nation." PhD diss., University of Southern California, 2011.

Savcı, Evren. "Revolting Grief." *Theory and Event* 19, no. 1 (suppl. 2016). https://www .muse.jhu.edu/article/610223.

Savcı, Evren. "Turkey's AKP and Public Morality." *Middle East Report Online*, December 26, 2014. https://merip.org/2014/12/turkeys-akp-and-public-morality.

Savcı, Evren. "Who Speaks the Language of Queer Politics? Western Knowledge, Politico-Cultural Capital and Belonging among Urban Queers in Turkey." *Sexualities* 19, no. 3 (2016): 369–87. https://doi.org/10.1177/1363460715613288.

Savcı, Evren. "Why Every City Needs a Center Square: On the Turkish Uprisings, Coalition Building and Coexistence." *Feminist Wire*, June 10, 2013. http:// www.thefeministwire.com/2013/06/why-every-city-needs-a-center-square-on -the-turkish-uprisings-coalition-building-and-coexistence.

Savcı, Evren. "The LGBTI+ Movement." Interview by Şebnem Keniş and İpek Tabur. In *Authoritarianism and Resistance in Turkey*, edited by Esra Özyürek, Gaye Özpınar, and Emrah Altındiş, 125–32. Cham, Switzerland: Springer, 2019. https://doi.org/10.1007/978-3-319-76705-5_13.

Schulman, Sarah. *The Gentrification of the Mind: Witness to a Lost Imagination*. Berkeley: University of California Press, 2013.

Scott, Joan W. "The Evidence of Experience." *Critical Inquiry* 17, no. 4 (1991): 773–97. https://doi.org/10.1086/448612.

Sedgwick, Eve Kosofsky. "Paranoid Reading and Reparative Reading; or, You're So Paranoid, You Probably Think This Essay Is about You." In *Novel Gazing: Queer Readings in Fiction*, edited by Eve Kosofsky Sedgwick, 1–40. Durham, NC: Duke University Press, 1997.

Şeker, Berfu, ed. *Başkaldıran Bedenler: Türkiye'de Transgender, Aktivizm, ve Altkültürel Pratikler* [Revolting Bodies: Transgender, Activism, and Subcultural Practices in Turkey]. Istanbul: Metis Yayınları, 2013.

Selek, Pınar. *Maskeler, Süvariler, Gacılar* [Masks, riders, "Gacı"s]. Istanbul: İstiklal Kitabevi, 2001.

Senses, Fikret. "Turkey's Experience with Neoliberal Policies since 1980 in Retrospect and Prospect." In *The Making of Neoliberal Turkey*, edited by Cenk Özbay, Maral Erol, Aysecan Terzioğlu, and Z. Umut Türem, 15–32. New York: Routledge, 2016.

Shah, Svati P. *Street Corner Secrets: Sex, Work, and Migration in the City of Mumbai.* Durham, NC: Duke University Press, 2014.

Shakhsari, Sima. "Weblogistan Goes to War: Representational Practices, Gendered Soldiers and Neoliberal Entrepreneurship in Diaspora." *Feminist Review* 99, no. 1 (2011): 6–24. https://doi.org/10.1057/fr.2011.35.

Shively, Kim. "Religious Bodies and the Secular State: The Merve Kavakci Affair." *Journal of Middle East Women's Studies* 1, no. 3 (2005): 46–72. https://doi.org/10.2979/MEW.2005.1.3.46.

Şık, Ahmet. *Dokunan Yanar (İmamın Ordusu)* [Whoever touches this will burn (Imam's army)]. Istanbul: Postacı Yayınevi, 2011.

Sirman, Nükhet. "Feminism in Turkey: A Short History." *New Perspectives on Turkey* 3 (fall 1989): 1–34. https://doi.org/10.15184/S0896634600000704.

Smith, Andrea. "Queer Theory and Native Studies: The Heteronormativity of Settler Colonialism." *GLQ: A Journal of Gay and Lesbian Studies* 16, no. 1–2 (2010): 41–68.

Solomon, Jon. "The Postimperial Etiquette and the Affective Structure of Area." *Translation: A Transdisciplinary Journal*, no. 4 (spring 2014): 171–201.

Spade, Dean. *Normal Life: Administrative Violence, Critical Trans Politics, and the Limits of Law*. Boston: South End, 2011.

Spivak, Gayatri Chakravorty. "Can the Subaltern Speak?" In *Marxism and the Interpretation of Culture*, edited by Cary Nelson and Lawrence Grossberg, 271–313. Chicago: University of Illinois Press, 1988.

Springer, Simon. "Neoliberalism as Discourse: Between Foucauldian Political Economy and Marxian Poststructuralism." *Critical Discourse Studies* 9, no. 2 (2012): 133–47. doi:10.1080/17405904.2012.656375.

Stockton, Kathryn Bond. *The Queer Child, or Growing Sideways in the Twentieth Century*. Durham, NC: Duke University Press, 2009.

Stokes, Martin. *The Republic of Love: Cultural Intimacy in Turkish Popular Music*. Chicago: University of Chicago Press, 2010.

Stoler, Ann Laura. *Race and the Education of Desire: Foucault's "History of Sexuality" and the Colonial Order of Things*. Durham, NC: Duke University Press, 1995.

Tahaoğlu, Çiçek. "Kadına Şiddette Suçlu Kim? Aile? Devlet? Toplum? Hepimiz?" [Who is guilty of violence against women? Family? State? Society? We all?]. KAMER, February 19, 2018. http://www.kamer.org.tr/icerik_detay.php?id=298.

Tarhan, Mehmet. "Zorunlu Askerlik ve Sivil Alternatif Hizmete Direniş Olarak Vicdani Red" [Conscientious objection as resistance to mandatory military service and alternative civil service]. In *Cinsiyet Halleri: Türkiye'de Toplumsal Cinsiyetin Kesişim Sınırları* [States of Gender: The Intersectional Limits of Gender in Turkey], edited by Nil Mutluer, 247–53. Istanbul: Varlık Yayınları, 2008.

Tekeli, Sirin. "Emergence of the New Feminist Movement in Turkey." In *The New Women's Movement: Feminism and Political Power in Europe and the USA*, edited by Drude Dahlerup, 179–99. Beverly Hills, CA: Sage, 1986.

Tüfekçi, Zeynep. *Twitter and Tear Gas: The Power and Fragility of Networked Protest.* New Haven, CT: Yale University Press, 2018.

Tuğal, Cihan. *The Fall of the Turkish Model: How the Arab Uprisings Brought Down Islamic Liberalism.* London: Verso, 2016.

Tuğal, Cihan. *Passive Revolution: Absorbing the Islamic Challenge to Capitalism.* Stanford, CA: Stanford University Press, 2009.

Tuğal, Cihan. "'Resistance Everywhere': The Gezi Revolt in Global Perspective." *New Perspectives on Turkey* 49 (2013): 157–72.

Turam, Berna. *Between Islam and the State: The Politics of Engagement.* Stanford, CA: Stanford University Press, 2007.

Valentine, David. *Imagining Transgender: An Ethnography of a Category.* Durham, NC: Duke University Press, 2007.

Wacquant, Loïc. *Punishing the Poor: The Neoliberal Government of Social Insecurity.* Durham, NC: Duke University Press, 2009.

Wacquant, Loïc. "Three Steps to a Historical Anthropology of Actually Existing Neoliberalism." *Social Anthropology* 20, no. 1 (2012): 66–79. doi:10.1111/j.1469-8676.2011.00189.x.

Wadud, Amina. *Inside the Gender Jihad: Women's Reform in Islam.* Oxford: Oneworld, 2006.

Ward, Jane. *Respectably Queer: Diversity Culture in LGBT Activist Organizations.* Nashville, TN: Vanderbilt University Press, 2008.

Weber, Max. *The Theory of Social and Economic Organization.* New York: Free Press, 1964.

Weston, Kath. *Families We Choose: Lesbians, Gays, Kinship.* New York: Columbia University Press, 1991.

White, Jenny B. *Islamist Mobilization in Turkey: A Study in Vernacular Politics.* Seattle: University of Washington Press, 2002.

Wikan, Unni. *Behind the Veil in Arabia: Women in Oman.* Chicago: University of Chicago Press, 1991.

Williams, Raymond. *Marxism and Literature.* Oxford: Oxford University Press, 1977.

Willse, Craig. *The Value of Homelessness: Managing Surplus Life in the United States.* Minneapolis: University of Minnesota Press, 2015.

Wilson, Ara. *The Intimate Economies of Bangkok: Tomboys, Tycoons, and Avon Ladies in the Global City.* Berkeley: University of California Press, 2004.

Wittig, Monique. *The Straight Mind and Other Essays.* Boston: Beacon, 1992.

Wolf, Sherry. *Sexuality and Socialism: History, Politics, and Theory of LGBT Liberation.* Chicago: Haymarket, 2009.

Wyers, Mark David. "*Wicked" Istanbul: The Regulation of Prostitution in the Early Turkish Republic*. Istanbul: Libra Yayıncılık, 2012.

Yalçın-Heckman, Lale. "Kurdish Tribal Organization and Local Political Processes." In *Turkish State, Turkish Society*, edited by Andrew Finkel and Nükhet Sirman, 289–312. New York: Routledge, 1990.

Yardımcı, Sibel, and Özlem Güçlü, eds. *Queer Tahayyül* [Queer imaginary]. Istanbul: Sel Yayıncılık, 2013.

Yazıcı, Berna. "The Return to the Family: Welfare, State, and Politics of the Family in Turkey." *Anthropological Quarterly* 85, no. 1 (2012): 103–40. https://doi .org/10.1353/anq.2012.0013.

Yeşilyurt-Gündüz, Zuhal. "The EU and the AKP: A Neoliberal Love Affair?" In *Silent Violence: Neoliberalism, Islamist Politics and the AKP Years in Turkey*, edited by Simten Coşar and Gamze Yücesan-Özdemir, 269–94. Ottawa: Red Quill Books, 2012.

Yildiz, Yasemin. *Beyond the Mother Tongue: The Postmonolingual Condition*. New York: Fordham University Press, 2012.

Yirmibeşoğlu, Şerife Gözde. "Women and Trade Unionism in Turkey: The Impact of the European Union." In *Gender and Society in Turkey: The Impact of Neoliberal Policies, Political Islam and EU Accession*, edited by Saniye Dedeoğlu and Adem Yavus Elveren, 205–21. London: I. B. Tauris, 2012.

Yıldırım, Fügen. *Fahişeliğin Öbür Yüzü: On Beş Kadının Tanıklığı* [The other face of prostitution: Accounts of fifteen women]. Istanbul: Metis Yayınları, 2002.

Yoltar, C. "When the Poor Need Healthcare: An Ethnography of State and Citizenship in Turkey." *Middle Eastern Studies* 45, no. 5 (2009): 769–782.

Yonucu, Deniz. "Devlet Şiddeti ve 'Mimli' Mahalleler" [State violence and "marked" neighborhoods]. *Express*, no. 138 (2013): 31–33.

Yücesan-Özdemir, Gamze. "The Social Policy Regime in the AKP Years: The Emperor's New Clothes." In *Silent Violence: Neoliberalism, Islamist Politics and the AKP Years in Turkey*, edited by Simten Coşar and Gamze Yücesan-Özdemir, 125–52. Ottawa: Red Quill Books, 2012.

Yücesan-Özdemir, Gamze, and Simten Coşar, eds. *Silent Violence: Neoliberalism, Islamist Politics and the AKP Years in Turkey*. Ottawa: Red Quill Books, 2012.

Zabcı, Filiz. "Internalisation of Dependency: The AKP's Dance with the Global Institutions of Neoliberalism." In *Silent Violence: Neoliberalism, Islamist Politics and the AKP Years in Turkey*, edited by Simten Coşar and Gamze Yücesan-Özdemir, 251–68. Ottawa: Red Quill Books, 2012.

Zengin, Aslı. "Devletin Cinsel Kıyıları: İstanbul'da Fuhşun Mekânları" [Sexual shores of the state: Places of prostitution in Istanbul]. In *Cins Cins Mekân*, edited by Ayten Alkan, 264–83. Istanbul: Varlık Yayınları, 2009.

Zengin, Aslı. *İktidarın Mahremiyeti: İstanbul'da Hayat Kadınları, Seks İşçiliği ve Şiddet* [Privacy of power: Prostitutes, sex workers, and violence in Istanbul]. Istanbul: Metis Yayınları, 2011.

Zengin, Aslı. "Sex for Law, Sex for Psychiatry: Pre-Sex Reassignment Surgical Psychotherapy in Turkey." *Anthropologica* 56, no. 1 (2014): 55–68.

Zengin, Aslı. "Violent Intimacies: Tactile State Power, Sex/Gender Transgression, and the Politics of Touch in Contemporary Turkey." *Journal of Middle East Women's Studies* 12, no. 2 (2016): 225–45.

Zengin, Aslı. "What Is Queer about Gezi?" Hot Spots, October 31, 2013. *Cultural Anthropology* website, https://culanth.org/fieldsights/what-is-queer-about -gezi?fbclid=IwAR0tH83edAhTE_lk1Brr1aRoFIxCKRUGdfQ4J7sdqCWq6p _8HUeTnoXkbMs.

Index

headscarf debate (*continued*)
  personal choice or human right vs. religious entitlement, 42; petition, identity politics, and, 36–40; politics of cruelty vs. politics of rights and, 38–39, 47–52; private sphere and, 49–51; securitization, 34; *Teke Tek* talk show and rights framework, 40–43; Turkish secularity, modernity, and, 32–35
Hendricks, Muhsin, 50, 176n49
homolingualism, 12–14, 148–50, 166n64
homonationalism, 8–10, 69, 166n64
homonormativity: headscarf debate and homosexual rights as litmus test, 36, 41–45; honor killing framework and, 67–68; Lambdaistanbul and, 114; neoliberalism and, 7
homophobia discourse: of cultures, 3, 8; headscarf debate and, 46–48; Islam and, 68–69; Middle East and geographies of, 69; securitization and demand to be protected from, 8
homosexuality: as *haram* (forbidden in Islam), 49–50, 71; as illness vs. sin, 29–30, 40, 46–47
Hong, Grace, 105–6
honor killing framework: critiques of, 66–67; East/West binary, stranger danger myth, and, 67–68; Kurds and, 73–74, 76; national dynamics and, 54; *töre cinayetleri* (custom killings) and backwardness trope, 74; Yıldız murder and, 53–55
houses of light (*ışık evleri*), 84

identity politics. *See* sexual subjectivities; subjectivities and minority categorization
Iğsız, Aslı, 57
Independent, 53–56, 60–61, 65
individualization, neoliberal, 91
Iran, 160n17, 171n2
işgal (occupying), 88
Islam: AKP's polarization of Muslims, 48; Alevis, 183n17; alternative modernity trope, 57, 145–46; cast as other by Kemalism, 33; charity associations, 34–35; culturalization of, 146; de-leftification and de-radicalization of, 17, 84; faith as fearlessness vis-à-vis authority, 71–73; homonationalism and, 8–9; honor killing framework, homophobia, and, 66–69; la-

bor repression and Erdoğan's evocation of, 127; Mahmood on female piety and, 72; morality, Islamic, 20–22, 104, 130, 134–35; "Muslims to themselves" vs. "Muslims to everyone" and, 36–39, 41, 45; Revolutionary Muslims, 136; Turkish-Islamic synthesis, 16–17, 84, 204n31; utopia, Islamic, 49; victim of imperial West framework, 3–4. *See also* neoliberal Islam
Islamic matrimony (*imam nikahı*), 53, 70, 177n3
Islamic State, 75–76
Israel, 9
İstiklal Street, Istanbul, 136

Jackson, Peter, 144
justice (*hak*), 38–39, 47–48, 180n61

Kabahatler Kanunu (Law of Misdemeanors), 80, 86–91
KADEM (Kadın ve Demokrasi Derneği; Association for Women and Democracy), 128
Kadınca women's club (pseud.), 114–21, 152
KaosGL, 35
Kaplan, Caren, 61–62
Kaplan, Hilâl, 37–40, 46–52
Karakaya-Stump, Ayfer, 201n71
Kauanui, Kēhaulani, 161n20
Kavaf, Selma Aliye, 29–30, 35, 43–45
Kavakçı, Merve, 34
Kelley, Robin D. G., 185n34
kendine Müslüman ("Muslims to themselves"), 36–39, 41, 45
Kennedy, Elizabeth Lapovsky, 195n17
killjoy, feminist, 121
Kırmızı Şemsiye (Red Umbrella), 98
Kocadağ, Hüseyin, 189n83
Koğacıoğlu, Dicle, 74
koli houses, 94–97, 188n67
kontrgerilla (counterinsurgency), 189n84
Kozakoğlu, Hayri, 84
Kurdish language, 19, 169n112
Kurdish opening, 35
Kurds, Kurdishness, and Kurdish politics, 22, 73–77
Kuzu, Burhan, 36, 40

labor repression, 126–27, 198n49. *See also* trans sex workers

neoliberalism: bare life, 106–7; difference, neoliberal, 105–6; Harvey on, 170n118; homonormativity, homonationalism, and securitization, 7–11; individualization and, 91; Lambdaistanbul politics and, 114; precarities, bare life, and, 106–8; schools of, 161n28; states of exception, neoliberal, 128, 199n54. *See also specific topics, such as* securitization

Öcalan, Abdullah, 75
Occidentalisms, 55–59, 124, 142
Öğüt, Süheyb, 46, 49–52
Oran, Baskın, 190n86
Orientalisms, 55–59, 69, 142, 146
Ottoman exceptionalism, 123, 196n33, 197n38
outness: outness/closet binary, visibility, and, 63–64; Yıldız murder and, 59–65
Öz, Yaşar, 189n83
Özal, Korkut, 186n49
Özal, Turgut, 18, 92, 124, 168n100, 176n2, 197n40, 204n31
Özbay, Cenk, 164n51
Özkan, Çiğdem, 40–43, 174n33

Parla, Ayşe, 140
particularism. *See* universal/particular binary
Pembe Hayat (Pink Life association): constitutional reform and, 35; hate crime legislation, demand for, 104, 107; job applications protest, 189n77; trans women and, 80, 91, 97–99
pinkwashing, 9–10
PKK (Partiya Karkerên Kurdistanê; Kurdistan Workers' Party), 17, 51, 75, 84
police force: historical background, 83–85; as indirect actors in violence, 101; marginality and terrorism language, deployment of, 100; trans sex workers, violence and fines against, 80, 85–86, 100; Turkish Police Duty Law, 184n31
political critique. *See* critique, limits of
political prisoners, 183n20
Potuoğlu-Cook, Öykü, 140
pride marches: AK LGBTİ and, 159n7; as deeply political, 113; embraced then banned by AKP, 1–2; Gezi protests and, 137; growth of, 19; Ramadan logic used against, 104; Trans Pride March and LGBTİ+ pride march, 159n6
prisoners, political, 183n20
private/public binary, 49–51
privatization, 22, 92. *See also* gentrification
pronouns and gender in Turkish, 196n22
Puar, Jasbir, 8–9, 69, 152, 164n54–165n55, 166n64
public/private binary, 49–51
public space: ability to define as unlawfully occupiable, 88; gentrification of, 88–89, 101, 103, 126; police role in defining, 83–84; privatization of, 92; trans sex workers, Law of Misdemeanors, and, 81, 88–91, 92. *See also* commons
Puri, Jyoti, 184n28

queer studies: anti-social turn, 193n4; critique, language, and, 112; English-centered, 14; Foucauldian omissions of coloniality and capitalism, 143–46; neoliberalism and Islam, separation of, 142–50; political economic and geopolitical shift in, 7–8; productive paradox of neoliberal Islam for, 2–3; securitization and decentering of US imperialism in, 10–11; self-correction and naming practices in, 193n5; translation as queer methodology, 4–5, 11–16, 150. *See also* critique, limits of

race, queer critique of family and, 61–62
rahatsız etme (disturbing), 88
Ramadan, 104, 136
Red Umbrella (Kırmızı Şemsiye), 98
re-enchantment and disenchantment of politics, 111, 121–22, 131–39
reforms, republican, 32–33, 57, 171n4
rent boys, "good" vs. "bad," 164n51. *See also* sex work
respectability politics: class and, 116; containment of bad publics and, 90; deep citizen violence and, 103; expansion of marginality and, 23, 103; Gezi commons and, 134; hate crime law demands and, 82, 107–8; Islam and, 48; trans sex workers and, 87, 92–93, 105
Return to the Family project (SSCPA), 180n55

www.ingramcontent.com/pod-product-compliance
Lightning Source LLC
Chambersburg PA
CBHW020856270326
41928CB00006B/727